ENGAGEMENT AND DEVELOPMENT

India's Northeast and Neighbouring Countries

ENGAGEMENT AND DEVELOPMENT

India's Northeast and Neighbouring Countries

Edited By

C. Joshua Thomas

AKANSHA PUBLISHING HOUSE

NEW DELHI

AKANSHA PUBLISHING HOUSE
R 37-B, Vani Vihar, Uttam Nagar
New Delhi-110059
Email: ektabooks@yahoo.com

Showroom
4649/21B, Ansari Road
Darya Ganj
New Delhi - 110 002
Ph.: 23269193 / 9811582579

ENGAGEMENT AND DEVELOPMENT:
India's Northeast and Neighbouring Countries

First Edition 2006

ISBN 81-8370-090-X

[Neither the ICSSR-NERC nor the Editor nor the Publisher necessarily takes any responsibility for views expressed by the authors of various articles.]

PRINTED IN INDIA

Published by M.P. Misra for Akansha Publishing House, New Delhi and Printed at Aryan Enterprise, Delhi.

Preface

With the paradigm shift from state-centricism to interdependence and global cooperation, the Indian state has been sensitized about the geo-economic potential of its Northeastern Region (NER) as its gateway to Southeast Asian countries. India's Look East Policy, introduced in the early nineties, is, therefore, aimed at gradual integration of the NER with the thriving market across the borders, and thereby, opening up to the emerging opportunities in the Southeast Asia. The NER, because of its geographic location cradled by five Asian countries – Nepal, Bhutan, Tibetan-China, Myanmar and Bangladesh, has natural geo-economic advantages to become the economic bridgehead of South East Asia. The implications of India's relations with her north and northeastern neighbours for NER are far deeper than any other regions of the country. Hence, the prospect of development of NER lies in the strong, stable and mutually beneficial relationship between India and her north and northeastern neighbours.

Keeping this background in focus ICSSR North Eastern Regional Centre invited diplomats, journalists, academics, administrators, research scholars and social activists to a *National Seminar on Partnership for Development: Holistic Approach to Northeast* to deliberate upon the essence of bilateral relations between India and her northern and northeastern neighbours. The Indian Council of Social Science Research, New Delhi sponsored and funded the two-day seminar that was held at Gangtok, Sikkim on 8 and 9 May 2002. This volume is the outcome of that Seminar. We profusely apologize for bringing out this volume so late due to some unforeseen and unavoidable reasons. However, the message of the seminar is as relevant today as it was four years ago. The views expressed in the papers presented and in the discussions that followed have been put together in this volume under the rubric: *Engagement and Development - India's Northeast and Neighbouring Countries.*

There are a number of officials, scholars and friends who have directly and indirectly helped in organizing this seminar and also bringing out this volume. We would like to put on record our deep appreciation for all their help, assistance and encouragements. But some of them deserve to be mentioned here.

We are grateful to ICCSR, New Delhi for extending financial support to this Seminar and we appreciate much Professor Andre Beteille, Chairman, Professor T.C.A. Anand, Member-Secretary and Dr. Vinod K. Mehta, Director of the ICSSR, for giving us the privilege to edit this volume and bring out in this present book form and without their timely intervention and encouragement this book would not have seen its light.

Special thanks to Professor Mrinal Miri, former Vice-Chancellor, North Eastern Hill University (NEHU) and Chairman, ICSSR-NERC, Shillong for his key note address in the seminar and also for his encouragement. Professor David Reid Syiemlieh, Department of History, NEHU and former Honorary Director, ICSSR-NERC deserve our thanks for helping in many ways in the organization of the seminar. Professor P. Tandon, Vice-Chancellor, NEHU and Chairman, ICSSR-NERC for his constant attention to the activities of the NERC.

A word of appreciation to all the paper presenters for accepting our invitation to prepare their research paper and also personally making it a point to present their papers in the seminar at Gangtok and they are: Ambassador C.V. Ranganathan, Mr. B.G. Verghese, Dr. P.D. Shenoy, Dr. Walter Fernandes, Professor Sujata Miri, Mr. Sanjay Hazarika, Mr. Subir Bhaumik, Dr. Gurudas Das, Professor Sajal Nag, Dr. Partha S. Ghosh, Professor A.C. Sinha, Dr. Samir Kumar Das, Professor R. Gopalakrishnan, Dr. Konsam Ibo Singh, Dr. Udai Bhanu Singh, Professor L.S. Gassah, Professor Bimal Pramanik and others. We are also grateful to Dr. V. Bhattacharjee of Gangtok and Dr. Sujata Dutta Hazarika of

Indian Institute of Technology, Guwahati for their assistance in the seminar.

Mr. Sanat Chakrabarty, Editor, *Grassroots Options*, Shillong deserve special thanks for sparing his valuable time to do the copy-editing for this volume.

We are fortunate to have a small team of talented young supporting staff in the Centre and their ungrudging help and cooperation, which made the entire work both during the seminar and also during the editing process much easier to accomplish. Their unassuming services deserve to be recorded here: Ms. Christine Blah, Ms. Narisha Kharbuli, Ms. Cerilla Khonglah, Mr. Romauldo Pasi, Mr. T. Aier, Mr. Rupert Momin and late Mrs. Jean M Blah.

Dr. Gurudas Das, formerly, Reader, Department of Economics, NEHU and currently Head, Department of Humanities and Social Sciences, National Institute of Technology, Silchar, who literally shouldered most of the preparatory works of the seminar deserves a big thank. Mr. M.P. Misra, Akansha Publishing House, New Delhi, has been a friend of NERC's publications and we are grateful to him.

Last but not the least both Kalai and Lind deserve special thanks for their love and understanding.

July 2006 **C. JOSHUA THOMAS**

Contents

SECTION V
LOOK-EAST POLICY, SECURITY ASPECTS - IMPLICATIONS FOR NORTHEASTERN REGION

Contributors

A.C. Sinha, 7331, Sector D-1, Vasant Kunj, New Delhi 110 070, *Email:* acoomarsinha@yahoo.com

A.N.S. Ahmed, Director, OKDISCD, Sapta Swahid Path, Sarumo-toria, Dispur, Guwahati 781 006, *Email:* dkdscd@hotmail.com

Bimal Pramanik, Director, Centre for Research in Indo-Bangladesh Relations, 107 Jadhpur Park (Ground Floor), Kolkata 700 068, *Email:* cribr@vsnl.net

B.G. Verghese, Centre for Policy Research, Dharma Marg, Chanakyapuri, New Delhi 110 021, *Email:* bgverghese@sag-7.org

C.V. Ranganathan, IFS (Retd.), Former Ambassador to China & France, F-26, I.F.S. Apartments, Mayur Vihar Phase-I, Delhi 110 091, *Email:* rangi@nda.vsnl.net.in

C. Joshua Thomas, Acting Director, ICSSR, North Eastern Regional Centre, Upper Nongthymmai, Shillong -793 014, Meghalaya, *Email:* joshuathomas67@hotmail.com

Gurudas Das, Head, Department of Humanities & Social Sciences, National Institute of Technology, Silchar 788010, *Email:* gurudas_das@yahoo.co.in

Konsam Ibo Singh, Associate Professor, Department of Political Science, Manipur University, Canchipur, Imphal, Manipur, *Email:* kibosing@yahoo.co.uk.in

L.S. Gassah, Department of Political Science, North Eastern Hill University, Shillong - 793 022, Meghalaya

P.D. Shenoy, IAS, Former Secretary, DoNER, Government

of India, Vigyan Bhawan Annexe, New Delhi - 110 011

Partha S. Ghosh, OKDISCD, Sapta Swahid Path, Sarumotoria, Dispur, Guwahati 781 006, *Email:* dkdscd@hotmail.com, *Email:* parsarg@hotmail.com

R. Gopalakrishnan, Department of Geography, NEHU, Shillong 793 022.

Sujata Miri, A-39, South Extension, Part-I, New Delhi 110 049, *Email:* sujatamiri@hotmail.com

Sajal Nag, Department of History, Assam University, Silchar, Asom, *Email:* sajalnag@rediffmail.com

Samir Kumar Das, Reader, Department of Political Science, Calcutta University, Kolkata, *Email:* skdas17@rediffmail.com

Sanjay Hazarika, Managing Trustee, Centre for North East Studies and Policy Research, D6, 6143/3, Vasanth Kunj, New Delhi 110 070, *Email:* sanhaza@yahoo.com

Subir Bhumick, BBC Eastern India Correspondent, 63-C, Ibrahimpur, Kolkata 700 032, *Email:* sbhau@yahoo.com

Udai Bhanu Singh, Research Fellow, Institute for Defence Studies and Analysis, New Delhi 110 067, *Email:* udaibhanusingh@ vsnl.com

Walter Fernandez, Director, North Eastern Social Research Centre, Khaguli Road, Guwahati 781 004, Assam, *Email:* nesrc1@ sancharnet.in

Introduction

—C JOSHUA THOMAS

Stability of a political system and economic development seem to be positively correlated. In an international system of States, especially in the era of globalization, no particular State can realize these twin goals in isolation. All modern nations, therefore use various international and regional fora to strengthen international support and enhance their 'national interest'.

Foreign policy of a country and its adept political and economic diplomacy are the effective instruments to promote its national interests, protect its sovereignty and territorial integrity and enhance its economic development. Modern States view the conduct of foreign relations as a dynamic exercise, which enables them in building national capability in order to respond optimally to new opportunities and challenges in a fast changing world. While the art of conducting foreign relations has far-reaching implications for national development, it is no less important for the development and security of the bordering regions.

It is important to understand as to how India's Northeast, being surrounded by Bangladesh, Bhutan, China and Myanmar is being affected by India's conduct of relations with these countries. The development interest of Northeastern region, as determined by its geo-strategic location, lies in greater interaction with the markets across the international borders. It may be noted that about 33 per cent of the country's total international border falls in NER involving five out of seven countries having border with India. As NER shares 98 percent of its borders with the neighbouring countries and merely two per cent with the mainland India, its cross-border dimensions form an important parameter in its development strategy. Moreover, NER shares substantial common resources with areas across its international borders. The historically developed pattern of production and communications are also oriented towards markets across the border. As a result the utilization of natural resources of NER calls for greater cross-country sub-regional development cooperation.

It is also important to examine the role of the national government in promoting this development interest of NER through its conduct of external relations since Independence. It has already been pointed out that the implications of India's relations with her north and northeastern neighbours for NER are far deeper than any other regions of the country. The prospect of development of NER lies in the strong and mutually beneficial relations between India and her north and northeastern neighbours.

Keeping this background in mind the Indian Council for Social Science Research - North Eastern Regional Centre (ICSSR-NERC) organised a two-day National Seminar on 'Partnership for Development: Holistic Approach to North East' at Gangtok, Sikkim on 8th and 9th May 2002. The main objective of this exercise was to deliberate upon the essence of bilateral relations between India and her northern and northeastern neighbours. A study of the nature of engagements, the substance of bilateral relations, structure of reciprocity, and built-in tensions will be of immense help in articulating the policy direction, which will have implications for the development of the frontier region, i.e. NER.

The seminar had five academic sessions and there were 18 research papers presented by distinguished diplomats, journalists, academics, and social activists. Each session had vibrant discussions. We are indeed pleased to present the revised and modified papers with minor editorial touch under the title, *Engagement and Development: India's Northeast and Neighbouring Countries.* We have organised these papers in this volume and divided them into five sections.

Section I entitled **Northeastern Region and the Regional Organisations**, comprises four papers. Dr. Gurudas Das in his paper, *Security, Engagement and Development: Development Interest of India's Northeast and the Art of Conduct of India's Relations with the Neighbouring Countries*, articulated the idea of "development interest of NER" and then went on to analyse as to how India's conduct of relations with the neighbouring countries has delimited the external perimeter as well as inner content of development of the NER. He emphasised that the geo-economic and geo-strategic location of the region is such that cross-border factors are determinants for development of Northeast region. He further outlines three phases of India's relations with her neighbours covering 1947-1962, 1963-1991 and 1992 onwards. The first phase in which the idea of 'Asianism' as an element of India's foreign policy was compatible with the geo-economic potential of NER, but the same could not be utilised due to Nehru's tribal policy, which did not favour any structural change in the economy of Northeast region. Following the 1962 Sino-Indian conflict, the overriding security concerns had negatively influenced the public sector investment in the NER. The second phase, which included the liberation of Bangladesh in 1971, brought promises to Northeast region particularly because the resource structure of the Northeast matched the demand structure of Bangladesh. In spite of the promises, Das feels, in retrospect, India's diplomacy failed to synergise the development interest of NER and the security interest of the country which had led the Indian State to intervene in favour of the liberation movement in Bangladesh. However, Das indicated that from 1992 onwards, with the onset of globalisation, new strategic partnership among neighbouring countries is being forged. It is important to harmonise these developments with the strategic location of the Northeast region.

In the second paper, *Unfinished Business in Northeast*, B.G. Verghese, mentioned that the Partition of India in 1947 caused extreme geo-political isolation for Northeast, making it emotionally, though not quite physically, South Asia's third land-locked area along with Bhutan and Nepal. The post-Independence period also brought other pulls and pressures into play, which strained the integration of the loosely administered or *excluded* frontier regions. This gave rise to a situation where the people of diverse tribal origins sought to differentiate themselves in order to prevent their identity from being submerged in the vast ocean of Indian humanity. According to him the problem of Northeast can be dealt by first recognising that Northeast is a part of India, which is composed of people from a different racial stock, namely, *Mongoloid India* and culturally part of South East Asia.

This is primarily because this huge land mass somewhat shaped like an elephant's ear is connected to Indian heartland by a 37 km wide Siliguri corridor whereas the external boundary of Northeast runs over 4500 km, contiguous with five countries, viz., Nepal, Bhutan, China, Myanmar and Bangladesh.

He highlighted the necessity of making a distinction between Boundary and Border. He says the words border or frontier and boundary represent very different concepts. While *boundary* would simply refers to the line demarcating the external political jurisdiction of a State, a border or frontier refers to transitional zones or bands of territory that lie on either side of the boundary. Border people share ties of culture and commerce and most often exhibit commonalities of race, people, language, religion, etc. Although India, like any other nation, must be concerned with the determination and inviolability of its sovereign boundaries, however, in its preoccupation with boundary fixation and related issues of border management, the government appears to have lost sight of the importance of developing an appropriate border policy.

Verghese says, the government's indifference towards bilateralism and intellectual failure to differentiate between boundary and border has alienated the Northeast region further, despite positive geo-political changes in the neighbourhood. It is not that nothing happened across or around Northeast borders, but instead of regional cooperation that should have fostered connectivity, trade facilitation and people to people exchange, these borderland witness insurgency, smuggling of drugs narcotics and spreading of HIV/ AIDS, and trafficking in women and illicit immigration.

He thus stressed the need for a more holistic approach to device development strategies that are sustainable and socially just, taking into consideration their unique, livelihood and value system.

Sujata Miri, in her paper, *The Paradox of Development,* examined the concept of development, which she feels is popularly equated with economic development. In her opinion, there is a growing realization in the Northeast that radical economic changes cannot be contemplated without corresponding cultural and political reorientation. Thus, according to her, what is needed is not mere economic development but a cultural and political transformation of the society duly assisted by modern technology. Northeast being home to various great cultures with a history of mutual interaction and exchange makes this difficult as a vitality of these cultures lead many to think that they can appropriate the powerful forces of modern economy while retaining their cultural and social specificity.

This monster of cultural identity often threatens the formation of national identity and mass communication has succeeded in generalising a form of collective identity to some extent. This national identity is seen as a necessary component for the process of modernisation. Although Northeast has been carved out on the Indian side with similar guideline in mind, we have not exactly achieved a level of solidarity between different cultural identities dashing our hopes for acquiring what is called modern development. She finally concludes by saying that the forces of change that impel us are also liable to uproot us and can also provide us with resources which can create for us the collusion that this uprooting is not uprooting at all, that now our roots have only found new sources of energy.

The last paper in this section is on *Shortages, Ethnic Conflicts and Economic Development in NE India*. In this paper, Walter Fernandes felt that lack of any sustainable development has increased the sense of alienation in this region, which has then led to political upheaval and insurgency. He writes that although this region experiences political upheaval, we often forget the reasons behind it - the main reason being the imposition of control that people outside the region exercise over its economy and the effort to impose a single culture on its people, which threatens both their livelihood and identity. Moreover being highly educated and identity conscious, the population find itself more and more being used as a source of raw material extraction for development rather than being equal partners in the national development process.

Thus according to Walter, power plants and multi-purpose projects for the Northeast are set up for power supply to the rest of the country, whereas people in the region face displacement and dispossession. He further argues against the concept of development more popularly adopted in the Northeast, that is, infrastructure development without any sustainable rehabilitation plan. We need to understand that *land* is very closely linked to their traditional identity, and any development effort, which lacks respect for local culture by alienating them from their land, is bound to fail. He suggested that development models in the Northeast should make an effort to convert *land* into a production resource, and communities into cooperatives. Therefore he concluded that only an economic approach is not enough; what is required is a combination of economic and social investments.

In the second section on **Indo-China and Bhutan Relations - Implications for Northeastern Region**, there are three papers. In the first paper, *India's China Policy: Implications for the Security and Development of the Northeast Region,* C.V. Ranganathan, former Ambassador to China and France apprises the group of Sino-Indian relations from the late 1950s to 1976 under the Mao Tse Tung regime where Sino-Indian relations at that time were misperceived. The boundary conflict has been widely documented. Both sides gradually adopted provocative posturing until 1962 when the trauma was witnessed. He describes the present situation to be a *status quo* since both sides have a matured relation and they are engaged in a mutual understanding of each other's position. This has promoted a situation of a non-violent nature. Even though until recently, China has not recognised the merger of Sikkim with India, the positive aspect is that, administratively, there is no hindrance from China. It is possible to foresee that there is no conventional security threat to India from China. While the Chinese support to Pakistan is a negative feature, bilateral relations are leverage on the issue.

He emphasises certain aspects noteworthy in the context of China. China has successfully pursued external forces to promote development and this development has been used to promote its position in international relations. There is a synergising of both external forces and domestic forces for the purpose of establishing a conducive neighbourhood. Another notable feature is of China's evolving attitude to the ASEAN. China has accorded recognition to every member of the ASEAN, and the latter has enmeshed China in such a network that it cannot provide military support to dissident movements very easily. There is enough evidence to prove that China does not support dissident movements in the Northeast region. China has built land-border connectivity with its borders, thereby using geography to its advantage. Through the Western Regional Development Programme (WRDP), it has concentrated development of specific regions in the country. The question is how we can leverage the Chinese developments to benefit the Northeast region. It is possible, Ranganathan concludes, by enlisting methods of using Sino-Indian relations advantageously – peaceful resolution of territorial disputes, confidence building, intensification of exchanges, cooperation on international forums etc.

A C Sinha, in his paper, *Ethnic Engagement in Bhutan and its Regional Consequences*, covers the ethnic background, the land tenure and feudal social structure of the region. The focus of Sinha's paper is on the ethnic conflict in Bhutan and how to tackle the problem. He identifies three circles of the Bhutanese foreign policy – the Indian circle, the regional circle and the multilateral circle. He observed that the Indian silence on the ethnic conflict in Bhutan is too eloquent to be ignored.

P.S. Ghosh, the author of the last paper in this section, *Bhutan and India: Partners in Progress,* highlighted the fact that Bhutan represents a good example of how Indo-Bhutan relations can do well for the Northeast. Ghosh said that India plays a significant role in the economic development of Bhutan, such as funding its two Five-Year Plans in the sixties. Other major endeavours in this direction involve the setting up of Penden Cement Project and the Chukha Hydroelectric Project in Bhutan. India provided 60 per cent of the grant for Bhutan major hydroelectric project. Bhutan now not only meets its domestic needs, but also export both cement and power to India.

Ghosh further stated that India has also played a vital role in assisting the foreign trade of Bhutan. He pointed out that Bhutan, in the second half of the seventies began trade with other Third World Countries and India provided transit facilities. Indo-Bhutan trade was further renewed in 1990, and in 1995. The result was that Bhutan's economy registered a commendable growth rate of 6.7 per cent. Besides primary products like coal and dolomite, secondary products were also on the export list.

The third section of this volume focuses on **Indo-Bangladesh Relations - Implications for the Northeastern Region.** There are five contributors. Sanjay Hazarika in his paper, *Bangladesh and the Northeast: Facing Migration, Ending Rhetoric, Embracing a Realistic Strategy for Change,* examines the issue of migration and its impact on the neighbouring Northeastern region, especially from Bangladesh. The speaker drew the attention of the participants to the substantial growth in the Muslim population of Assam through the process of migration. At the same time the growth of the Hindu population in Bangladesh is on the decline. Migration, he reiterates, is a *survival strategy* for the Bangladeshis, but the use of law to solve the migration problems, as is the present practice in India, has not worked. He further points out a realistic workable strategy for change and progress in Assam-Bangladesh relations. Marketing vegetable produce, processed food minerals and providing scope for tourism were some of these strategies. Hazarika also suggested setting up of a National Immigration Commission to take a detailed look at the laws that exist on the issue of immigration. The issue of identity cards to Indian Nationals should be mandatory, he further stressed.

Samir Kumar Das, in his paper, *Ethnicity and Security in Assam: A Plea for Greater Indo-Bangladesh Partnership,* highlights the fact that India and Bangladesh share many a commonality in its culture and language, but these commonalities turn out to be a symbolic threat to the nationhood of both these countries. He grounded his argument on the old English proverb that "familiarity breeds contempt". Das, briefly dealt with two relatively different yet interconnected parts. The first part drew attention to two major threats born out of the commonalities, i.e., immigration and insurgency. The second part shows that bilateralism may not be the panacea for solving the problems of insurgency faced by the two neighbours. It also outlines the framework of a future partnership regime as a step towards resolving these problems and threats.

While elaborating on issues of immigration, Das points out certain alarming trends. Firstly, that immigration is not haphazard and sporadic; in fact, it is very organised. The role of early settlers coming from the same village or district of Bangladesh is important in getting the latecomers settled and economically rehabilitated. In fact, immigration is so organised and planned that it defies any easy detection resulting into an official fall in immigration figures. Secondly, immigrants seem to flock in areas where their brethren are already in substantial number. Thirdly, these immigrant pockets seem to turn fast into hotbeds of fundamentalism and insurgency, because the newly ascended Islamic fundamentalism has acquired an organised and militancy character.

In the paper, *Partnership in Indo-Bangladesh Economic Development: The Case of Jaintia Hills in Meghalaya*, L.S. Gassah traces the trade and commerce activities between the peoples of Jaintia Hills in Meghalaya and Bangladesh. He also pointed out the pre-independence and post-independence trade and economies of both the countries from a historical point of view. He further discussed the border trade agreement between the two countries and argues that what is urgently needed today is the perception on partnership for the overall development of the economy of the areas along the Indo-Bangladesh border.

A.N.S Ahmed, in his paper, *Indo-Bangladesh Relations and its Implication for Northeast India* stresses on the long historical relations shared by India's Northeastern region and eastern Bengal, now Bangladesh. With the end of the Cold War and changing regional and international scenarios, the past experience of regional cooperation between Northeast and Bangladesh has provided clue for a futuristic paradigm for cooperation on a number of issues. Ahmed believes the major problems, such migration, which hampers regional cooperation, can be tackled by active security patrolling and border fencing. However, the issues like minority problems, harbouring rebels from Northeast and cross-border militant activities, remain contentious and require greater political consensus and will to address them.

He hoped that in spite of these unresolved issues, India and Bangladesh could work together on issues of mutual benefits, such as, environmental protection and bilateral trade. In fact, he believes, the bilateral trade between the two neighboures could transform the economy of the entire region. Ahmed emphasised on the need for the promotion of SAPTA as a long-term solution to the entire issue of trade relations.

The last paper in this section by Bimal Pramanik entitled, *Plight of Minorities in Bangladesh with Special Reference to Their Exodus to Northeast India and the Related Issues* highlights the pitiable conditions of the minority communities, which are subjected to unmitigated terror and torture quite frequently in Bangladesh. He expressed concern over the gradual Islamisation of Bangladesh politics, which is fanning the virus of communalism and anti-Hindu sentiments. He cited extensive statistical accounts to show the increasing trend of Hindu migration to India. He also advocated that a national immigration authority should be set up to look into the migration issues. It is mandatory to define and distinguish between a refugee and an illegal migrant and also there is a need to make a distinction between old and new migrants, which in many cases have led to conflict situations.

The fourth section dwells on **Indo-Myanmar Relations - Implications for Northeastern Region** and consisted of three papers. Subir Bhaumik in his presentation on *Burma*

Policy and its Impact on its Northeastern Region, analysed the impact of Indo-Burmese policy on the Northeast and highlighted India's primary concern for Northeast and how the *China* factor actually led to the formulation of Indo-Burma Policy. Apart from the *China* factor, India's interest in Burma has much to do with the security of her own sensitive Northeastern region, her desire to access markets in South East Asia including Burma, her concern to stop the inflow of drugs and weapons from Burma's turbulent frontier region, and to ensure the safety and security of the people of Indian origin who continue to live in Burma.

Bhaumik examined how each of these concerns has influenced India's Burma Policy since 1950s and sought to assess the impact of that policy on India's Northeast. He traced out the entire process of military cooperation between India and Burma's military regime from as far back as 1960s, which suffered a setback only when India grew suspicious of Burma's growing relation with China from early 1980s. Although when the student uprising started in 1986-87, India's support to the pro-democracy movement became evident in the shelter India provided to hundreds of Burmese students who fled the country. However, by late 1990s, again India and Burma had reviewed the military alliance in order to tackle cross-border terrorism and drug trafficking.

Bhaumik argued that the thaw in the Indo-Burmese relations would have three-fold impact. Firstly, growing Indo-Burmese military cooperation could effectively deny the rebel groups to one of the longest and safest base areas. Secondly, better bilateral economic ties between the two countries could provide the necessary boost to industrialisation of Northeast India. Thirdly, growth of bilateral trade could improve local economies of the adjoining region. However he agrees that all this will happen only at the cost of India's support for Burma's pro-democracy movement.

Konsom Ibo Singh, in his paper entitled *Indo-Myanmar Relations since 1988: Its Implications on India's Northeast* observes that although initially, India supported the pro-democracy movement of Burma spearheaded by its students, it remained silent when the western democracies and Japan condemned the State Law & Order Restoration Council (SLORC) for its undemocratic and repressive measures; India did not join them. He said since 1991, India's policy towards Myanmar has been guided by two imperatives: Firstly, that Myanmar should not form an exclusive area of influence of other great powers and secondly, Myanmar being geo-strategically important to India as it borders China and Bangladesh, Singh feels that, Indo-Myanmar cooperation is necessary to counter drug trafficking, insurgency and insecurity of the Northeast.

Uday Bhanu Singh in his paper entitled *Geo-Economic and Geo-Strategic Importance of Myanmar in India's 'Look East Policy'* highlighted that India's Look East policy made an effort to strengthen India's relations with South East Asia in early 1990s and the evolving relationship with Myanmar has been an integral part of that process. He emphasises not just on the historico-cultural component of this relationship but also on the more pragmatic economic and strategic considerations, which could form the basis for a reliable partnership. He pointed out that India's look east policy coincided with its economic liberalisation program and Myanmar's endeavour to assimilate with the international community. His suggestions are: firstly, greater Indian participation in investment and financial sectors in Myanmar and secondly, opening up of land routes through the Northeast, would provide an alternative to the sea route to reach out to the larger South East Asian region.

In section five on **'Look East Policy', Security Aspects - Implications for Northeastern Region** three papers were presented. P D Shenoy in his paper on the *Importance of Northeastern Region in India's Look East Policy* discussed on the development scenario in the northeast, the various initiatives taken by the Government of India to accelerate development in the northeast; to contain militancy in the northeast and strengthen India's ties with the SAARC nations. In another paper on *India's Eastern Neighbours and Insurgency, Small and Heavy Arms Proliferation and Narcotics in Northeast India*, Sajal Nag describes the Northeastern region as one of South Asia's most disturbed regions due to the prevailing insurgency all over the region and the massive influx of small arms and narcotics in northeast India. He also identified the routes by which drugs and small arms are smuggled into the region and also the linkages between small arms, narcotics and insurgent groups. In the last paper on *Some Geo-Political Aspects Concerning Internal Security in Northeastern India*, R Gopalakrishan stated that insurgencies, militancy, terrorism, etc. are all symptoms of socio-economic crisis and political uncertainty and he explains the present day conflicts and the internal security problem in the northeast India. Gopalakrishan asks why despite the various development programmes in the Northeast, insurgency continues and even spread further to other parts of the region. Is this due to the location and numerous neighbours that the region has? Or is due to the political, social and economic predicaments, which the region has found itself into? Or is it a geopolitical heritage? These aspects need to be enquired into for an understanding of the region, which is in a state of revolt.

The papers presented in this volume were read in 2002 and now it's 2006. Four long years has passed and during these four years there are three major changes that took place in the Northeast: *one*, China has recognised Sikkim as part of India; *two*, Northeastern Council has Sikkim as the eighth member, and *three*, NEC has undergone a thorough structural changes. These aspects of course we could not include in this volume, however, we would like to take up the same, perhaps, in our next volume on ***India-China Border Trade: A Strategy for Frontier Development.***

In conclusion, it is clear from the presentations collected together in this volume, *Engagement and Development: India's Northeast and Neighbouring Countries*, earnestly attempts to deepen the understanding of the issues that the region is faced with and calls for accelerating the engagement process with the Governments of the neighbouring countries and opening of the borders for trade and people to people contact, which will be beneficial both for India's Northeastern region and its neighbouring countries.

SECTION I

NORTHEASTERN REGION AND THE REGIONAL ORGANISATIONS

1

Security, Engagement and Development: Development Interest of India's Northeast and the Art of Conduct of India's Relations with the Neighbouring Countries

—GURUDAS DAS

Foreign policy of a country intends to promote its national interest, protect its sovereignty and territorial integrity, and ensure security. Modern states view the conduct of foreign relations as a dynamic exercise that enables them in building national capability in order to respond optimally to new opportunities and challenges in a fast changing world. While the art of conducting foreign relations has far-reaching implications for national development, it is no less important for the development and security of the bordering regions.

I am grateful to Omeo Kumar Das Institute of Social Change and Development (OKDISCD) for offering me a position of Visiting Faculty for the year (2000-2001), during which the idea expressed in this paper was developed and material used here were collected. I am also grateful to Amlendu Guha, A.C. Bhagabati, Atul Goswami and A.N.S. Ahmed for commenting on it while presented this idea in the form of a talk at OKDISCD in July 2001.

Although it is of utmost interest to study as to how India's relations with her immediate neighbours affected her pace of development in past 58 years, we do not propose to undertake this ambitious task here. Our objective is far narrower.

We, rather, intend to focus on the implications of India's security concerns in the eastern border for the development of the bordering Northeastern Region (NER). That is, as to how the development prospect of NER has been affected due to security concern arising out of hostile relations between India and neighbouring Pakistan and China. How India's conduct of foreign policy in relation to her neighbours delimited the external perimeters of development for NER. Being surrounded by Bangladesh, Bhutan, China and Myanmar, it is only natural that unlike any other regions, NER will be directly affected by India's conduct of relations with these countries. A state-centric traditional security perception tends to consider the bordering regions as vulnerable to external threats. This perception, in turn, informs the other state-led development actions in the bordering areas. Thus, the conduct of India's foreign policy not only sets the outer perimeter of development for NER, it also largely determines the inner content of development.

The development interest of NER, as determined by its geo-strategic location, lies in greater interaction with the markets across the international borders. The length of the land border between NER and the neighbouring countries is shown in Table 1.

Table 1

Detail of the length of the land border between the Northeastern States and the neighbouring countries

(In km)

1. NER-Myanmar	1,643
2. NER-China	1,000
3. NER-Bhutan	650
4. NER-Bangladesh	1,956
Total	**5,249**

Source: Das & Purkayastha, 2000. Note: Lengths are not precise. Annual Report, 1999-2000, MOD, Government of India.

It may be noted that about 33 percent of country's total international border falls in NER involving five out of seven countries having border with India. As NER shares 98 per cent of her border with the neighbouring countries and merely two per cent with mainland India, cross-border exchange forms an important parameter in its development strategy. Moreover, NER shares substantial common resources with areas across the border. And the historically developed pattern of production and communications are also oriented towards markets across the border. As a result, the utilization of natural resources of NER calls for greater cross-country sub-regional development cooperation.

It is our utmost interest to examine the role of the Indian State in promoting this development interest of NER through her conduct of external relations since Independence. It has already been pointed out that the implications of India's relations with neighbouring China, Bangladesh, and Myanmar for NER are far deeper than any other regions of the country. As the region is surrounded by these countries, and inhabited by the social groups having affinities with their counterparts across the borders, and being isolated from the "mainland of India", having traditional markets across the border, non-cooperation from the neighbouring countries would put the region in a suffocating situation without any hope for it to grow and develop. Thus, the interest of the region and its long-term security lie in strong and mutually beneficial relationship between India and her eastern neighbours. Although, the same also holds good for the national interest, but for NER it is a precondition for her survival. It is from this point of view we shall look at India's conduct of foreign policy in relation to her neighbours.

As the conduct of foreign relations is a dynamic process and keeps on changing in commensurate with the global change, it may be of some conceptual value to divide the temporal space of India's relations with her neighbours into three broad phases. *Phase-I* starts from independence and extends up to 1962, the year in which Sino-Indian border conflict took place. This border conflict not only brought a change in India's foreign policy, but also a significant policy-shift towards NER having far-reaching effects on its future evolution. *Phase-II* covers the entire time-span starting from 1963 to the end of the cold war in 1991, the year in which erstwhile USSR had collapsed. This phase is characterized by two Indo-Pak wars of 1965 and 1971. The emergence of Bangladesh as an independent country in 1971 has significant bearing on the security and development of NER. *Phase-III* covers the period since 1992 characterized by onset of globalization paradigm where India is increasingly seeking forward engagement with her neighbours.

Phase-I (1947-1962): From Asian Solidarity to Hostility

The concept of "Asiatic-Federation" and the notion of "Asianism," as mooted by Indian National Congress even prior to Independence (Bandopadhyaya, 1991: 80-81) as part of its anti-colonial struggle, and later articulated and operationalized by Jawaharlal Nehru, as the first Prime Minister of India, was fully compatible with security and development concern of India in general and NER in particular. The idea emphasized the need for close cooperation among the post-colonial Asian societies, having common experience of colonial exploitation and suffering, for their future progress. But this perspective of 'Asianism' was destined to crumble with the sharpening of competitive and overlapping interests between India vs Pakistan and China in South Asian region. India, interspersed between West and East Pakistan, has always been perceived as the principal threat to the territorial integrity and national security of Pakistan. In fact, Partition of the country on the basis of the religion, and formation of Pakistan without any territorial contiguity has instilled in it an in-built threat perception from India. However, in 1948, on Kashmir issue, the two neighbours took arms against each other, fell apart, and became archrivals, which rendered the first blow to the "Asian Solidarity" movement.

Nehru tried to advance this movement by befriending China and sidelining Pakistan. The Treaty of 1954 between India and China, and the Bandung Conference of Afro-Asian countries held in 1955, in which Nehru and Chou-En-Lai played the leading roles, seemed to have restored the credibility of the movement to some extent. But the overlapping interest of both India and China in the Himalayas and their competitive claims for regional power had brought Sino-Indian honeymoon to an abrupt end. The Chinese occupation of Tibet in 1950 made India alert of her northern security. It also panicked the Himalayan kingdoms of Nepal, Bhutan and Sikkim. These Himalayan states had been a part of British India's defense system as the buffer states between India *vis-a-vis* China and Russia. In relation to these kingdoms, British India adopted a forward policy whereby they enjoyed internal autonomy but their external relations were directed by British interest (Lamb, 1960:260). Independent India adopted the same policy for Bhutan and Sikkim. The Treaty of Peace and Friendship signed between India and Bhutan in 1949 and Indo-Sikkim Treaty of 1950 were a mere continuation of the British legacy. In order to restrict the Chinese advance beyond Tibet, both India and Nepal entered into a Treaty in 1950. As part of her forward policy in the Himalayas, India, throughout the Fifties, pushed her administration to catch up the McMohan Line in the north. Like India, China also had security interest in the Himalayan Kingdoms. In fact, China viewed Tibet to be her palm and Nepal, Bhutan, Sikkim, Ladakh and NEFA as its five fingers (Thapliyal, 1999: 193). This conflicting interest in Himalayas appeared to have led to the Sino-Indian border conflict in 1962. India was taken aback by the sudden Chinese attack, and, in absence of any defense preparedness, had to swallow a humiliating defeat. The story is well known and we do not intend to repeat it here. What is important for us is the significance of 1962 border conflict for India in general and NER in particular.

Firstly, there had been divergence of views among the Indian policy makers on the possible security threat to our northern and northeastern borders. Sarder Patel, the first Union Home Minister warned Nehru against the security threat arising out of Chinese annexation of Tibet and urged to review our border policy and security and favoured speedy development of communication/transportation infrastructure. But Nehru's idealist assessment of Indo-China relations and his conviction to settle scores with China through dialogue led him to underestimate the threat perception. This underestimated security perception coupled with Nehru's policy towards tribal development (Das, 1995: 78-82) had a significant bearing on the slow pace of development in NER during Nehru's regime (1947-64).

Secondly, the 1962 border conflict put the last nail in the coffin of the Asian Solidarity movement. 'Asianism' as an element of India's foreign policy had built in promises for the land-locked and isolated NER. With the unfolding of future, NER could have been more focused to the market networks of neighbouring countries, which would have helped in breaking her isolation. The potential the region derives from her geo-strategic location to act as the gateway not only to South-East Asia but also to Central Asia, remained unexplored.

Thirdly, Government of India's handling of the 1962 crisis and its failure to protect the lives and properties of people had generated tremendous psychological shocks in the minds of the people of the region. India's role in protecting the interest of the region was viewed as inadequate. This deeper feeling of being dumped at the moment of crisis helped anti-India forces within and strengthened their position in disengaging people from Indian state.

Fourthly, India's defeat in 1962 had largely tarnished its image in South Asia and her small neighbours started drifting towards China in their bid either to assert against her or to gain more by siding with the more powerful rival. This had made it difficult for India to immediately advance her interest through the improvement of bilateral relations after the collapse of Asiatic perspective.

Fifthly, in order to fill the 'population vacuum' near Sino-Indian border in Arunachal Pradesh, a massive resettlement program was launched after 1962. A sizeable section of East Pakistan Chakma refugees were rehabilitated in Khagam, Miao, M'pen, Kharsang and Chowkham areas of northeastern Arunachal Pradesh in subsequent years (Das, 1995: 83). This has created the breeding ground for the festering Chakma-Arunachalee conflict.

Sixthly, India's defeat in 1962 encouraged Pakistan to seek a military solution to Kashmir problem. After Nehru-

Liaqat Ali pact of 1950, Pakistan had improved its security position significantly by signing Mutual Defense Assistance Agreement in 1954 with the United States and joining the SEATO (1954) and CENTO (1955). With the establishment of USA-Pakistan-China axis following the 1962 Indo-China border conflict, Pakistan's attempt to forcibly occupy Kashmir had led to Indo-Pak war of 1965. The implications of this war for the security and development of NER were obvious. With growing Indo-Pak animosity, not only the NER's traditional market in East Pakistan remained inaccessible, the political space therein had also been freely used to destabilize the region. Both the Naga and Mizo rebellions that started during 1950s and 1960s respectively were nurtured, sheltered and nourished by Pakistan through its eastern wing. The internal insecurity of the region grew tremendously with China's backing the Naga and Manipuri insurgents. Sandwiched between China and East Pakistan, not only the external security threat to NER had increased manifold, its internal insecurity also became a prime concern. This fast deteriorating security environment had a negative bearing on the development prospect of the region.

Phase-II (1963-1991): Replication of Cold War in South Asia

Beset in a cold war paradigm and besieged by Pakistan-China-USA axis, India had limited diplomatic options to address her security threats. India took a pro-USSR position to thwart any future threat to her security arising out of her rivals and adopted an "inward looking" strategy for national development. It may be noted as a digression that the mixed economy model characterized by public sector dominance in basic industries and infrastructure and private participation in consumer goods and services reveals the state's concern for speedy national development. The realization that "without development there can be no security" loomed large in the minds of the policy makers. What is important to us is to note that the use of scarce resources was strictly guided by the criteria of its maximum spread effects and inter-sectoral growth impulses. The fact that any major investment in NER, due to her geographical location, would result into less spread effects compared to other regions in the mainland, did not merit any large-scale public sector investment in the region. As a result, the state-sponsored development had largely bypassed the region.

Be that as it may, the outbreak of liberation movement in East Pakistan (1971) provided India with an opportunity to break her "cordoned off" security environment. Throwing the garb of "non-alignment", India entered into a treaty with USSR (1971), used bipolar world contradictions in her favour, intervened in favour of liberation movement in East Pakistan, and played a decisive role in bringing Bangladesh as an independent nation. This event has far-reaching implications for India's security concern in general and security and development of the NER in particular.

Firstly, India relieved off permanently from Pakistani threat to her security in the eastern border. A friendly Bangladesh would also improve internal insecurity conditions in the NER by debarring insurgents to use Bangladesh territory against India.

Secondly, a scope has emerged to re-establish NER's traditional markets and communication networks which had been snapped due to partition. As Bangladesh needed corridors through Indian land to ease out movement of goods and people from one part to another interspersed by Indian territory, India's land-locked Northeast also needed corridor through Bangladesh. There exist mutually beneficial grounds for cooperation in this regard.

Thirdly, Bangladesh economy after long years of colonial exploitation, followed by 24 years of internal colonial exploitation by Pakistan, and then ravaged by the liberation war, was in a bad shape. It was only natural for Bangladesh to look up to India for necessary financial and technological help creating a space for Indian industries and trade in Bangladesh economy. Since the resource structure between Bangladesh and the Northeastern region is of complementary in nature, it was expected that the NER's resource-oriented products would find a vent in Bangladesh leading to a close cooperation particularly between eastern region of Bangladesh and NER.

Fourthly, there arose a hope that the issue of immigration and influx from erstwhile East Pakistan into ethno-sensitive Northeast would be amicably resolved. The north-eastern societies would get away with the burden of war-refugees.

Fifthly, the victory against Pakistan in 1971 would improve India's image in South Asia, which she lost in 1962, to a large extent, and would enable her to advance the national interest in the neighbouring countries through bilateral channels.

Sixthly, with improved external security environment in the north-eastern border, India would be in a better position to address the internal insecurity dimension in NER arising out of ethnic insurgencies, inter-ethnic schisms and underdevelopment.

With the emergence of Bangladesh, India's threat perception in her Northeastern border and her national interest in Bangladesh in terms of trade in general and NER's trading interest in particular had improved to some extent. But this Indo-Bangladesh honeymoon was short lived. Bangladesh followed a pro-Indian foreign policy during 1971-75 period, followed by anti-India position during 1976-1988, and then a strategy of cooperation since 1989. As the image of dominating India was always permeating the consciousness of Bangladesh, the shifts and swings in Indo-Bangla relations might well be explained as Bangladesh's efforts to come out of the Indian influence. Bangladesh's perception of her security threat from India increased significantly following the incorporation of Sikkim into Indian Union in 1975. The interfering attitude of Indian state in internal matters of her small neighbours, the socio-political compulsions at home arising out of Hindu-Muslim relations in South Asia, and the cold war paradigm that had been replicated in South Asia, following Indo-Chinese conflict in 1962 and Indo-Pak war in 1965 - all had a strong bearing behind the drift of Bangladesh towards China-USA axis in the post-Mujib era.

So far the interest of NER is concerned, opening up of overland trade, although in a very limited way, gave some respite. Mineral products and forest products from Meghalaya, Mizoram and Tripura found ready markets in Bangladesh - which otherwise would have not been cost-effective. However, the potential of border trade between NER and Bangladesh largely remained untapped primarily because of inadequate engagement of both the governments in this regard. As Bangladesh was facing escalating deficit trade balance with India, and seeking its redressal through higher imports (by India), she (Bangladesh) as a result was not much encouraged to utilize the border trade potential in full, which would only further complicate her balance of payment situation. As "border trade" is a strategic-parameter having a great significance for the development of Northeastern economy, Indian government could have accommodated it in a far better way by adjusting its overall bilateral trade interest with Bangladesh. Either the growth generating significance of border trade was underrated, or the economic diplomacy in this case was not informed by geo-political wisdom of the Indian state.

However, the issue of NER's access to her traditional communication channels through Bangladesh, e.g., Tripura's access to Calcutta through Bangladesh, did not materialize. Moreover, the threat of infiltration across the border loomed large throughout with growing political uncertainty in Bangladesh characterized by frequent flood, poverty, over population and utter underdevelopment. Besides this identity threat to indigenous societies, real or perceived, the use of insurgent groups by Bangladesh for bargaining other wider issues with India, particularly during strain bilateral relations, remained as a built-in threat to the internal insecurity of the NER.

While India's relations with Bangladesh has a direct bearing on the security and development interest of the Northeastern States of Tripura, Meghalaya and Assam, the Indo-Myanmar relations has similar implications for Manipur, Nagaland, Mizoram and also partly for Arunachal Pradesh.

India's security interest in Myanmar is evident from her geo-strategic location. Myanmar shares an equally significant border with both India and China. The northern frontiers of Myanmar constitute a tri-junction with Bangladesh, China and the eastern frontiers of India. Myanmar is also an important country lying on the rim of the Bay of Bengal. The southeastern coast of Myanmar is close to the Nicobar and Andaman islands. Moreover, Myanmar is also the corridor through which India can reach out to "extended neighbourhood" regions of South-East Asia. Hence, the presence of any hostile power in Myanmar is viewed inimical to Indian interest. As far as the interest of NER is concerned, people living in the States of Manipur, Nagaland, Mizoram and Arunachal Pradesh besides having ethno-cultural affinities with the people across the border, had developed traditional trading relations. Their access to markets across the border is much easier than the markets even in Assam plains. As a result, sharing of resources and communication channels including traditional trade routes across the border is an essential precondition for their future development. Moreover, because of commonality in ethnic origin and historically developed cultural ties between the people across the NER-Myanmar border, the possibility of spilling over of social discontents across the international boundary has made the internal security of NER vulnerable.

Thus India's Myanmar policy has direct bearing for the security and development of NER. India's Myanmar policy is largely informed by her threat perception from China. The threat of communism from China brought India and Myanmar closer to each other during the 50s and 60s. In order to accommodate the interest of Myanmar, Nehru had even gone to the extent of giving up the Indian claim on Kabow Valley, with which sentiments of people of Manipur were strongly associated. The 1951 Treaty of Peace and Friendship institutionalized the bilateral relations. Several Treaties followed thereafter in order to strengthen mutual economic, technical, and cultural ties. But with the realization of Myanmar that instead of pro-Indian position, its security interest will be better served in adopting a neutral policy between India and China, and with the signing of Treaty with China in 1960, Indo-Myanmar relations started losing its warmth. During 1962 Sino-India conflict, Myanmar took a neutral position and subsequently tilted towards China.

In post-1962 period, until the breakdown of the cold war paradigm, India's Myanmar policy was largely informed by her antagonistic relations with China. While China was increasingly engaging herself in constructive cooperation with Myanmar in terms of building roads and other infrastructure, and thereby strengthening her economic and security interest in Myanmar, India maintained studied silence. Increasing supply of the Chinese arms and ammunitions into Myanmar, alleged access of the Chinese naval force to Myanmar ports, the Chinese assistance to Naga and Manipuri insurgents, use of Myanmar territory by the insurgents as bases for conducting subversive activities against India—all added to India's anxiety without any adequate response. Thus, India's disengagement in Myanmar and its failure to evolve any counter strategy not only harmed the Indian business interest in Myanmar, this has alarmingly escalated the internal insecurity in NER and blocked its prospect of development. However, the situation started improving since early 90s to which we shall come back later. Although the Asian Solidarity Movement died a premature death in 1962, the geo-economic compulsions for such regional cooperation became stronger with the unfolding of time leading to the launching of South Asian Association for Regional Cooperation (SAARC) in 1985 with Bangladesh, Bhutan, India, Maldives, Nepal, Pakistan and Sri Lanka as its members. Pregnant with tremendous scopes for the development of the South Asian region, SAARC has a special promise for enhancing development interest of the NER.

Firstly, the programme of trade liberalization among SAARC members brightens up the possibility of utilization of full potential of "border trade" between NER and Bangladesh.

Secondly, with the growth of cooperation among the member countries, it might have been possible to link up Indian communication system, i.e., roadways, railways and waterways, to that of Bangladesh, which could have broken the geographic isolation of north-east to a large extent providing the necessary vent for the products of NER in Bangladesh markets.

Thirdly, the idea of sub-regional development and the concept of growth zones mooted in SAARC Expert Group report have tremendous implications for the development of NER. The Expert Group has identified three sub-regions, north-eastern sub region, consisting of parts of Nepal, Bhutan, India and Bangladesh, the southern region consisting of a part of India, Maldives and Sri Lanka, and the north western region consisting of India and Pakistan, for initiating sub-regional development programmers (SAARC Survey 1998-99:72). The NER is covered in SARRC's first growth zone area, i.e., Northeastern sub-region. Since the basic idea of development cooperation at the sub-regional level is to put development in the sub-region on a faster track, SAARC's zonal growth approach has the potential to address the development interest of the NER.

Fourthly, once the sub-regional cooperation takes off in the SAARC's north-eastern sub-region, it is possible to gradually supplement the mainland of India as the principal source of manufactured exports to NER through various joint ventures particularly between NER, Bangladesh and Bhutan. This will lead to the increasing utilization of NER's natural resources on the one hand, and equally enable Bangladesh and Bhutan to improve their trade balance vis-a-vis India (Thapa 1999: 175) on the other.

Fifthly, the proposal for the creation of an Asian Energy Grid mooted at the Trilateral Business Summit in Dhaka in 1998 by the Prime Ministers of Bangladesh, India and Pakistan has a great relevance for the development of NER. In spite of having the highest potential for generating hydro-electric power in the country, which has been estimated at 31857 MW out of 84044 MW available for the country as a whole, i.e., 38 per cent of total, only about one per cent had so far been utilized (CEA, 1997) in NER. With Asian Energy Grid in operation, demand would not pose any further barrier in utilizing this huge untapped power potential. The revolutionizing role of power in economic development of the region hardly needs any clarification.

However, the promise embedded in SAARC for NER does not appear to turn into reality in foreseeable future. Bilateral relations among the member countries, time and again, over shadowed the collective interest of the group. SAARC deliberations were disrupted in 1985 and 1990, because of tensions between India and Sri Lanka on the Tamil ethnic problem, again during disputes between Nepal and Bhutan on the question of the Nepalese whose citizenship rights in Bhutan were questioned by the Bhutanese government, again following the destruction of the Babri mosque in 1992 and the resultant agitations in Bangladesh and Pakistan against India and now the military coup in Pakistan in 1999 led to India's reluctance to participate in SAARC meetings in which the military regime of Pakistan is also a member (Dixit: 2001).

In its 16 year lifespan, the only worthwhile achievement of SAARC in the realm of economic cooperation has been the creation of Preferential Trading Arrangement among its members (SAPTA). If the gains from trade liberalization were any indication, this regional grouping had generated much frustration than hopes. The share of intra-SAARC exports in total SAARC exports has risen from 3.16 per cent in 1990 to 4.25 per cent in 1996. And the share of intra-SAARC imports has increased from 1.91 per cent to 4.06 per cent during the same period (SAARC Survey, 1998-99: 51). Achievements are, no doubt, abysmal. Needless to say that unless the two big powers, India and Pakistan, who play the dominant role in SAARC affairs, shrug off their myopic state-centric positions in favour of regional cooperation, it is hard for SAARC to take off. This realization, perhaps, has led the member countries to look beyond SAARC for partnership in their development strides. India's engagement in other alternative regional development forums and her adoption of "look east" policy, which will be taken up next, become more meaningful while viewed from this perspective.

Phase-III (1992 onwards): Globalization and the Era of Forward Engagement

With the collapse of Soviet Union in 1991, the cold-war paradigm came to an end. Bi-polar world became unipolar with United States of America at the helm of global affairs. The launching of the globalization programme by the USA and its allies has completely changed the spectrum of cold-war strategic partnerships. The international system, greatly relieved of bipolar tensions, has generated a tremendous scope for the states to forge new partnership in order to strengthen their security environment and enhance national interest. Responding to these new challenges Indian state is being formulating new approaches towards the conduct of her foreign policy. Some of these new policy shifts particularly in relation to neighbouring countries and regions having direct bearing on the security and development of the NER are of our particular concern.

India's China Policy started changing from isolation to engagement following the visit of the then Prime Minister Rajiv Gandhi to China in 1988 and reciprocal visit by Chinese Premier Li Peng in 1991, after a gap of 31 years of such state visits. The successive visits by the President and the Prime Minister of India to China in 1992 and 1993 respectively and the reciprocal visit by the Chinese President in 1996 had considerably released the tensions in Sino-India relations. The "Agreement on the Maintenance of Peace and Tranquility along the Line of Actual Control (LAC) in the India-China Border Areas", signed on September 7, 1993, during the visit of India's Prime Minister to China, has laid down the framework for maintenance of peace and tranquility along the LAC between India and China. Under the agreement, the two sides agreed to resolve the boundary question through peaceful and friendly consultations. Both the countries committed not to use force against other by any means. Pending an ultimate boundary settlement, both agreed to "strictly respect and observe" the LAC between the two sides and not to overstep it by any activity. Where there are differences on the alignment of the LAC, the experts from both countries would "jointly check and determine" where the LAC lies. Both the countries agreed to undertake a series of Confidence Building Measures (CBMS), including the reduction of military forces deployed along the India-China border in conformity with .the principle of "mutual and equal security" (Annual Report, MOD; 1993-94:4). Besides this, the "Agreement on Confidence Building Measures in the Military Field along the Line of Actual Control in the India-China Border Areas", signed in November, 1996, during the visit of Chinese President Jiang Zemin to India, *inter alia* stipulates that neither side shall use its military capability against the other side, and includes provisions for negotiating the reduction of limitation of forces from mutually agreed geographical zones along the LAC, the prior notification of military exercises, and service to service contacts (Annual Report, MOD,1996-97:5-6).

These two agreements followed by the visit of the India's President Mr. K. R. Narayanan to China in 2000 and the visit of the Chinese leader Mr.Li Peng to India in January, 2001, have significantly scaled down the elements of mistrust in Sino-Indian relations that had aggravated further following the Pokhran II explosion in May 1998. Notwithstanding the Chinese involvement in Pakistan's nuclear weapon and missile programmes that remains as a major concern for India, the role of China in Indo-Pak war on Kargil in 1999 seems to be an indicator of shifts in China's India policy as well.

Be that as it may, the compulsions arising out of the forces of globalization, challenges faced by the nations in evolving a new global order, and forging new strategic partnership seem to have largely informed the remaking of foreign policy of both India and China towards each other since 1990s. Although no durable structure of cooperation between them has yet evolved, China's realization of the fact that the "common ground" between India and China "far outweighs" the differences between them, and the need "to elevate Sino-Indian relations to a new height in the 21st century" for "peace and development in Asia and the world at large" seem to enhance the possibility of establishing a constructive partnership of cooperation" between these two Asian neighbours in foreseeable future (Li Peng, 2001).

Like India's China policy, the Indo-Myanmar relations also started improving since early 1990s. Removal of idealistic elements and injection of more sense of pragmatism in formulating India's policy towards Myanmar have led Indian policy makers to realize that India's support to pro-democracy movement led by Aung San Sụ Kyi against the military regime would in no way enhance India's security and national interest in Myanmar. As there was no sign of relinquishing power to the Suu Kyi led National League for Democracy, which emerged victorious following 1990 election, by the Myanmar military regime, India had little choice other than to come to terms with the ruling junta. Informed by China's intensive engagement in Myanmar, growing insecurity in Northeastern region arising out of various insurgent activities, and the strategic importance of Myanmar in India's "Look East policy," India had adopted a more pragmatic Myanmar policy setting aside its interest in democracy in Myanmar, one of the major irritating factors that strained Indo-Myanmar relations for so long.

The visit of Vice Foreign Minister of Myanmar, Mr. U. Baswe, to India in 1992 helped both the countries to clear their misconception about each other. Both entered into agreements for the development of areas along the international border and for working together against the forces of destabilization, militancy and insurgency. A border trade agreement was signed in 1994 allowing trade to flow through selected customs posts along Moreh (Manipur)-Tamu (Myanmar) and Champhai (Mizorarn)-Hri (Myanmar), sectors. Although only the Moreh-Tamu sector has been officially opened for trade pending the infrastructural development in the other sector, this Agreement, no doubt, has profound importance for the NER. As part of India's further engagement in Myanmar, the Indian government has already constructed the Tamu-Kalemayo road. This road is expected to be a part of the ambitious Asian Highway Project conceived to link up Singapore with New Delhi via Kualalampur, Ho Chi Minh City, Phnom Penh, Bangkok, Vientiane, Chiang Mai, Yangson, Mandalay, Tamu, Dhaka and Calcutta (Dhar:2000). This Asian Highway, once comes into reality, will remove the communication bottleneck of the land-locked states of Manipur, Mizoram and Nagaland to a large extent and will pave the way for their integration with the South-East Asian region. Besides economic opportunities, improved Indo-Myanmar relations also have direct bearing on the security environment of NER. Increasing cooperation between the security forces of India and Myanmar in dealing with cross-border insurgent activities has compelled many of the Northeast insurgent groups to shift their bases from Myanmar. The visit by General Maung Aye, Vice President of the Myanmar Government to India in November 2000, has opened up the scope for India's multi-faceted and comprehensive engagement in Myanmar, which will enable India to address her concerns about security and development in the NER in a far better way.

The Indo-Bangladesh relations also started improving since early 1990s. The 'Gujral Doctrine' and return of democracy in Bangladesh largely facilitated normalization of bilateral relations. India's forward engagement started with the visit of External Affairs Minister Mr. I.K.Gujral to Bangladesh in 1990. Within a short span of time a number of irritants like the issue of providing Tin Bigha Corridor to Bangladesh, sharing of the Ganga water and repatriation of the Chakma refugees to Bangladesh, were effectively resolved. India provided the Tin Bigha Corridor to Bangladesh in 1992. The accord on sharing of the Ganga water was signed in 1997. And the problem of Chakma refugees was solved with their repatriation from camps in Tripura to Bangladesh in 1998. This repatriation of Chakma refugees has, no doubt, a great significance for ethno-sensitive psyche of the people of Northeast. This achievement in India's Bangladesh policy would appear to have reduced inter-ethnic schism arising particularly out of Mizo-Chakma conflict in Mizoram and Arunachalee-Chakma conflict in Arunachal Pradesh in more than one ways by scaling down the threat of further Chakma ingression in Mizo and Arunachalee territories respectively.

Look East Policy

Besides improving relations with the neighbouring countries, since early 1990s India has adopted "look east" policy as part of her response to post cold-war global situation. The aim of this policy is to forge forward-looking engagement with South East Asian Countries, ASEAN as a group as well as with the members of the group. This policy aims at recuperating India's loss of market in erstwhile USSR by gaining from the growing South East Asian economies. India was accorded the status of "Full Dialogue Partner" of the ASEAN Forum (ARF) in 1996. India sees the ARF, the only security dialogue forum in the Asia-Pacific region, as a desirable initiative for fashioning a new pluralistic and cooperative security order in tune with the diversity of the region and in consonance with the transition away from a world characterized by blocs built around military alliances (Annual Report, MOD, 1999-2000: 7). The ASEAN-India Joint Cooperation Committee Meeting held in New Delhi in April, 1998 provided important mechanisms for implementing various decisions. The visit of President K.R. Narayanan to Singapore in 2000 and of Prime Minister A.B.Vajpayee to Vietnam and Indonesia in early 2001 and reciprocal visits by the leaders of ASEAN countries are gradually adding content and structure to India's Look East Policy. There has been an appreciable rise in India's two-way trade with the South East Asian Countries. While the share of Indian exports to South East Asian Countries has increased from 11.44 per cent during 1990-91 to 18.12 per cent during 1999-2000, the share of India's imports from these countries has gone up from 13.46 per cent to 19.40 per cent during that time (The Economic Times: 22:01.01).

Bangladesh, India, Myanmar, Sri Lanka and Thailand Economic Cooperation (BIMST-EC)

What is important from the NER's point of view is India's growing engagement in different sub-regional level development initiatives involving the neighbouring Asian and South-East Asian countries. The launching of BIMST-EC in 1997 involving Bangladesh, India, Myanmar, Sri Lanka and Thailand, has a profound development and security implications for the NER. BIMST-EC is the first grouping of its kind in which two ASEAN members have come together with three countries from South Asia to form an association for economic cooperation. The forum aims at utilizing the untapped resource potential in the sub-region for mutual benefits. It has already identified the priority areas such as communications, infrastructure, energy, trade and investment, tourism and fisheries for cooperation, with each country assuming a specific responsibility for coordination. Important projects, which are currently under consideration by the forum include: the Asian Highway Link (which has already been mentioned earlier), Asian Railway Network and a Natural Gas Pipeline Grid (Annual Report, MEA, 1998-99: iv). All these projects have tremendous implications in removing the communication isolation as well as utilizing the untapped resources of NER. While the NER will have access to the proposed Asian Highway through the Imphal-Tamu feeder road, as indicated earlier, the railway system of India and Myanmar will be linked at Dibrugarh railhead. This will enable the NER to have access to the Asian Railway Network.

Bangladesh, Bhutan, India and Nepal Growth Quadrangle (BBIN-GQ)

Besides BIMST-EC, another cross-country sub-regional initiative having wider ramifications for NER is the Growth Quadrangle involving Bangladesh, Bhutan, India and Nepal (BBIN-GQ). Although this initiative is still in embryonic form, working modalities for cooperation have already been finalized in the second meeting of foreign secretaries of the four countries at Kathmandu held on 17 July 1998. The BBIN-GQ is to follow a project-led approach to cooperation in the core economic sectors of multi-modal transportation and communication, energy, trade and investment, tourism, utilization of natural resources and environment. These projects will be supportive of and complementary to national plans of the countries in the Growth Quadrangle. The projects will make best use of neighbourhood synergies and the resources and expertise within the sub-region will be given priority in their implementation. A prioritized, practical, action oriented, time-bound and incremental approach will be followed in selection, development and implementation of projects having immediate impact as well as large infrastructure projects with long gestation (Annual Report, MEA, 1998-99: 19).

Nepal, besides looking after the overall sub-regional cooperation efforts, will also coordinate projects in the areas of tourism and multi-modal transportation and communication. Bangladesh will coordinate the projects involving energy and utilization of natural resources. Bhutan and India will coordinate projects involving environment and, trade and investment promotion respectively (Annual Report, MEA, 1998-99:19). Once the BBIN-GQ takes off, it will provide yet another space where development interest of NER can be accommodated.

The Mekong-Ganga Initiative (MGI)

Another cross-country sub-regional cooperation programme having long-term implications for the development interest of NER is the Mekong-Ganga initiative (MGI). This Initiative traces its origin in "Mekong Basin Project" involving Myanmar, Cambodia, China, Laos, Thailand, and Vietnam. Later, this project has been widened to accommodate India. The inaugural Ministerial Meeting on MGI took place in Vientiane at the initiative of India and five South East Asian countries in November 2000. The Vientiane Declaration upholds the common desire of the member countries to develop relations and better understanding among themselves for enhancing friendship, solidarity and cooperation. Tourism has been identified as an immediate priority area having significant potential for development in the sub-region (Baruah: 2001). For tourism development, studies are to be conducted into joint marketing, facilitating travel in the region and expanding multi-modal communications and transportation links. Although this initiative is still under process, its future unfolding will have significant impact on the NER, which is India's gateway to Mekong Basin Region.

Kunming Initiative

Besides these institutionalized cross-country sub-regional development initiatives, opinion across the countries is getting crystallized for the formation of another growth quadrangle involving China, India, Myanmar and Bangladesh - which has found an expression in the "Kunming Initiative" articulated in an international conference at Kunming, the capital of Yunnan Province of China, in August 1999. The basic objective of this initiative is to promote cross-country sub-regional development cooperation among contiguous regions of eastern/north-eastern region of India, southwest China, northern Myanmar and Bangladesh.

Conclusion

Thus, the opportunities arising out of post-cold war global scenario and India's positive response to these, have created a favourable external condition for the development of the NER through cross-country development initiatives. The geo-strategic location of the region necessitates an integrated cross-country sub-regional cooperation for development. This can only be achieved by placing the NER in a larger South Asian as well as South East Asian canvass. For so long this perspective was not in the consciousness of the Indian State. As a result, India's conduct of foreign policy towards her neighbours was not much informed of the development interest of the NER prior to 1990s. Moreover, the underestimation of external security threat to north-eastern border prior to 1962 and overestimation of the same at least during 1962-1971 appears to have negatively influenced the central public sector investment decisions in this region. The development interest of the NER had, thus, become a hostage to state-centric mindset. Due to the failure of economic diplomacy of the Indian State, even after 1971, to promote development of the NER through forward engagement with Bangladesh and Myanmar had further added more life to the disabilities of the region. Even the SAARC framework, which could have been utilized to remove some of the predicaments of the NER, has largely remained inoperative primarily due to Indo-Pakistan rivalry. The external perimeter of development as defined by India's relations with the neighbouring countries is, thus, not in harmony with the geo-strategic location of the NER. The resultant underdevelopment partially caused by this disharmony entangled with other ethnic aspirations has substantially added to internal insecurity environment of the region

REFERENCES

Bandopadhyaya, Jayantanuja, 1991, (reprint), *The Making of India's Foreign Policy*, Allied Publishers, New Delhi.

Buruah, Amit, 2001, "Vietnam for dynamic ASEAN-Indian ties", *The Hindu*, January 10.

Central Electricity Authority (CEA), 1997, *Fourth National Power Plan, 1997-2012*, Government of India.

Das, Gurudas, 1995, *Tribals of Arunachal Pradesh in Transition*, Vikas, New Delhi.

Das Gurudas and R K Purkayastha (eds.), 2000, *Border Trade: North East India and Neighbouring Countries*, Akansha Publishing House, New Delhi.

Dhar, M.K., 2000, "The Mekong-Ganga Initiative," *The Sentinel*, December 3.

Dixit, I.N., 2001, "South Asia's weak Link," *The Telegraph*, January 18.

The Economic Times, January 22, 2001.

Government of India, *Ministry of Defence (MOD), Annual Report*, 1993-94, 1996-97, 1999-2000.

Government of India, *Ministry of External Affairs (MEA), Annual Report*, 1998-99.

Lamb, Alastair, 1960, *Britain and China Central Asia*, Pall Mall Press, London.

Li Peng, 2001, Speech delivered, as Chairman, National People's Congress of China, at India International Centre, New Delhi, on January 13, (as published in *The Assam Tribune,* January 24, 2001).

SAARC Survey of Development and Cooperation 1998-99, Research and Information System for the Non-Aligned and other Developing Countries, New Delhi.

Thapa, Surya Bahadur, 1999, "The Future of South Asian Cooperation: A Partnership for the Twenty-first Century," in *South Asian Survey,* 6(2), Sage Publications, New Delhi.

Thapliyal, Sangeeta, 1999, "Nepal and Bhutan", in P R Chari, (ed), *Perspective on National Security in South Asia,* Manohar Publications, New Delhi.

2

Unfinished Business in Northeast*

—B.G. VERGHESE

I first visited the Northeast in 1951 shortly after commencing a career in journalism with the Times of India in Bombay. I had an invitation from a friend, but more than that it was the allure of a motoring holiday from Guwahati to Kohima and Imphal that drew me there. I was fascinated by this new frontier - the mighty Brahmaputra, lovely tea gardens, the deep forests and enormously diverse people- and have returned again and again ever since.

In 1955, I was witnessed to the inauguration of the Naga-Tuensang Hill Area and was able to fly around the North East Frontier Agency or NEFA, today's Arunachal Pradesh.

In 1962, I went to Bomdila and Se La as a war correspondent just a couple of days before the Chinese broke through to the foothills. Tezpur was a ghost town on the fateful night of November 20 and 21 as the administration and civil population evacuated the north bank and the security forces pulled back to Guwahati. The local State Bank currency chest and official papers at the District Collectorate had been burnt. The doors of the mental hospital were opened and the inmates

*An earlier version of this paper was presented in the Seventh Kamal Kumari Memorial Lecture delivered at Guwahati on April 19, 2002.

released. Those lost souls alone remained behind along with 11 journalists, myself and another Indian, Prem Prakash, among them. As we kept vigil, around midnight the Chinese declared a unilateral ceasefire and pull back to its Himalayan claim line. It was a truly eerie experience. A month later I returned with the civil administration to Bomdila having meanwhile enjoyed the unpaid hospitality of Tezpur's Planters' Club whole unattended store of tinned fish and beer sustained us with something more than survival rations.

In 1966, I had barely joined the Prime Minister's Office as Information Advisor when I flew to Aizawl following the MNF uprising. Two years later I toured the entire Northeast extensively and wrote a series of official papers on integrated development of the Northeastern region and the harnessing of its immense water resources. I'm not sure it was read by anybody. That vision remains to be implemented.

In 1980, I was off and on in Guwahati for many weeks on behalf of the Gandhi Peace Foundation. I was engaged in a bid to broker an accord between the young AASU leadership and the Centre through the Governor on the thorny issue of safeguarding Assam's identity in the face of the influx of Bangladesh immigrants. Like other efforts, it did not work and led to much grief.

Through the 1980s and 1990s I travelled extensively throughout the Northeast once more to research two books that were to follow: Waters of Hope, on water resource development and India's Northeast Resurgent, the thrust of which is summed up in the sub-title, "Ethnicity, Insurgency, Governance, and Development". Finally, in 1997, I was a member of the Shukla Commission that submitted to the Government a report entitled "Transforming the Northeast". I am currently associated with the ADB in an endeavour to promote the concept of a South Asian Development Quadrangle embracing Nepal, Bhutan, Bangladesh and Eastern/Northeastern India alongside a Track II effort in parallel to conceptualize regional cooperation between Bangladesh, Eastern/Northeastern India, Bangladesh and SW China in a so-called BCIM Forum.

I recount this personal history, partly as nostalgia but also because it highlights that are not easily forgotten. There is much unfinished business in the Northeast.

The Partition of India in 1947 caused the extreme geo-political isolation of the Northeast, making it emotionally, though not quite physically, South Asia's third landlocked state with Bhutan and Nepal. The loss of connectivity and market access all around set its economy back by at least a quarter century. The impact of this was not fully understood.

The coming of Independence also brought contrary pulls and pressures into play. There was an understandable drive to nationally integrate the hitherto loosely administered or constitutionally "excluded" frontier regions. Per contra, the extraordinary diverse mosaic of tribal peoples who had lived alone and aloof in their little village republics sought to differentiate themselves in order to prevent their identity being submerged in the vast ocean of Indian humanity. This was part of the pains of transition towards a new nationhood rather than an inevitable clash between integrative and secessionist tendencies.

Three forces were at work. At one level a few ethnic groups sought independence from India with the departure of the Raj. At another level, several groups sought separation from Assam, but within India, in view of their own linguistic and ethnic particularities. Finally, certain smaller groups have continued to seek autonomy within the several North Eastern states to safeguard their interests and protect their way of life. The founding fathers wrote the Sixth Schedule in the constitution to accommodate the Northeastern diversity. Nevertheless, the interplay of these forces is still at work. The Northeast has seen the emergence of new states and a variety of autonomous and apex councils.

Despite much criticism and seeming failures, this has been a most creative exercise of nation-building and state formation that has few parallels anywhere in the world. That there is still much discontent that is manifest in multiple insurgencies signifies the trauma of continuing transition rather than failure. There is no reason for despair.

While Assam has been recognised into smaller units, the geo-political reality of the Northeast still eludes common understanding. This huge landmass, shaped something like an elephant's ear, is attached to the Indian heartland by the narrow, 37 km wide Siliguri corridor. As against this, the external boundary of the Northeast runs over 4,500 km and is contiguous with five countries. Nepal, China, Bhutan, Myanmar and Bangladesh. Everything north and east of Siliguri must be defined as part of the Northeast - Sikkim, the Darjeeling-Gorkha Hills Area (DGHA) and North Bengal included. This is Mongoloid India and culturally part of Southeast Asia.

Equally, the entire Northeast must be treated in all strategic respect as a single, unified entity, a federation within a federation. While the distinctive identities and concerns of the Seven Sisters plus Sikkim, the DGHA and North Bengal and the autonomous sub-units within them, must be respected in every way, they cannot prosper without regional integration. This alone will ensure cohesion, overall development, coordination and economies of scale. This understanding too has to dawn fully on all concerned.

This calls for a total restructuring of the North Eastern Council in both its planning and security dimensions with its locus in Shillong rather than in Delhi. It also calls for a new administrative ethos with the restoration of the former Indian Frontier Administrative Service in place of unwilling cadres of unhappy misfits. A different set of planning norms needs to be applied, relying on the peculiar circumstances and genius of the region. The effort must be to build on what is best in traditional community institutions which have been either thoughtlessly or too hastily set aside in the name of some mythical all-India norm or accounting practice.

It is obvious that the Northeast cannot ignore its immediate neighbourhood, which is far more international than national. Trans-border trade with the countries beyond (including Bangladesh now) was the lifeblood of whole communities in Sikkim, the DGHA and the Northeast. These ties were severed by the Partition, war, insurgency and diplomatic strains and tensions over periods of time. Fortunately, we now live in better times and relations with all our neighbours have improved. Unfortunately, the country's diplomatic and trade policy in relation to the region and emerging opportunities therein remains wedded to past shibboleths and a continuing inwardness of approach. I would argue that the path to closer integration of the Northeast lies in opening up the region to its external neighbourhood, including Southeast Asia, China and especially Bangladesh.

The Northeast should be seen as a bridge to lands and opportunities beyond rather than as a *cul de sac* in a troublesome extremity of the country. Moreh and Lekhapani, the Indian termini of the Burma Road and the Stilwell Road, should, like Bombay, have a Gateway of India facing the East. Border trade can be the first step to restoring trans-border community and commerce, providing a stimulus to inter-country trade not merely as a transit corridor but as a source of local manufacture. What is now considered and sees itself as peripheral, with all its emotional implications for national integration, will thereby gain centrality and visibility. Regional cooperation will be fostered by and can in turn foster connectivity, trade facilitation, regional cooperation and people to people exchange. Unfortunately, the Government prefers bilateralism and views multilateralism with suspicion.

India, like any other nation, must be concerned with the determination and inviolability of its sovereign boundaries. However, in its preoccupation with boundary fixation and the related issue of border management against illicit traffic and other crimes or threats to national security, the Government appears to have lost sight of the importance of developing an appropriate border policy. Although the words border or frontier and boundary are interchangeable used in common parlance, they represent very different concepts. While "boundary" refers to the line demarcating the external political jurisdiction of a state, border or frontier refer to transitional zones or bands of territory that lie on either side of the boundary. Border regions most often exhibit commonalities of race, peoples, language, religion, natural systems, environment, culture and ways of life. Border peoples share ties of culture and commerce.

These human and natural ties are not necessarily severed by national boundaries and it is a matter of regret and concern when this occurs. The Government's indifference or mistrust of bilateralism is in part a by-product of a wider intellectual failure to differentiate between boundary and border, between governments on the one hand and man and nature on the other. This infirmity has had a negative impact on the Northeast despite positive geo-political changes in the neighbourhood.

It is not that nothing happened across or around the country's Northeastern borders. These are unquiet borderlands and witness to cross-border insurgency, gun-running, narcotics and AIDS, smuggling, money laundering, trafficking in women, and illicit immigration. These manifestations tell of the porosity of and vigorous negative activity across these borders. Rather than shrink behind a defensive siege mentality, the object of policy should be to convert this vicious circle into a virtuous cycle. The Northeastern States are willing and anxious to open up. The Centre has to be more responsive. Slow and stately movement is compounding the lost opportunities of either wasted years.

Sub-regional cooperation offers a good starting point. When SAARC was stymied by the Indo-Pakistan deadlock, the smaller partners suggested sub-regional cooperation. Thus was born the idea of the South Asian Development Quadrangle. This is essentially based on the Ganga-Brahmaputra-Meghna natural resource region, embracing Bhutan, Nepal, Bangladesh and Eastern and Northeastern India. This concept has long been frawned upon by the Government of India but has not fortunately won its approval. SADQ may be a sub-region of SAARC but in terms of population it is larger than the European Union, ASEAN or NAFTA. This is no disqualification. Nevertheless, it is as well to recognize that SADQ, a macro sub-region, comprises many mini and micro agro-climatic and socio-cultural regions with problems and opportunities of their own.

It would be useful to plan for such mini-micro sub-regions as well, some of them even extending beyond the confines of SADQ into Myanmar and Tibet in due course. A few such mini-regions spring to mind. One could be a Meghalaya-

Mymensingh/Sylhet sub-region; another, the Meghna-Feni-Karnafuli (MFK) natural resource region comprising Mizoram, Tripura, Manipur, Cachar in India and the Chittagong Hill Tracts, Chittagong, Noakhali, Comilla and Sylhet districts of Bangladesh (to which parts of China Hill and Rakhine districts of Myanmar could be added later). A third sub-region that suggests itself would be could be a Himalayan grouping including Sikkim, the DGCA and parts of Arunachal, Bhutan and eastern Nepal.

The MFK sub-region has many hill-plan-ocean and plantation-market-export complementarities that await exploitation with Chittagong as an entrepot. It has strong ethno-cultural links and could if brought together offer attractive economics of scale that would translate its very substantial energy (hydro/hydrocarbon), plantation and eco-tourism possibilities into major market opportunities. The Northeast needs outlet to the sea at Chittagong and/or Akyab/ Sittwe in Myanmar. Likewise, if Bangladesh aspires to build a deep water port at Chittagong - a sore need for the upper Bay of Bengal littoral - this will be a non-starter or a puny effort without the hinterland, larger market and investment and infrastructure that the Northeast and Eastern India would provide. The great inland waterways that inter-connect the region could also be revivified in conjunction with Bangladesh for inter-modal transport. The mutual benefit is obvious. In all these matters it is necessary to think and act concurrently, and not sequentially, in order to deprive synergy.

The idea of BCIM regional cooperation, to which reference has been made earlier, is also worth pursuing as one among many formations that might ultimately interlock in a larger South Asia, Southeast Asia and East Asian network. The Mekong-Ganga Cooperation and Association and BIMST-EC are already there. The recent inauguration of flights from Guwahati to Bangkok from the Guwahati International airport is an augury of the future. The Moreh-Tamu-Kalewa highway leading on to Mandalay, built by the Border Roads Organisation as an Indian-aided project, has opened another door. The proposed Guwahati international air cargo facility will mark yet another step towards establishing new cross-border links. This, however, is hastening far too slowly without any concerted planning about how the facility is to be used - for what, by whom. Here is a supreme example of sequential planning.

All these varied tasks cannot be done by Government or in the public sector alone. Private investment is essential, bringing with it capital, technology, management skills, flexibility and innovation. Turning down or delaying foreign investment on grounds of the Northeastern sensitivities can no longer be unquestioningly accepted. There is certainly a strong case for fashioning policies that ensure that the region enjoys value-addition in terms of employment and income generation and is not merely used as a raw material base or transit zone. The days of large plantatïons in "garden" and "estates" are over. There is neither the land nor social acceptance to permit this any further. However, the smallholder experiment has worked well either through co-operativisation or in partnership with large manufacturers. Small tea growers along with Arunachal foothills sell their produce to the big garden factories in the adjacent areas of Assam.

There is huge scope for small-holder cultivation of plantation crops and in horticulture, herbiculture and floriculture with technical inputs, planting material, processing and marketing being provided by large units. Small-holder lands can be invested as equity, with the state or community as a third partner in joint ventures, if so desired. The same can be said about sericulture and weaving. Various incentives have been announced and limited counter-guarantees can be offered. Local entrepreneurs and industries need to be encouraged to cater to the Northeast's defence market for fresh and processed foods, boots, blankets, uniform material, parachutes and so forth.

Land ownership patterns are often cited as inhibiting land acquisition for infrastructural and industrial requirements. Meghalaya has developed the concept of "tribal interest" as a supervening doctrine. With the steady shortening of the jhum cycle for a variety of reasons, many areas have suffered ecological regression. Nagaland's Environmental Plan for Economic Development (NEPED) is an imaginative example of upgrading jhum cultivation through the protection and promotion of bio-diversity to restore the kind of sustainable agro-forestry practice it once was.

Very large areas of *jhum* fallow can be reclaimed for plantation and horticulture with appropriate cadastral surveys and improved land use planning. These can be made available for tripartite joint ventures on the lines described with small holders organized around larger corporate or cooperative mother units. The NDDB can play a pioneering role here on the basis of the Amul pattern, which is applicable not only to dairying but to other areas of agricultural endeavour as well. The small rubber and tea growers of Tripura are waiting for this to happen.

Larger infrastructure such as railheads, utilities, cold storages, warehouses, industrial area, export processing zones and educational and medical facilities and the townships that inevitably develop around them require substantial tracts of flat lands. So will installations associated with the large water regulation and hydro-electric storages planned in the Northeast such as Kameng project and Dihang and Subansiri cascade in Arunachal, the Tipaimukh dam in Manipur and other schemes in Meghalaya and Mizoram. These could transform the region and make it an energy powerhouse that attracts collateral investment and infrastructure. These water resource projects will also carry a requirement for the resettlement and rehabilitation of persons displaced by them.

Once possible solution lies in creating "trusteeship areas" along foothills tracts around the Brahmaputra and Barak Valleys that are in dispute between Assam and the hill States carved out of it. Could these be placed under Central trusteeship for, say, 50 years and be used for development of the kinds of infrastructure and investment described?

Displaced persons, including the Chakmas in Arunachal Pradesh, could be relocated here in new non-farm jobs that could be created. Formulas for revenue-sharing between the concerned States can be worked out. Assam might feel it is getting a poor deal as it will be "sharing" what it regards as its land with everybody. Not so, Assam is greatly in need of water regulation to moderate floods, improve its agricultural calendar, prevent erosion of Majuli and other char lands and to get the plentiful cheap electricity that would propel its industrialization and counter educated-unemployment problem.

Peace is needed for Development and Development for Peace. There is no given sequence; both go hand in hand. Both ends of the equation must be worked on simultaneously. I have thus afar addressed problems of development. What of Peace? There is considerable evidence that the people in the Northeast are fed up with violence, extortion and the disruption of daily life. They want both Peace and Development. The current ceasefire and the ensuing dialogue being conducted initially between the Government of India and the NSCN-IM faction holds out promise. There is now a clear vested interest in peace among all Nagas. The Naga Reconciliation Movement is seeking to end internecine strife and unite all the Naga tribes and factions in the search for an honourable and just settlement. The Naga peoples' claim is that they were never part of India and are therefore neither separatists nor secessionists. They too regained their freedom with the departure of the British and, moreover, marked this with their own declaration of independence. Yet, in all the discussions and in the documents recently produced by them, the word "sovereignty" is not used. The emphasis is on the "acknowledgement of the Naga history".

With the official NSCN-IM-Government talks now moving from modalities and monitoring to substantive issues, the question arises as to how the circle can be squared with honour to all and in keeping with current realities. One way out would be for the united Naga factions to renounce for sovereignty even while recalling their past as a free people and then to reaffirm their accession to the Union of their volition. Simultaneously, the Government of India could acknowledge the Nagas' sense of their history. It could then explain its inability to reverse history and undo any part of the Union, which consists of a vast plurality of free and equal peoples living together as fraternal partners in a sovereign, democratic Republic.

Nagaland already enjoys a special position under Article 371-A of the Constitution. The degree of Naga "self-determination" within the Indian Union can be sought to be expanded in ways that enhance the distinctive identity of all the Naga peoples in Nagaland and contiguous areas. The Naga way of life and cultural and economic bonds can surely be strengthened without derogating from the integrity of any other Indian State. The instrumentality of the Naga Ho Ho (assembly) is already available and at work for such purposes.

The Bodoland problem seems to be moving towards resolution with broad agreement on the constitution of Bodoland Territorial Council under the Sixth Schedule. This would empower the Assam Governor to safeguard Bodo interests in respect of all transferred subjects.

The problem now is to ensure that the other ethnic groups within the BTC area enjoy equivalent safeguards to protect their special concerns. A Naga accord in particular will have a salutary effect throughout the Northeast. The other insurgencies must be similarly approached with a mixture of understanding, accommodation and firmness. Many problems are essentially psychological and can be prevented and cured by tactful handling. In many matters, style counts for as much as substance, possibly more.

Assam has made a number of interesting political forays in creative federalism. The non-territorial Apex Councils established to protect the Tiwa, Rabha and Mishing identity follows the earlier creation of new Autonomous Councils for Karbi Anglong and North Cachar Hills. Some would argue that these have not worked to everybody's satisfaction. Yet they represent bold experiments on which one can build.

The principle of non-territoriality can also be used to diffuse and thereafter resolve the thorny issue of outsiders in the region. Those so defined may be granted electoral rights in specially designated non-territorial constituencies. This would enable them to elect a certain number of members to the State Assemblies, and even to Parliament if necessary. They would thus no longer hold the balance in a large number of constituencies as at present. Shillong and Dimapur represent two such "general" constituencies that are larger than most in Meghalaya and Nagaland. Similar non-territorial constituencies can be set up in special export processing zones or in the trusteeship areas outlined earlier.

The mechanism of the Upper Houses can also be used to give appropriate representation to special groups and ethnic minorities and even to "outsiders".

The problem of "foreigners" has to be treated differently. There is no way either cohorts of illicit immigrants are going to be deported except through due process which may be redefined if necessary. Those established to have entered India after the presently stipulated cut-off date should enjoy all civil and economic rights but may be denied electoral rights until legitimately brought on the rolls. They should be eligible for naturalisation after five or more years as may be determined and their children accorded citizenship by birth. All births, deaths and property sales should be registered. None of this will be easy. But a beginning has to be made to plug loopholes and facilitate a permanent settlement.

The future ingress of illicit immigrants, especially from Bangladesh and Nepal, has to controlled by better border management and accelerated development of those countries, a task that India must assist in its own enlightened self-interest. Over and beyond that, entry must be regulated by authorized work-permits for designated jobs in specified areas. Such protocols must work both ways, with Indians eligible to go to Bangladesh on similar terms whenever opportunity arises.

What is the role of the media, especially the regional media, in all of this. The Fourth Estates sets the agenda and shapes social discourse. It has to abandon cynicism and carping criticism even as it focuses on incompetence and malfeasance. It can ensure transparency and accountability within parameters of responsible journalism. It needs to reinforce success by reporting on the many positive things, small and big, happening around the region. It must interpret the Northeast to the rest of India and the greater Indian reality to the Northeast.

There is much more that one can say of the Northeast. I certainly see better days ahead. The country is now more conscious of the Northeast and is genuinely anxious to assist its development and resurgence. But the Northeast cannot just wait for something to turn up. It has to exert itself and put its house in order. The way ahead is not going to be easy. There is much to be done. It's time to get on with the job.

3

The Paradox of Development

—SUJATA MIRI

The concept of development, extremely complex as it is, is in popular parlance, equated, in different degrees of sophistication, with economic development. The image of the Northeast as an underdeveloped region is one of economic stagnation, poverty, unemployment, lack of modem infrastructure, absence of a spirit of economic enterprise and adventure and so on. The developmental plans specially devised for the region, have either not produced the desired results or, in many ways, have made things worse. There is now the growing realization that radical economic changes cannot be contemplated without corresponding cultural and political reorientation. The traditional cultural practices are unable to cope with the forces of rapid industrial development. What is needed is thus, not merely economic development, but a cultural and political transformation of the society, a transformation process duly assisted by modem technology.

However, the matter obviously is not as simple as that. The Northeast is home to a great variety of cultures and languages with a history of mutual interaction and exchange, where trade certainly was an important element; but surely not the only one. There was a great deal of mutual learning from one another, mutually life-enhancing communication. Some of these cultures still retain their vitality and springs of action of their own, which lead many to think that they can appropriate the powerful forces of modem economy, while retaining their cultural and social specificity in a very large measure. This has led, on the one hand, to an increasing curiosity about one's own cultural roots, and on the other, to a ruthless politically instrumental use of the idea of cultural identity by people who fish in the troubled waters of the economic mess of our country.

The renewed interest in traditional systems of governance, in the old ways of organizing life and finding meaning in it, as evidenced in the large number of publications relating to the cultural heritages of communities, can be taken as an expression of faith in the potency of the traditional way of life of these communities. But almost always this expression of faith remains just that; it is hardly ever backed up by actions and engagements, which can even remotely justify this faith.

Nonetheless, it may be worth dwelling upon briefly some of the ideas, which inspire this faith. There is a great variety in the Northeastern personality just as there is a great variety in the cultures of the people. Clearly the different groups are regionally and personally different from each other. Yet, until very recently, in the history of this region, the life of the people of the region generally was informed by the belief that that we are all related, that harmony was mandatory condition of nature itself.[1] Moreover, their sense of place -of space- was largely determined by the manner in which they saw themselves in relation to nature. Space was seen as an embodiment of events, beings and powers. Their experiences of space were infused with the meanings of the products of their material and "nonmaterial" cultures - the woven cloth that covers one as well as binds one to others, the instruments for making music, dances, songs, houses, weapons of war and hunting, tales of heroic and shameful deeds, the deeply felt continuum between man and nature and so on. These experiences emanated from each landmark of every group's immediate environment, giving meaning to the life of peoples who cannot conceive of themselves as apart from their land.

One of the distinctive features of the development of the modern world has been the dissolution of local economies into national economies, clearly paralleling the development of national culture. Unlike in the past, goods and services are not geographically focused but are simultaneously available to an anonymous crowd of potential buyers. The transport of goods is making it possible for the manufacturers to market their goods on a mass scale, to Kohima, Itanagar, Tura and so on. The developments in media communications have not only made all aware of the goods but have, with ever increasing sophistication and attractive contrivances, created desires for them, the fulfillment of which is made to appear as the primary goal and meaning of human life. The message delivered is clear: the only culture that can serve as stable and practical is the modern culture of ever-increasing desires and the invention of new technologies for their fulfillment. So far what we have been living with has been ambiguous, uncertain or simply lack of knowledge. Only when we reach the level of modern mass culture will we be living with clarity and meaning.

What of our relationship with nature? The answer is again loud and clear: Nature as the reverse of culture has now to be viewed with fear and distrust. The ambivalence of our attitude to nature does not merely relate to spaces on the edge of society and how we draw those boundaries but also on how we seek to enshrine differences between ourselves and with other life forms. When man-made boundaries can be asserted and sustained with conviction nature can confidently exist as a resource for exploitation. In brief, there is a strong indication that for the entire region under consideration westernization is the motivating programme providing the concerned communities with a core of agreed beliefs or perspectives. There has now to be a drift towards global culture in which particular cultural identities are becoming increasingly less important stimulated by parallel trends in the production and marketing of consumer goods.

But paradoxical as it may sound, while the spirit of globalization is the unification of culture, globalization has also been instrumental in the organized assertion of differences. The difficulties of resisting the aggressive promotion of mass consumerist culture are matched by the use of the very same technologies which are pressed into service for such promotion, e.g., the incredible changes in the methods of communication and dispersal of goods, to, on the one hand, resist the attempted obliteration of differences, and, on the other hand, to regenerate old differences and create new ones. Only think of the highly sophisticated networks of communication, which sustain what we call "fundamentalisms" of various kinds, and the transformations that have taken place in the celebrations of "folk" festivals - the *bihu* of the Assamese people, for instance. While the new forms of mass entertainment do certainly act as a unified controlling power, they may also be viewed as emancipatory and welcome innovations, which can be used to counter the fear that our culture is loosing its authority and our people are turning away to alternative beliefs. Consequently there is a chaos of meanings. The traditional institutions and forms through which their life was customarily given meaning have also started to lose their effectiveness. The elder's authority in relation to all matters is being questioned by new modes of productions, innovations and appreciation, which fall outside the canons of traditional cultural institutions. (This is partly illustrated by the emergence of large-scale student movements in the region). The chaos of meanings is well reflected in the contradictory pulls and pressures, which inform our political life and practice-particularly of the leadership. In personal and family lives, there is an easy acceptance of the idea of global uniformity, but the pursuit of power requires politicians at least to appear to challenge the anonymity of mass culture by reminding the society-by subtle or by crude means-of the multiplicity of its own forms of social life.

One item of clothing or dress, for instance, which links the community to its past can be seen always on the body of the leaders as and when they grace public functions. Immaculately dressed in western clothes one can spot a shawl or a jacket hung loosely over the leader's shoulders, signifying the continuity between novelty and tradition. The shawl on a western suit symbolizes the "synthesis" between the emerging forms of mass society with the spectacles of entertainment and consumption on the one hand, and the organization of difference as a political end.

For many, political "commitments" are focused on cultural topics, especially "cultural identity". Most politicians raise slogans concerned with raising consciousness or pride in identity, campaign for rights to difference and for the utter otherness of the "other". The new rulers use the language of pluralism to ignite those who feel genuinely neglected. Such talks frequently achieve the intended result: damaging the traditional harmony between groups and communities and replacing it with competition and even enmity.

More seriously, the intensely cultural representations of identity after independence have generated both freedom as well as new tensions of insecurity. Central to the dislocation caused by modernity has been the uprooting of culture. Culture is becoming de-territorialized. Earlier it appeared reasonable to presume that a form of life is tied to a territory in a precise and a specifiable way. Here culture traditionally defines a lived environment as well as a world of acquaintance and familiarity. A hundred years ago, in each village, the everyday world was contained and highly predictable. The arrival of a stranger was by and large viewed as a threat or an intimation of disorder. With the advent of large scale infiltration from neighbouring countries (specially Bangladesh) the North-easterners have been forced to seeing strangers in their midst as normal. After a painful period of struggle, there appears now a normalization of awareness of strangers leading to the development of urban societies and metropolitan culture. Both sides of the border see the development of metropolitan-based mass communication and entertainment networks that provide a level of cultural homogeneity. Nevertheless the awareness of diversity leads often to anguished questions of identity.

A consolatory thought for someone who is resolutely committed to modernity is that modem sensibility itself must enable us to confront the implications of living in multi-cultural social formulations. Since we are in the process of transition, we should take for granted that there are a variety of ways of arranging social themes. Any form of social order is a pragmatic construction. That our group alone was divine in origin was a myth, born of our ignorance. The confidence of a group in its own distinctiveness must give way to the emergence of what is called modem attitude which, besides other things, causes the realization that society is a human creation.

The words of Whitehead are prophetic for this region. "It is the business of the future to be dangerous," he said. "The major advances in civilization are processes that all but wreck the societies in which they occur." Today we witness in the people, a mixture of traditional and the modern, with a decline in the first hand experience of their own "past", resulting in a reactionary mentality. This explains to some extent, the extraordinary intensity of communal affiliation in the region. People who had lived in harmony for generations have turned on their neighbours looking at them with suspicion and sometimes more seriously wishing that they did not exist at all. The imminent possibility of new struggles, underground movements of all colours, illustrates the effect of the conflicting demands of modernization and ethnicity in the context of an increasingly global culture. Every single minority community feels threatened by the encroaching mass culture and desperately tries to cling to its hegemony in its small part in the Northeastern region.

All said and done, and in spite of the monster of cultural identity threatening the formation of national identity, mass communication has succeeded in generating a form of collective identity. The people by and large are aware of not only the boundaries of their states, but have also come to grasp the new invention called the international border. The boundaries of the known world, let us say, for a Khasi in a single village, have expanded beyond his grasp. "I know everybody and everybody else knows me too" has been supplanted by a more abstract imagination of a world shared in common. "I a Khasi, just as the Mizo, am member of the Indian Nation".

Nation "builders"- some of them at least- aspire for the formation of just this kind of an identity which they call the "national identity", which they believe is a necessary component for the process of modernization. (A natural goal of nationalist movements has been to attain and maintain autonomy, unity and identity on behalf of a population deemed by some of its members to constitute an actual or potential nation. Across the border Nations have been constructed equivalent in as many respects as possible, to cultures, which have an identity through being distinctively different. Though the seven States have been carved out on the Indian side of the border with a similar guideline in mind, we have not exactly succeeded in achieving a level of solidarity between different cultural identities dashing our for acquiring what is called modern development. The elite encourage cultural essentialism in which attempts at intimate cohabitation are spurned. Thankfully, this is counteracted by the emergence of a 'new elite' such as, doctors, engineers and other professionals, whose membership of these new professions gives them an identity, which marks them off from the traditional forms of professionalism. Their occupations give them a higher social status and sometimes they are able to exercise authority over the political leadership. However the number of such professionals is till date relatively small. Consequently, the nexus of police, politicians and bureaucrats dominate most areas.

My concern, in this brief presentation, has been to show the utter lack of clarity of the terrain that in a seminar like this we are trying to explore. The forces of change that impel us are also liable to uproot us, and the same forces of change provide us with resources which can create for us the illusion that this uprooting is not uprooting at all, that now our roots have only found new sources of energy. In politics this illusion is used for the selfish ends of power and for most people on the ground, it is an intimation of loss of meaning and despair. I did not wish to end on such a pessimistic note; but it does seem to me that a degree of pessimism is healthy for the truly human spirit.

NOTE

1. This is contrary to the view of Edward Gait (A History of Assam-1905) who, influenced by the British imperialist ideology believed that it is only the British intervention in Assam that put an end to hostile incursions and internal discussions and thus for the first time brought stability in the region.

4

Shortages, Ethnic Conflicts and Economic Development in Northeastern India

—WALTER FERNANDES

Most people in India know the Northeastern States only for political upheaval, which some view as secessionist while others interpret as a result of real or perceived threats to their culture and livelihood. Though also Sikkim is a member of the Northeastern Council, this paper will limit itself to the "Seven Sisters" of Assam, Arunachal Pradesh, Nagaland, Manipur, Meghalaya, Mizoram and Tripura. That there is political upheaval in the region is beyond doubt. It is often forgotten that basic to it is the control that people from outside the region exercise over its economy and the effort to impose a single culture on its people. It threatens both their livelihood and identity. As a result of such control the people of the region experience alienation of their livelihood resources. Linked to it is high educational status and absence of investment in productive jobs. A consequence is resentment, which takes the form of competition for the scarce resources. In the context of shortages it takes the form of an effort to protect their identity and livelihood from outsiders and their neighbours.

In these States such resentment has given birth to the debate on the indigenous question. In this region the issue has taken three forms. Firstly, each group decides a cut off date that suits it. Some want their identity to be linked to the 1826 British-Burmese treaty that ceded the Northeast to the colonialist. Others link it to 1947, the year of Indian independence and others to the 1951 census. Those who came to the region after it would then be non-indigenous. To the indigenous status they link the right to political and economic decisions and land ownership because their alienation is seen mainly in the form of land acquisition for tea estates and petroleum in Assam and for Defence all over the region. So protection of their identity is linked to the protection of their land. The late comers, whether owners or labourers, are linked to its alienation. The identity takes a new form in each region. In every case it leads to ethnic conflict. Women feel its negative impact more than men do.

The Background of the Study

In this context in a recently completed comparative study of six tribes, "Changing Women's Status in the Northeast" we looked at the stage of economic development in the region, the constraints it faces and its impact on different tribes, with focus on the gender issue. We tried to see whether the tribal societies of the region are able to deal with the changes and help women to become an integral part of the developmental process. If not, why not? We analyzed the economy also in the context of ethnic conflicts and the indigenous issue. In this longitudinal study of a 30-year comparison between the past and the present, we chose a sample of 825 families, 56 of them non-tribals. Here we discuss only the 769 tribal families, 170 of them Angami from Nagaland, 169 Adivasi, 58 Boro and 23 Garo from Sonitpur district and 106 Dimasa in the NC Hills of Assam, 200 Garo from East Garo Hills, Meghalaya and 43 Aka from Arunachal Pradesh (Fernandes and Barbora 2002).

Its starting point was the assertion in feminist studies that modernisation in its present form strengthens patriarchal values at the cost of women. On the other side, tribal women have traditionally enjoyed a higher status in their society than non-tribal women have, without being equal to men.

The Northeastern tribal women seem to be better off even than their caste society counterparts in the region and much more so in comparison with the rest of India. So the shortages and the conflicts have special implications for them because the situation is changing against them especially with regard to the ownership pattern of common property resources (CPRs). Studies show that where women retain some control over the productive resources, their social standing too is better than that of the communities in which they have lost all control (Menon, 1995). When individual ownership and commercialization take over, traditional institutions often get transformed in such a manner that patriarchal rules get strengthened. Women experience its negative impact more than men do.

The six tribes we studied represent a continuum in the process of modernisation. The Aka have been somewhat isolated till recently. The Adivasi were brought into the region from Jharkhand in eastern India beginning from the mid-19th century as indentured labourers to work in the tea gardens. Most of them have retained their Jharkhand language and culture but have for all practical purposes lost their tribal identity. The local population considers them outsiders and they perceive themselves as people of Jharkhand. But some in their younger generation question this identity (Ekka, 1990). The Bodo (Boro) who were the rulers of much of lower Assam, have today been pushed to a few districts (Butola 1997) western Assam where too they compete for the land and forest resources with the Adivasi and others whom they consider outsiders. The Dimasa were Hinduized by the Bengalis who came into the region as the administrators of the British. The local language of education, market and religion is Bengali. Today they are trying to return to their own identity. The Garo are a matrilineal tribe that is modernising itself. There are signs it favours men and goes against women (Marak 1997). The Angami led the resistance to the British in the 19th century, to the Japanese in the 1940s and were in the forefront of the Naga Nationalist Movement after 1947. However, during the last 3 decades they have gained access to education and other modern inputs. Today there is some ambiguity among them about their involvement in the nationalist struggle (Misra, 2000: 11-17). When Nagaland was formed in 1963, a Constitutional amendment introduced Article 371A to give priority to their customary law.

From the beginning there has been a demand for protective measures in the Northeast against the intrusion of outsiders who could threaten their livelihood. As a result, three of these tribes, viz. the Aka, Dimasa and Garo came under the Sixth Schedule of the Constitution that recognises, among others, community control over land and political autonomy in the form of district autonomous councils. Their land may not be alienated to outsiders. The Naga come under Article 371A. Thus their autonomy is protected in theory but the practice may not always tally with the legal status (Barbora 2002). Today the Boros too are demanding an autonomous council and the Sixth Schedule in their area. It causes more conflicts with the others, particularly the Adibasi whom they consider outsiders.

The People of the Northeast

The population of these States in 2001 is given in Table 1. The rest of the data come from 1991 since data from 2001 were not available at the time of writing. 8.14 millions of India's 67.76 million tribals lived in these States in 1991. Except for a few plains tribes like the Boro, they inhabit the hills, while the plains are dominated by non-tribals. Four States have tribals as their political leaders but the urban centers, where economic decisions are taken, are dominated by non-tribals from outside.

Some tribes are small and others numerically strong. The Adi are 26.9% and the Nishi 21.74% of the Arunachal tribals while the Aka are only 0.63%. The Mishing are 11.24% and the Boro-Kachari a third of the Assam tribals. The Garo are 50% and the Khasi 47% of the Meghalaya population. The Mizo are 87.3% of the tribals in their State. In three States tribals are more than 80% of the population and in one, two thirds. But their proportion is low in the populous States of Assam, Manipur and Tripura. The Bodo-Kachari, numerically a third of the tribals in the region, are only 3.7% of Assam's

Table 1

Total and Tribal Population, Urban/Rural in the North Eastern States

State	Population 2001 Total	% 1991 Urban	% 1991 Rural	Tribals 1991 Total	As % of Urban	As % of Rural	% of total
Arunachal	1091117	12.80	87.50	550351	05.84	94.16	63.66
Assam	26638407	11.09	88.89	2874441	03.38	96.62	12.81
Manipur	2388634	27.52	72.48	632173	08.42	91.58	34.41
Meghalaya	1774778	18.60	81.40	1517927	13.56	86.44	85.53
Mizoram	891058	46.10	53.90	653565	45.21	54.79	94.75
Nagaland	1988636	17.21	82.79	1060822	12.04	87.96	87.70
Tripura	3191168	15.30	84.70	853345	01.65	98.35	30.95

Source: Registrar General and Census Commissioner 1994: 13-17 and 2001: xi

population. Besides, the proportion of tribals has changed in Tripura from more than 56% in 1951 to around 30% today (Sen, 1993: 13). That causes many conflicts. Another group in conflict is the more than 40 lakh Adivasi whom the British brought to Assam from Jharkhand in the 19th century to work in the tea gardens. They are not included in the Schedule and most other tribes oppose their inclusion for fear that the inclusion such a big group will lead to competition for the few jobs available and for the depleted natural resources (Fernandes, 1999).

Dependence in the Primary Sector

Another point to be noted is the almost total dependence of the Northeast in general and of the tribal communities in particular, on agriculture. Most tribes, especially those practising shifting cultivation have traditionally kept a division between the domestic and social spheres. Men controlled their community resource (CPRs) and the woman was in charge of the domestic economy. So the division of work was less unfavourable to women. In settled agriculture based societies the man took decisions both in the family and society and decided the division of labour in agriculture (Fernandes and Menon, 1987: 72-74). As long as the community owned the resource the woman exercised some control over it as the one in charge of the family. With modernization integral to which is individual property, she loses the control over the livelihood (Menon, 1995). Globalization intensifies this process since it is more destructive of the natural resources. We asked ourselves whether this situation could be remedied. In this context we studied the nature of development in the region.

A study of their transition to modernization given in table 2 shows firstly that the access of most tribes to education has been relatively high. Many Northeastern States have made substantial progress in literacy in the 1980s. In Arunachal Pradesh 71.08% were literate in 1991 and in Mizoram 94.22%. Low urbanization is another feature of the tribals in particular, Mizoram being an exception (Fernandes, 1999). Another feature of the economy is the predominance of the tertiary sector. In 1994 the whole of Northeast has 214 major and medium industries, 166 of them in Assam. Even an industrially

Table 2

Economic Profile of the North Eastern States, 1991

	Industries		Workforce Participation		% in Each Sector			Per Capita Income		
States	1991	Total	Male	Female	Primary	Secondary	Tertiary	80-81	85-86	90-91
Arunachal	17	45.22	63.66	36.34	67.44	8.66	23.90	1561	3274	5046
Assam	166	31.19	80.64	19.33	73.99	5.56	20.45	1200	2313	4114
Manipur	6	38.55	58.57	41.43	70.00	9.66	20.34	1429	2362	3893
Meghalaya	7	40.32	62.83	37.17	74.81	3.73	21.46	1361	2250	4530
Mizoram	1	42.09	61.32	38.68	65.99	5.07	28.94	1289	2658	NA
Nagaland	16	42.29	58.54	41.46	75.26	3.48	21.26	1448	2591	5006
Tripura	1	29.09	83.07	16.93	64.08	6.41	29.51	1323	2074	3430
All India	NA	37.64	51.52	27.06	67.53	11.97	20.50	1625	2749	5054

Source: D'Souza 1999; NEC 1995: 149; Dubey and Gangopadhyay 1998.

"backward" State like Orissa had 374 units in 1995. Thus the dependence is on the primary and tertiary sectors. The primary sector includes agriculture, forestry, fisheries and mineral extraction. In 1996, 75.26% of the Nagaland workforce was in this sector against an All India average of 67.53%. The "secondary" sector i.e. industry employed only 3.48% against an All India average of 11.97%. The "tertiary" sector includes fields like commerce, tourism and information technology that are weak in much of the Northeast. So here it includes mostly employment in the administration. In 1996 around 23.9% of the workforce of Arunachal Pradesh was in this sector, so also 20.45% of Assam, 21.46% of Meghalaya and 21.26% in Nagaland against an All India average of 20.5%, (D'Souza 1999; Dubey and Gangopadhyay 1998; NEC 1995: 149).

This summary of the nature of the economy has several implications. The primary sector is saturated and cannot offer avenues for the educated youth. Many tribes sustain themselves on shifting cultivation (*jhum*). Efforts are being made to stop this form of agriculture but no alternative is provided. Investment in industry is very low. So the spectre of unemployment follows from a saturated primary sector. But the tertiary sector is unable to expand further.

Contested Claims and Conflicts

Table 2 also confirms our claim that in the Northeastern context land and agricultural practices are the mainstay of the economic and political choices that a community makes. Agriculture is the main source of income. However, also the difference in agricultural practices matters a great deal for women's status and access to wealth and resources. Where subsistence agriculture, in the form of jhum exists, there is a greater degree of dependence on allied forest resources. It has great significance in areas where the forest resources are dwindling. That is one more reason why we focus on the land and forest resources rather than on income. The economy of the Northeast can thus be summarized as extraction related. Tea, though called an industry, in reality belongs to the primary sector (Barbora, 2002). The other resources extracted are oil and coal.

This situation in the region as a whole is the setting within which contested claims and conflicts can be understood. It can also give one an idea of changing women's status. Hence, one need not dwell on statistics alone to state that society in the Northeast is an area with educated youth with very few avenues of employment. That is why we focus less on income than on access to and control over productive resources. Calculation of income in monetary terms can at best be approximate in a semi-monetized subsistence economy. Some of the tribes we studied, for example the Aka, are only now beginning to come face to face with the market forces and depend on a semi-monetised economy. So income calculated in monetary terms is not relevant to them and others in a similar situation. It is true particularly about women. Secondly, a high income does not in itself ensure a woman's high status. As seen in the case of women in Haryana, Punjab and other prosperous States, it may even result in the deterioration of their status (UNDP, 1997).

An issue at the centre of ethnic conflicts is the identity of the tribe. In their effort to protect it or acquire a new one, tribal leaders often forget that it can become. male centred and also result in class division in their egalitarian society. We saw it in the demographic status. The average number of persons in the respondent families is 5.7 and the sex ratio 953, against the national average of 933. However, both the family size (5.08) and sex ratio (889) are low among the Adivasi who have been impoverished and have for all practical purposes lost their tribal identity. It is the lowest in the 10-19 cohorts. Because of their poverty they send girls away as domestic helpers in middle class families, to work in exploitative conditions. Among the Boro too the sex ratio is 890 and family size 5.33.

The sex ratio is 1,096 among the Aka because of polygamy as such not necessarily a sign of high women's status. Because of the same reason their family size is 6.05. Out of 1,345 persons in the 223 matrilineal Garo families there are 681 females and 664 males at a sex ratio of 1,026. It confirms our hypothesis that, while being patriarchal, matriliny confers a higher status on women than even the patrilineal tribes do. At 924 the sex ratio is low among the Dimasa. We could not find any specific reason for it. Their family size of 5.48 is close to the national average. Of the 1,032 members in the 170 Angami families, 504 are females and 528 males at a sex ratio of 955. Thus the overall status of the Angami woman as seen in the demographic data is not as bad as that of the Adibasi but is not as good as that of the Garo. There is difference in the different cohorts but we shall not go into it.

Education and Gender Bias

It is in this context that we looked at the educational and occupational status of the respondents. The data substantiated the overall situation of the neglect of some and advancement of others. One saw the appalling educational status of the Adibasi. Their high illiteracy is one more indication of the impact of impoverishment on girls and women in particular. Out of 859 members in their families 41 girls and 44 boys are below 5. Of the remaining 774 (361 females and 413 males), 308 (39.79%) are illiterate 169 (46.81%) of them females and 139 (33.69%) males. 38 out of the 70 (54.29%) girls between 5 and 10 are out of school against 8 of 54 boys (14.82%). Thus one sees both the neglect of the tribe as a whole and a gender bias, which continues in the remaining cohorts too. 21 girls (40.38%) in the 10-14 age group are illiterate against 15 boys (21.43%). Female illiteracy is 39.40% in the 15-19 group against 22.2% for boys. In the 20-29 age group 37.1% of women are illiterate against 35.21 % of men. Female illiteracy climbs to 54.39% in the 30-39 cohorts against 41.67% for men. Of the members above 40,62.96% of women and 51.92% of men are illiterate.

Fifteen out of 17 (88.24%) Aka girls and 10 out of 22 (45.45%) boys below 10 are illiterate since their children begin school later than at 5. So most of them may not remain illiterate. 4 out of 16 (25%) girls and 6 out of 20 boys (30%) are illiterate in the 10-14 cohorts. In the 15-19 age group 2 out of 3 boys and 3 of 10 girls are out of school. The proportion of illiterates rises after it to 50% among men and 56.67% among women in the 20-39 cohorts, but comes down to 35.29% for men in the 30-39 age group but is at a high 84.21 %

among women. Illiteracy in the cohorts above 40 is 85% for men and 90% for women. The Aka who have remained isolated are only now joining the "mainstream" and its impact is seen in the improvement in literacy among them during the last 20 years. One is not certain that gender equity is attended to. Our visits to some schools showed that there are few girls than boys in them. For example, a private school opened four years ago has 51 boys and 19 girls.

Illiteracy is the lowest among the Angami. Only 3 out of 47 boys (6.38%) and 2 of 37 girls (5.41%) below 10 are out of school. They are close to 5 and will probably begin school soon. In the 10-14 age group, there are only three illiterates in a total of 136 and the 15-19 age group has 3 out of 131. They are 14 out of 242 (5.79%) in the 20-29 group and 13 out of 112 (11.61%) in the 30-39 cohort. For those above 40, the illiteracy rate is 18.07% among men and 17.07% for women. It is the highest in the 60+ age group. 32 out of 80 or 40% are illiterate. One sees a close link between Christianity and education. Though most of them became Christians before the 1950s, there is substantial change in their educational status during the last 30 years. Many schools and two colleges have been built in the area in the 1980s and one sees its effect in the 68 Angami graduates, 43 of them women, mostly in the 20-39 cohorts. We know from the demographic data that many graduate women have left the region. But their proportion remains high even among those who have remained behind.

Though living in the same region as the Adibasi, there are only 3 illiterates among the Boro in the age groups below 15, all of them in the 5-9 cohorts. They are around 5 years old and will probably begin school soon. Most illiterates are above 30. Among them more women than men are illiterate. Of the 57 (23.46%) illiterates above ten, 47 are above 30. Thus they have made much progress in the last 30 years but only two of them, both men, have completed high school. So while illiteracy is low, so are their prospects of going beyond reading and writing to vocational courses or higher education.

Among the Dimasa too 11 out of 13 illiterates below 20 are in the 5-9 age group and we shall ignore them since they will probably go to school soon. Illiteracy is high in the age groups above 30, particularly among women. 70 out of 123 (58.33%) illiterates in these cohorts are women though they form only 42.28% of the age group. As many as 81.08% of women is illiterate, against 32.67% of men. 80% of those who have completed high school are below 30, so are the 6 who have completed class 12. Thus they have made substantial progress during the last few decades but have stopped at reading and writing. Only 30 have completed high school and two are 2 graduates, both men.

As for the Garo, 246 of the 1,034 (23.79%) family members above five are illiterate. Twenty-one of the 173 (12.14%) girls in the 10-19 age group are illiterate, so are 16 of the 174 boys (9.2%). This difference could have been ignored as not being representative because of their small numbers if the data for the age groups above 20 did not show that while there is near equality in the number of boys and girls, discrimination exists against women in education. 17.56% of the women in the 20-29 cohorts are illiterate against 11.72% of men. Their number goes up to 40 out of 88 (45.45%) against 25 out of 76 (32.89%) for men. In the 40+ cohorts, 56 out of 114 (49.12%) women and 44 out of 150 (40%) men are illiterate. 13 out of 19 graduates are in the 20-29 age group, 33 of the 45 who have completed class 12 are below 30, so are 27 of the 47 who have completed class 10.

Thus much progress has been made during the last 30 years. The data reinforced the fact that the facilities created recently are bearing fruit. This progress itself can add to unrest among them if they remain at this level with no technical training and no job prospects. In reality, investment in productive jobs is low and the illiteracy rate shows a class and gender bias even among the Garo. To understand it one may go back to our earlier analysis of tribal societies keeping a separation between the domestic and social spheres. The woman had a higher status than her caste counterparts did because of the control she exercised over the family sphere. But even in a matrilineal society in which the woman's power went beyond the family to some control over the resources through inheritance, the man continued to represent the family in the social sphere. Education being a social reproduction system and meant to take the person towards the larger society thus belonged to the man's world. So when western education reached them through the Church, men were the first to get its benefits.

However, the Angami have passed through a process of a struggle for their rights. Unrest among them has been called secessionist. Whatever its nature, the point we are making here is that it was a political process which has made it possible for them to internalize an ideology of equality because their nationalist movement was primarily a reaction to the outside control of their economy and imposition of a single culture on them (Sanyu, 1996: 90-93). In other words, it was for the protection of their economy, culture and identity, all of which, they felt, were being threatened. However, this ideology has not gone beyond it to gender equality. As a result the few jobs that are available often go to men. Besides, we found a deficit of women among them in the 20-29 age group. Our field notes show that it is because a large number of educated of this age group migrate away from the region in search of jobs. Besides, women are better educated than men. There are 41 women among 68 graduates among them. Many of them remain unmarried because their social norms demand that the man at least as educated than the woman, if not more.

Occupation and Development

What this shows is that education alone cannot change a society. The State, the Church and other non-governmental agencies have made education available but access to it depends on their social norms. As a result, more boys than girls gain access to school even in a matrilineal tribe. A political process helps as one can see from the educational status of the Angami. However, social norms take over when it comes to jobs and marriage. Besides, our hypothesis was that modernization expressed in commercialization, changing land relations and new cropping patterns strengthens individualism and patriarchy and results in the deterioration of women's status. Studies show that the tribal communities, particularly those practising shifting cultivation, kept a division between the domestic and social spheres. The man controlled the community resources (CPRs) and the woman was in charge of the domestic economy. So the division of work was less unfavourable to women. In settled agriculture based societies the man took decisions both in the family and society and decided the division of labour in agriculture (Fernandes and Menon, 1987: 72-74). Thus as long as the community owned the resource the woman exercised some control over it as the one in charge of the family. With modernization integral to which is individual property, she loses this control over their livelihood (Menon, 1995). Globalization intensifies this process since it is more destructive of the natural resources. We also hypothesised that some negative effects can be overcome with inputs such as women's organization for economic control, social assertion and education.

To understand this situation we studied the occupational pattern of all the members of the respondent families. That too showed a gender and class bias. The two most important occupations among the Adivasi are daily wages and plantation work. A small number is in salaried jobs. In a total of 650 family members above 10, as many as 225 (34.62%) depend on the tea garden for their livelihood. There is a bigger number of women among the plantation workers while there are more men among other salaried persons. Equally important is the fact that five children below 15 are working in the plantations, four of them girls. One may contrast it with the number children of this age group at school. Out of 52 girls only 15 (28.85%) are at school against 32 boys out of 70 (45.71 %). To this number should be added the "missing girls" of this age group. Because of poverty many girls are pulled out of school to work as domestic helpers in middle class families. One can thus see that poverty and not ensuring access to school and to equality, goes against women. They feel the impact of poverty more than men do. Thus one sees both a class and a gender bias in their occupations.

Similar is the situation of the Boro whose literacy rate is better than that of the Adibasi, particularly among girls. Fewer girls than boys are at school but 18 out 28 girls (64.29%) of the 10-14 age group at school compare fairly well with 15 out of 20 boys (75%) studying. However, all four children of this age group involved in agriculture are girls. Unemployment is lower among the Adivasi than among the Boro. 106 out of 528 (20.08%) Adivasis above 15 are unemployed against 66 out of 174 (37.93%) Boros. The main reason seems to be that the former have some jobs in the plantations though on exploitative terms. The latter do not have such a livelihood option and there is low investment in other sectors. That agriculture cannot maintain all of them is confirmed by their small number working in the fields against the big number of the unemployed and daily wage earners.

These two tribes may be contrasted with the Aka who are only now emerging from their tradition, and the Angami who have had access to education and have also experienced the political process of insurgency. Among the Aka 100 out of 237 persons above 15 (42.19%) are involved in agriculture. Women (53) among them are marginally more than men (47) thus indicating some control over *jhum* cultivation. There are 2 daily wage earners and 4 salaried persons among them, 3 of the latter men. Though small in number, they may indicate the beginning of class formation that renders some unemployed and also that modem inputs give preference to men in jobs in the formal sector. 10 boys and girls each are at school in the 5-9 age group and 12 and 9 respectively above 15.

That education can make a difference is seen from the fact that as many 167 of the 734 (22.75%) Angamis above 15 have salaried jobs and 38 (5.18%) are in business. Of equal importance is the fact that all the boys and all except two girls in the 10-14 age group are at school. But only 37 (22.16%) of the 167 persons having salaried jobs, mostly in the administration, are women, thus showing a bias against them though they are better educated than men. Similarly only 7 of the 38 persons involved in business are women. Little wonder then that 51 of the 86 (59.3%) unemployed persons above 15 are women though they are 355 of 734 (51.63%) persons in these cohorts.

The Angami confirm our hypothesis that despite education women's status can remain lower than that of men if adequate measures are not taken in this regard, employment in the secondary sector being the most important. Economic decision-makers have taken no such measures. So the primary sector continues to be the livelihood of 142 women out of 199 (71.36%) family members in this sector. It cannot cater to this highly educated tribe. Besides since their social norms have not changed with the times women cannot receive the type of social support they require. The Dimasa too show the trend visible among the Angami. 42 out of 59 persons having a salaried job (71.19%) are men though they are only 156 (46.43%) out of the 336 family members above 15. On the other side, 84 out of 140 (60%) of those involved in agriculture are women. Unless new jobs are created, unemployment can rise among them. The few jobs available may then be monopolized by men.

While the number of Garo males and females involved in agriculture is almost equal, the other occupations show a male bias also in this matrilineal society. There are only 22 women holding salaried jobs in a total of 83 (26.51%). 165 out of 836 (19.74%) family members above 15 live on daily wages, 60 (36.36%) of them women. Little wonder then that 124 out of 173 (71.68%) unemployed persons are women. 22 are housewives who do not work outside their home. Moreover, there are only 157 girls at school against 180 boys. That shows a polarization between the family and social spheres. The woman had greater control over the domestic sphere. But as the social sphere gets strengthened, men tend to acquire more power at the cost of women.

Women and Access to Wealth

Access to wealth resources has come to be accepted as a valid parameter to gauge women's status, as such an important variable contributing to its understanding. The data given till now point to the fact that many modern inputs can go against women and result in class formation if measures are not taken to ensure the access of all the classes and both the sexes to their benefits. An example of such a change is the matrilineal Garo society in which the issue of a woman's status has to be read alongside that of her male kin who wield considerably more power today than in the past. Though she is the heiress her husband manages the inheritance (Marak 1997: 58-61). The State recognises him as the head of the family and the village. Decisions on land transfer are, therefore, routed through him. In parts of the East Garo hills there has been a slow transition to cash crops that are not fully conducive to community control over land. Hence, land transfer to individuals is being encouraged with a distinct slant towards men who alone can deal with such crops. The decision to transfer land for commercial use is taken by the man, not the woman, the heiress. Since only a few moneyed persons can grow these crops it leads also to class formation in the process of modernization and commercialization.

The Basis of Ethnic Conflicts

In an effort to understand the totality we analyzed the changes in their economic status pertaining to their access and control over the natural and other resources and the extent to which commercialization has affected their role in the economy. We also looked at the power women and men enjoyed in the domestic and social spheres in the past and their situation today. This issue is closely linked to their access to the community's wealth producing capacities. We used the decision-making process in the family as an indicator to analyze gender-based changes in the power structure. To do it we looked at women's traditional role in their cultural and social systems and the result of recent economic and social processes. Through this analysis, we tested our hypothesis on tribal women's status and social standing in the Northeast in a society in a flux. As stated already, the data at our disposal indicate that Angami women have dealt with these changes better than the others have done. But their social system has not changed thus creating a new dichotomy between social and domestic spheres. Adivasi women are the worst victims, followed by the Boro of Balipara.

A sector we studied is the changeover from jhum to settled agriculture. The first factor that came out is the exclusion of women from decision-making in the latter. The second is land alienation and class formation through individual ownership. In every case there is a transition to individually owned land from the CPRs. Even among the Angami, 13 of the 170 families studied are landless but 24 own more than five acres of land, 29 more than 10 acres. Thus class formation is emerging among them. They are among the few tribes that practise a form of terrace cultivation that is technologically close to settled agriculture while retaining many features of shifting cultivation. For example, unlike in most other tribes, Angami women far from being barred from working the terraced fields with ploughs are expected to do so (D'Souza 2001). One does not make an absolute of ploughing because there is an opinion that barring women from it is a way of ensuring that they are not overworked. The point made is that class formation creates a gap between the better off sections and the poor among the Angami, control over division of work shifts to men. Equally important is the fact that most tribes go back to their tradition to justify male domination. The customary laws among the Angami and the Sixth Schedule among the others is interpreted by men, and the State deals only with them. They present as their interpretation of the indigenous status that gives them exclusive right over the resource. However, it is interpreted according to the interests of men from the elite.

One can see in Table 3 that land alienation is high among the tribes. In most cases it is lost through indebtedness because of growing poverty. In other cases it is sold for social needs or to educate children, many of whom remain jobless. It is in this context of land alienation, high dependence on agriculture and lack of productive investment that one can also situate many conflicts in the Northeast. As a result, the process of ethnic relations becoming antagonistic over the issue of access to resources is real. That, for example, is the basis of the Boro-Kokrajar conflict that is justified in the name of their right to the resources in the name of their indigenous status (Kar 1999), which is denied to the Adivasi. Unlike most other tribes the Angami have found an alternative to land alienation in the form of jobs in the tertiary sector. However, the number of educated persons is growing but employment generation is low. While a scenario of total

Table 3

Land Ownership by Tribe in Bighas*

Tribes	Landless	Jhum	0.1-0.5	0.6-3.0	3.1-7.5	7.6- 15.0	15.1-30	30+	Total
Adibasi	128	0	1	22	12	6	0	0	169
Aka	3	38	0	0	0	2	0	0	41
Angami	13	1	1	63	21	18	24	29	170
Boro	32	0	0	3	14	6	3	0	58
Dimasa	1	40	0	39	21	4	1	0	106
Garo	84	0	1	56	41	28	8	5	223
Total	261	79	3	183	109	64	36	34	769

*mone acre is three bighas

alienation may not become visible in the foreseeable future, there is sufficient cause for concern. The changes that are occurring can have a negative impact on the community as a whole and women in particular. It is true particularly about the Adivasi who are the most powerless group and can be rendered further powerless. Hence, there is the need to find alternatives to the processes that marginalize some communities.

Search for a Solution

The analysis can be extended to other aspects, such as, changing power relations in the family, the issue of succession, the role of the market and others. However, we do not need to go into every aspect studied because the data given point to the fact that modernization breaks up the community into classes and that the woman's status deteriorates. Commercialization introduces changes in favour of men from the elite. The spectre of impoverishment and unemployment as well as the attack on their identity and livelihood result in ethnic conflicts. Each tribe claims exclusive right over the use of the depleted resources and tries to exclude all others. We have also seen that when education combines with an awareness of rights, there is a possibility of the subalterns demanding equality and of developing protective mechanisms against their marginalization. That is difficult in the case of the powerless groups like the Adivasi. But the power structures do not always respond to their demands. Many aspirations of men as well as modern inputs do not necessarily go in the direction of equality.

It is in this context that we studied issues like inheritance and the market. We realize that we need to take a new look at the customary law. A constitutional amendment of 1963 protects their customary law under Article 371A. The Sixth Schedule plays a similar role for some other tribes. But the Boro and the Adivasi do not have any such protective mechanism. However, today though this demand comes in the name of identity, its primary objective is exclusive control over the depleted resources. The Adivasi-Baro conflict in Assam, the Naga-Kuki, as well as the Naga-Meitei conflicts in Manipur, are for land to which is linked their tribal identity.

It is in this context that we need to go back to the issue of lack of productive investment. Education is to be encouraged. However, today it has become a source of disillusionment and of unrest among the tribals, who are deprived of their livelihood. In the absence of productive investment they have to compete for the few jobs in the tertiary sector or continue to depend on the primary sector, neither of which is expanding. That has to be the first step to be taken. Drug addiction, criminalization and other escape mechanisms as well as the unrest whether in the form of ethnic conflicts or reaction to outsiders cannot be solved unless the highly educated youth can be offered hope of a new livelihood. They also need protection against attacks on the culture and identity.

In reality, that is not being done. Inaugurating a seminar on Prospects of Peace in Assam at Guwahati in late August 2001, Mr Tarun Gogoi, the chief minister of Assam said that the State needs two million new jobs. If that is true, then the estimate for the whole of the Northeast should be raised to three million new jobs. In reality there is no investment in the secondary sector. Several industries have closed down in the 1990s and hardly any new one has been opened. Besides, having that form of industrialization is not a solution to unemployment, which is a basic cause of unrest and competition for the scarce resources. Alternatives have to be found to it because the present form of globalization based investment and industrialization do not create jobs. According to estimates the GNP in the country as a whole has grown by between 5% and 6.5% but employment generation has been negative. According to ILO estimates 8 million jobs were lost in India by the mid-1990s and the figure has grown since then. Moreover, the cost of a new industrial job had gone up to Rs. one million by the late 1990s and must have increased further today. Thus the cost of solving the unemployment problem one needs at least Rs three trillion and such resources are not available.

What it means is that alternatives have to be found to the form of investment too. Offers are being made to the private sector, particularly to foreign investors to invest in the Northeast to solve the problems. In reality they cannot solve the problem. The Northeast requires employment intensive low capita based employment generation. It can be done only by going back to their livelihood i.e. land which cannot expand any more. The alternative is to expand its use in such a way as to make it more productive. Simultaneously loss of more of their livelihood has to be prevented. For example, plans are afoot to build more than 100 massive hydel dams in the Northeast, which is one of the 25 mega-biodiversity zones of the world. The objective is to sell power to other States. They will thus bring in some income to the States but not new jobs. In the process the livelihood of many more communities will be lost without replacement though not many may be physically displaced. All the studies on development-induced displacement and deprivation point to impoverishment and further marginalization of the already powerless. The same will be the situation in the Northeast.

What is needed is to find modes of making the present type of resources more productive by helping the community as a co-operative to invest in components like agro-industries. The communities need much training and support to turn themselves into production and marketing co-operatives. That is where educational institutions, the State and civil society have to work together. One needs in this region the type of education that can build up the confidence the communities require to take control of their local economy, to make their resources productive and market them. Most of these components are in the hands of outsiders and the local communities have to be trained in a new form of management of their livelihood.

Questioning Tradition

It has also to be done in such a way that their culture and identity are protected. In saying it we focus on the customary laws and the Sixth Schedule of the Consitution because these tribes present them as mechanisms essential to safeguard their identity that is under threat. This issue cannot be ignored in the name of national development. We have seen from the data given above that their livelihood is being alienated from them. The communities run the risk of being impoverished and marginalized because of it. So protective mechanisms are needed. But one needs to study some of its implication. For example, their customary tends to be interpreted by men from the elite in their own favour. It has created in the elite a vested interest both in class formation and stronger forms of patriarchy. That is what has happened in the case of inheritance and jobs. The changes that have come about through education are ignored in their customary law.

Besides, there is a tendency among many tribes to romanticize their community tradition and claim that all answers are found in it. This trend can be seen in the effort of the Naga to protect their customary laws. They demanded this right when there was a threat to their identity and needed to combine its protection with education. But they have not done enough to protect women's rights, instead have often used the customary law in the opposite direction. It shows that left to itself modernization strengthens a male dominated society. Their society adapts itself to these values and re-interprets their customary law to strengthen class formation led by men from the elite.

The other aspect that comes out is the hardening of the identities. It is closely linked to migration and external control over the resources. With the shortage of resources, many tribes demand exclusive control over the resources because they are indigenous to the region. They perceive their livelihood resources as being depleted by outsiders and often struggle against the State that they perceive as handing their economy over to outsiders. Thus the economic, social, cultural and other causes interact in the demand for an indigenous status. Because of it, "the three steps of defending their livelihood, protecting their identity and propounding a sub-nationalism specific to a cultural and ethnic group merge into one" (Fernandes, 1999: 3579). However, while protecting their indigenous status, they are not ready to share their resources with others who are not their exploiters but may be victims of the same system that marginalizes them. While hardening their indigenous identity, they also expand the definition of the "outsider" to include all the tribes that they perceive as being in competition.

This analysis shows the need for a new culture in the context of recent changes including commercialization and globalization. We have not given in this paper the perception of our respondents about changes in their status during the last three decades. The data we collected show that a majority of the respondents betray a sense of frustration and helplessness as well as strong resentment. That is the foundation of ethnic conflicts. That is the reason for a new culture which not to be interpreted as the externals of song and dance or language though they too are important.

The first effort is to protect their land, forests and the rest of their livelihood from outsiders. One has also to counter the tendency to accept the values that go both against the sustainable use of their livelihood and women. So in order to build a new culture of sustainable use of their livelihood that also makes it more productive, one cannot go to the externals of their tradition but to the value system that guided it. A study of most tribes shows that the three values that guided them are inter-generational and intra-generational equity and a relatively high status of women. A new culture has to begin with these values and modernize them, for example, by accepting equality rather than a relatively high status of women. Equity and sustainable use have to result in the maximization of land and forest resources without destroying them. That can give a new meaning to equity and sharing that can go beyond individual tribes that harden their identity in order to demand exclusive use of the resource, to sharing with all those who have gone through the common experience of alienation.

Conclusion

In this paper we have discussed some processes of alienation in the Northeast of India, with specific reference to the six tribes. We have mentioned the processes of alienation of their livelihood and culture that results in the present unrest. We have alluded to the role of culture. It cannot be understood as a 'given' condition of social life but is contingent upon various other factors. Political and economic developments influence it. This in turn is further articulated in its interpretation by various interest groups within the community. We have seen culture through the prism of social institutions and the manner in which individuals, especially women figure in the social relations within the social institutions. That showed us its role in social reproduction and the need to create a new indigenous culture and identity. We have seen that also the educational institutions have inculcated a spirit of awareness. However, the region needs more changes to help them to take control of their local economy in their region. In this context one has to look at various possibilities of change that education and other institutions can facilitate in their communities.

These issues are a challenge to persons in education, religious leaders and the civil society. When the culture, economy and very identity of the people they serve are under attack, their work has to strengthen their identity. It is also clear that no single component can give all the answers. Culture, education, religion and the economy have to combine in a common enterprise. Social leadership, the voluntary sector, religious leaders and educationists have to come together to develop alternatives to these processes that marginalize the people. To achieve it a new understanding of equity has to be built on their culture. One cannot go back to the past and maintain all their beliefs and practices intact. Instead educational and religious institutions have to join civil society in helping their social system to change to respond to the aspirations of equality. Thus social, cultural and economic changes have to go hand in hand to support a new indigenous identity based on class and gender equity.

REFERENCES

Barbora, Sanjay. 2002. "Ethnic Politics and Land Use: Genesis of Conflicts in India's North-East," *Economic and Political Weekly*, 37(13): 1285-1292.

Butola, B. S. 1997. "Crisis of Hegemony and Counter-Hegemonic Insurgency in Northeast India," in B. Pakem (ed). *Insurgency in Northeast India.* New Delhi: Omsons Publications, pp. 73-88.

D'Souza, Alphonsus. 1999. *Northeast India*. Jakhama: Kohima Region of the Society of Jesus.

D'Souza, Alphonsus. 2001. *Traditional systems of Forest Conservation in Northeast India: The Angami Tribe of Nagaland*. Guwahati: Northeastern Social Research Centre.

Dubey, Amaresh and Shubhashis Gangopadhyay. 1998. "Turbulent Intelligence," *The Telegraph*. March 23.

Ekka. Francis. 1990. "Linguistic Implications of Migration to the Tea Gardens," In: S. Karotemprel and B. Dutta Roy (eds). *Tea Garden Labourers of Northeast India: A Multidimensional Study on the Adivasis of the Tea Gardens of Northeast India*. Shillong: Vendrame Institute, pp. 143-155.

Fernandes, Walter. 1999. "Conflict in North-East: A Historical Perspective," *Economic and Political Weekly*, 34(51): 3579-3582.

Fernandes, Walter. 2001. "The Challenge of Peace amid Social Change in the Northeast," *Jnanadeepa Pune Journal of Religious Studies.*, 4(1, January): 87-100.

Fernandes, Walter and Geeta Menon. 1987. *Tribal Women and Forest Economy: Deforestation. Exploitation and Status Change*. New Delhi: Indian Social Institute.

Fernandes, Walter and Sanjay Barbora. 2002. *Modernisation and Women's Status in Northeastern India: A Comparative Study of Six Tribes*. Guwahati: Northeastern Social Research Centre.

Kar, R. K. A Panoramic View of the Tea and Ex-Tea Tribes of Assam. In: Thomas Pullopillil (ed), *Identity of Adivasis in Assam*. Delhi: Indian Publishers Distributors, pp. 21-46.

Marak, Caroline. 1997. "Status of Women in Garo Culture" in Soumen Sen (ed). *Women in Meghalaya*, New Delhi: Omsons, pp. 56-72.

Menon, Geeta. 1995. "The Impact of Migration on the Work and Tribal Women's Status," in Loes Schenken-Sandbergen (ed). *Women and Seasonal Labour Migration*. New Delhi: Sage, pp. 79-154.

Misra, Udayon. 2000. *The Periphery Strikes Back*, Shimla: Indian Institute of Advanced Studies.

NEC. 1995. *Basic Statistics of North-Eastern Region*. Shillong: Northeastern Zonal Council.

Registrar General and Census Commissioner. 1994: *Primary Census Abstracts: Scheduled Tribes Castes I, Part II-B (ii)*. Delhi: The Comptroller of Publications.

Registrar General and Census Commissioner. 2001: *Census of India 2001: Provisional Population Totals.* Delhi: The Controller of Publications.

Sanyu,Visier. 1996. *A History of Nagas and Nagaland: Dynamics of Tradition Village Formation.* New Delhi: Commonwealth Publications.

Sen, Sipra. 1992. *Tribes of Mizoram: Description, Ethnology and Bibliography.* New Delhi: Gian Publishing House.

UNDP. 1997. *India: The Road to Human Development.* New Delhi: United Nations Development Programme.

SECTION II

INDO-CHINA AND BHUTAN RELATIONS - IMPLICATIONS FOR NORTHEASTERN REGION

5

India's China Policy: Implications for the Security and Development of the Northeastern Region

—C.V. RANGANATHAN

The approach in this paper is to examine the Indo-China relations from interdependent perspectives involving some outstanding issues connected with security. However, the attempt is to deal with security from a more comprehensive angle than purely military or territorial aspects. And lastly, the potential benefits to the Northeast India, which either abuts the more populated portions of the long Indo-China boundary or the neighbours developing parts of China are looked at, given the recent welcome signs of a qualitative improvement of relations between the two countries.

Two sections of the Indo-China boundary run along the Northeast India, which are of great strategic value. The first section, the shorter one, includes the Sikkim-Tibet boundary. This is the only section of the long Indo-China boundary, which is not disputed. It has been peaceful except for a very few aberrations in times when relations between the two countries had reached a very low point. The lowest points in Sino-Indian relations from 1962, when the armed conflict took place till 1976, also marked a period of intense domestic turmoil in China. One needs only to recall the Mao Zedong inspired Great Proletarian Cultural Revolution, which lasted from 1966-1976 in this context. That era seems to be light-years away when one looks at how China has developed from the early eighties to the present. During these two decades and more, the emphasis in China's external strategies has been to work towards achieving a peaceful environment surrounding China in all directions, a situation which would enable it to concentrate on economic and social development. The results are there for all to see.

The second section of the borders of the Northeast India with Tibet comprises of Arunachal Pradesh's border with China. The Chinese claims to overwhelming portions of areas south of the MacMahon Line in Arunachal Pradesh pose vital strategic and diplomatic challenges to India. 1962 showed that it is possible to breach this trans-Himalayan mountainous frontier and the trauma to the national psyche still persists. The ecological and economic worth of Arunachal Pradesh to India hardly needs emphasis. Much of the waters that originate from the Tibetan region and irrigate India and Bangladesh, flows through the State. It is populated, it is resource rich and it is a frontier State guarding India's precious assets in the east Himalayan region. The value of this region for the territorial integrity of India and particularly its Northeast contrasts greatly with the other major area under Chinese claim in Ladakh.

Although disputed and fought over and pending the eventual solution of the boundary question, a status quo, which is favourable to India prevails in Arunachal Pradesh. India is in complete control of all areas to the south of the MacMahon Line in Arunachal Pradesh while the area claimed by China in Ladakh is under the Chinese control. A notional Line of Actual Control all along the Indo-China boundary has come into existence since 1962 and with very few exceptions peace and tranquility have prevailed along this line for over two and a half decades.

Pragmatism and maturity shown by the Governments and armed forces of both countries over these decades have characterized the management of the Indo-China boundary dispute. This management has contributed to the removal of the high degree of emotionalism, which marked discussions and parliamentary debates concerning the boundary dispute till a few decades ago. There are various landmarks in relations, which have brought about the tension-free management of the boundary dispute. The 1979 visit of Atal Bihari Vajpayee to China in his capacity then of External Affairs Minister, the return visit in 1981 of the Chinese Foreign Minister, the visit to China of former Prime Minister Rajiv Gandhi in 1988, followed by a steady stream of highest level exchanges between leaders of the two countries since.

In 1993 and 1996 two major agreements of political and military significance were signed, when former Prime Minister Narasimha Rao visited China followed by a reciprocal visit by Chinese President Jiang Zemin. These two agreements have far reaching implications for restoring confidence and trust to the relationship particularly in those sections of the military leadership in both countries where it is most needed. When implemented they would have a beneficial fall out on political and public opinion. Centred around mutual agreement on the delineation of the Line of Actual Control which separates the armed forces of both countries, there are a wide array of articles dealing with mutual withdrawals of troops and equipment, disengagement in agreed geographical zones, conduct of ground and aerial exercises, and a series of confidence building measures. Exchanges of official maps on large scales, an exercise which has commenced would help each side understand better the perceptions of the other side on the alignment of the Line of Actual Control. De facto peace and tranquility has prevailed along the Indo-China boundary over more than two decades where not a shot has been fired in anger. When Indian troops were engaged in Kargil in 1999 or mobilized in 2001 across the Pakistan borders, no diversionary Chinese troop movements across Arunachal Pradesh or Ladakh, which would cause concern, have been reported. An imaginative use of the provisions of the two Agreements of 1993 and 1996 would ensure that Indian and Chinese forces can guard the borders in a non-violent and non-provocative manner. The exercise of implementing the two agreements on the ground is without prejudice to the position of both countries on the substance of the boundary dispute. This should remove suspicions that the Line of Actual Control would eventually congeal into a permanent boundary agreement to the disadvantage of either side.

Given the fact that neither side has undertaken the important task of preparing public opinion for alienation of territory, a permanent boundary agreement between India and China is still a distant prospect. Exaggerated worries about the electoral prospect of political parties in India seem to be an inhibiting factor for both ruling parties or coalitions to squarely face the issue. Preoccupation with domestic matters and concerns about Tibetan reactions over deals involving original Tibetan claims to places in Arunachal Pradesh seem to be consideration-on the Chinese side. Without the exercise of the necessary political will in either country and the build up of a perception of mutual gains from a more vibrant overall relationship between India and China, the resolution of the boundary dispute would not be possible. But the maintenance of a tension free environment surrounding the boundary is a welcome sign that the relationship has acquired more maturity.

Forward looking and pragmatic approaches to the management of the Indo-China boundary have contributed to the abatement of the territorial dispute being a matter of deep security concern to India and China. While there is a *de facto* military stability along the Himalayan frontiers, however, there are certain residual Indian political concerns, which impede the full realization of economic opportunities for the border States of Sikkim and Arunachal Pradesh on the Indian side and to Tibet on the Chinese side. Non-acknowledgement of the accession of Sikkim to India by China is one such obstacle. Although China has not hesitated to deal with the reality of India's administrative authority in Sikkim or its military control in the Sikkim-Tibet border regions, China is perhaps the only country in the world that has not recognized Sikkim as one of the States of the Indian Union. The historic factors, which contributed to this situation, have lost their salience. Flexible solutions need to be found to this question if the age old trade and cultural ties between

Sikkim and Tibet are to be restored to the mutual benefit of these two entities. A leaf can be taken out of China's own example from the deep and intense economic relationship, which China and Taiwan enjoy in spite of an adverse and abnormal political relationship. The separation of politics from economics is what the Chinese practised for many years before the normalization of relations between China and a whole host of countries in her neighbourhood and elsewhere.

China's friendship with Pakistan and its assistance to Pakistan in building up its conventional and non-conventional capabilities is often seen by strategic thinkers in India as a threat to India's security.

September 11 has provided a sobering opportunity for India and China to carefully examine how the Pakistan factor in the Indo-China-Pakistan triangle can be dealt with. This may seem difficult to envisage in a situation where relations between India and Pakistan have reached a nadir by early 2002. However, with some exceptions, contemporary Chinese behaviour on some issues, which bedevil the Indo-Pakistan relations, provides room for optimism that the future evolution of the triangle could be beneficial to the region. From the Eighties when the prospects of Sino-Indian relations improved, China's position on Kashmir, which is seen as one of the litmus tests by both India and Pakistan of their relations with China, has become very nuanced. This must belie unreal Pakistani expectations, which do not take account of the real politics behind China's readjustments of policies towards the sub-continent.

The readjustment of China's relations in the Indo-Pakistan context and towards other countries in the South Asian neighbourhood is based not merely on the shifting contours of post-cold war geopolitics. Acknowledgement that India is the predominant power in the region is recognition of a reality that has existed for long. No outside power can displace India for its obvious impact on its neighbourhood, nor displace the interdependence within the region that geography compels.

China's support to the consolidation of the development of regional cooperation through the South Asian Association for Regional Cooperation (SAARC) is of a piece with its policies in South-East Asia and elsewhere. Multi-polarity in the international order which China desires as an alternative to the dominance of single powers could be achieved, in its prescription, through the emergence of autonomous regional groupings working together to realize common developmental objectives and through multilateralism. An important statement made in the Pakistani Senate by President Jiang Zemin in 1996 emphasized the importance attached by China to the success of SAARC for peace and development in the region. Then he went on to add that, "if certain issues cannot be resolved for the time being, they may be shelved temporarily so that they will not affect the normal State-to-State relations". His audience in Pakistan may not have relished the statement.

The Chinese took the opportunity of September 11 to provide a detailed official statement about the various pan-Turkic organizations, which were indulging in terrorism, subversion, sabotage and fomenting internal dissensions within Xinjiang in recent times. In a lengthy article prepared by the Information office of the State Council in January 2002, the ultimate aim of these organization was seen as the formation of a state of "East Turkistan" composed by those Muslim minorities who speak Turkic language and are spread across borders shared by Xinjiang and some Central Asian States. The historical precedent of a short-lived East Turkistan Islamic State set up in November 1933 in Kashgar in Xinjiang is recalled as an example of local extremists colluding with foreign forces to split Xinjiang from China in the colonial era.

Detailing the names of the various organizations and their anti-China activities, the article seeks to prove that China is also a victim of international terrorism. One organization in particular, "the East Turkistan Islamic Movement" whose aim is the setting up of a theoretic Islam State in Xinjiang has been seen as directly supported by Osama Bin Laden. He is reported as having advised the movement to link up with the Uzbekistan Islamic Liberation Movement and the Taliban in Afghanistan and as having provided financial and arms assistance to it. All these provide the rationale for supporting the international coalition against terrorism and the intelligence assistance provided by China to USA.

What should be of interest to India is that the article clearly acknowledges that the anti-Xinjiang terrorists based in Afghanistan and other areas on China's periphery have made a "strategic shift" by evacuating its members from these places to South Asia (Pakistan is not named) and other Central and West Asian regions after the military interventions in Afghanistan. The threat of their regrouping and continuing activities aimed at China is acknowledged. The more open, albeit indirect, admission that the Taliban in Afghanistan and its southern base could continue to pose threats is a common feature which India and China share.

If China is to be a constructive partner in the loose international coalition against terrorism, then the coyness with which she dealt with officially supported terrorism of the Taliban-type by Pakistan and other Gulf States needs to be given up *vis-a-vis* India. For some years before September 11, China was a victim of externally sponsored terrorist activities but her attempts at curbing such activities through quiet diplomacy with Pakistan and direct engagement of the Taliban regime, did not produce satisfactory results for China.

The agreement during Premier Zhu Rongji's visit to India in January 2002 to set up a mechanism to exchange views on terrorism is therefore a welcome development. Sino-Indian cooperation in this field has a much wider spatial significance for Asia than the subcontinent. With their growing economies, incomplete control over their peripheries, not fully developed financial and legal systems, both India and China must frankly deal with various complexities. Effective cooperation to diminish if not eliminate the opaque nexus of international finance with trans-border crimes, the spread of drugs, terrorism and other ills, requires better domestic systems of governance than they presently have. Frank recognition of these aspects should inform their separate and combined actions in combating international terrorism even as they build-up the confidence to cooperate with each other.

The emergence of a stable, modernizing, self-assured and moderate Pakistan is clearly in the interest of both India and China. Both have welcomed President Musharraf's address to the nation on 12 January, 2002 in this context. It would be churlish for Indians to be dismissive about Chinese claims that policies towards Pakistan have been readjusted. Yes, the Chinese posture that they seek to establish good relations with India without jeopardizing their long established friendly relations with Pakistan is not mere semantics. For a variety of reasons including the fear that American and western influence would become entrenched in Pakistan to China's detriment, the Chinese policies would continue to be oriented towards the maintenance of friendship with Pakistan.

How China is going to square the circle of seeking an improved relationship with India while assisting Pakistan strengthen itself in the conventional and non-conventional military fields, would remain a conundrum. Such assistance, it may be argued, minimized the strategic superiority of India *vis-a-vis* Pakistan. The contradictory strands of the Chinese approach have perhaps drawn more emotive reactions in India than the unresolved boundary dispute. The Pakistan card in the Chinese hands is seen by some in India as a deliberate attempt to restrict Indian energies to the sub-continent. Such thinking may overstate the realities. But they do draw attention to the need to find a proper equilibrium in the Indo-China-Pakistan triangular relationship with which all three can be comfortable.

On China's assistance in the nuclear and missile fields to Pakistan, India has no direct leverages to exert *vis-a-vis* China. India cannot accept at face value the bland assertions by China that it abides by international norms and non proliferation rules after her accession to the Non-Proliferation Treaty. However, after September 11 the situation has changed dramatically within Pakistan, which could work to India's advantage. China's own fears about weapons of mass destruction falling into irresponsible and wrong hands create some convergences with American positions on the subject. While USA-Chinese dialogues on the issue of China's proliferation have not satisfied the Americans that the Chinese are prepared to make firm commitments, there could be limited region-specific agreements, with respect to those regions which are proven hosts of terrorist havens. Further American ground presence in Pakistan enhances surveillance over clandestine or official transfers of material and technologies, which go towards development of non-conventional weapons of mass destruction. The confidence and trust in China's intentions for the further improvement of Sino-Indian relations to which leaders of the two countries have committed themselves, would be severely affected if continuing evidence of Chinese assistance to Pakistan in the non conventional fields surfaces as often as it does.

Myanmar's admission to the ASEAN some years back has made the ASEAN an immediate neighbour of India. Realizing that complementarities between Myanmar have to be exploited to the benefit of populations in Northeast India, India has made modest investments in building road links to connect Indian States to the western parts of Myanmar. Cooperation with Myanmar to cope with insurgency and drug smuggling is of vital importance to India. Promotion of Indian investments in infrastructure and industrial projects in Myanmar needs to be enhanced. The Hanoi Declaration of the ASEAN in July 2001 adopted the Initiative for ASEAN Integration (IAI), a bold plan for the integration of the markets of Cambodia, Laos, Myanmar, and Vietnam.

Initiated in Kunming, capital of Yunnan province in China in 1999, three rounds of academic level discussions have focused on possible multi-modal land connectivities, cross border trade and investments and cultural exchanges, involving Bangladesh, India, Myanmar and Yunnan province of China. The diverse ethnic populations of the Northeast India and Bangladesh have been cut off from mainstream developments on account of their geographical isolation and remoteness. Cross-border exchanges can go a long way to supplement developmental plans to improve the economic well being of populations in the peripheries. China's future plans involve massive infrastructural investments in Tibet, Yunnan, Sichuan, Xinjiang and other south western provinces to redress the serious regional imbalances, which have cropped up after economic reforms. All these areas are not distant neighbours of India and the Chinese investments to develop its neglected western region would have an impact on India in this ever shrinking world.

For the academic initiatives mentioned above to bear fruit it is time that governments either support or involve themselves in the exercise. Numerous areas such as effective border and security management, provision of infrastructure in roads and navigation links, facilities for cross border trade, banking and other amenities need to be attended to. In this as in other areas the required political will for sub-regional cooperation and imaginative approaches are required. If substance is to be added to the frequent announced intention of "looking east" in India's foreign policy, a beginning needs to be made with our immediate eastern neighbourhood before we look further a field. The active participation of the Chinese and the Myanmarese delegations in these initiatives would show that neither does Myanmar see itself as an exclusive area of Chinese involvement, nor does China exclude India and Bangladesh from expanding Myanmar's western links.

Historically, the great commercial and cultural movements in Asia had both a continental and maritime dimension within a Four Water Quadrant bound by the lower Ganga/ Brahmaputra to the South and the West, the Yangstzekiang to the North and the Mekong to the East. This quadrant, one of the most populated but poorest regions of the world straddles East Asia, South and South East Asia. Today cooperation between the sovereign entities that compose the quadrant are meant to be structured through an alphabet soup of organizations that have been formed on the basis of geographically contiguous regional and sub-regional groupings. This is an acknowledgement that there is a unity of shared geography, which has been converted into assets for development by modern technology and means of communications.

The vast regions of India from Uttar Pradesh to the Northeastern States have rich natural resources, which could be optimized only through trans-border cooperation and promoted by all the concerned States. The imperative of harnessing the potential of the river waters of India-Nepal-Bhutan-Bangladesh needs no reiteration. As for the Northeastern States, the Governmental Task Force on "Transforming the North East" has stressed the importance of restoring and augmenting the Northeast's historic cross-border links with Myanmar, Bangladesh, Tibet and South-west China, an idea whose time has come.

It is time that Governments and peoples of the SAARC region pay more emphasis to geo-economics than what has prevailed so far. Political parties and concerned NGO's, academicians need to be made aware of the inherent potential of what George Verghese and others have described as "land bridge architectures". Harnessing the abundant water and energy resources, promotion of cross-border multi modal communications, facilitation of cross border trade through transit links and construction of the required infrastructure in roads and ports should be the developmental priorities. Security for the sovereign States in South Asia needs to be understood in a more comprehensive sense than the narrow confines of conflict, power and military balance theories.

6

Ethnic Engagement in Bhutan and its Regional Consequences

—A.C. SINHA

State is a civil community having its own government and law. As per convention, it is attributed to have a definite territory, a population of citizens, a functioning government and its sovereignty of governance. It is entirely another matter that these ideal typical conditions are rarely found even in the case of most appropriate example of the State. Indian Union as a State is similarly no exception to the above generalization. What legally it claims as her territory is disputed by some of her neighbours. There are non-citizens residing illegally within her bounds. Its government does not govern in a similar way to all her regions and citizens. And in matters of sovereignty, its helplessness gets occasionally exposed when the terrorists mount attacks with impunity. Northeast India provides an example to the utter negation of all the above attributes of an ideal Indian State. But one cannot wish it away as it is. In case, we seriously consider the region for a meaningful understanding, we have to look closely across the territorial limits to the neighbouring countries. One such country is Bhutan, which is more exclusive, different, distant and dissimilar to India. Yet, the Bhutanese scenario has far reaching implications for Northeast in particular and South Asia in general.

We assume that the claimed State system of Bhutan is sacrosanct. Similarly, the territorial limits, legal citizens, and her functionaries provide us with given parameter. Bhutan, located on the eastern Himalayan ranges on the northeastern boundary of India, has been painted as an ideal system of its own. Its monks, forts, snow, and the royalty were all described as other-worldly. It was a blissful Shangri-La away from din and bustle of the crowded metropolis. It had a few people and plenty of space; dense forests with roaring wild creatures; perennial snow-fed rivers and lamaseries with monks and nuns perched on the hanging snowy slops. This ideally and other worldly image of the Druk kingdom is totally shattered today, because of the on-going ethnic strife. The country is undergoing a phase of low intensity conflict, a new phenomenon for her, but with a serious potential for a regional conflagration. This paper is an attempt to trace out the background of the ethnic conflict and its consequences to the Indian region in particular and the South Asian Association of Regional Co-operation (SAARC) in general.

Ethnic Background

The Drukpa State of Bhutan is the creation of the Tibetan immigrants. Shabdrung Ngawang Namgyal (1594-1651), one among them, laid the foundation of this unique polity in the first half of the 17th century. Some of the significant aspects of this polity may be identified with the theocratic legitimacy based on incarnation, ubiquitous oligarchic conflict, duality of authority, and extremely fragile and limited economic base (Sinha, 1998). This mode of government continued up to 17th December 1907, when Ugyen Wangchuk (1861-1926) founded the present ruling dynasty, when he was crowned as the Maharaja of the Bhutanese princely State under the tutelage of the British. Ugyen Wangchuk's rise in 1880's also coincided with the arrival of another ethnic group of the Nepalese (who were later designed as the Lhotshampas) on the southern Bhutanese Duars as lumbermen, herdsmen and farmers.

Ugyen Wangchuk and John Claude White, a British political officer at Gangtok, struck a good working relationship. So much so that the latter was invited after his retirement in England to introduce tea plantation and timber farming in the southern Bhutanese foothills. Much earlier in life, White was impressed with the industrious Nepalese and it was he who was instrumental in introducing them to develop southern Sikkim. He was in close contact with the Bhutanese agent,

Ugyen Dorji, who was appointed in 1898 the chief of Haa region (in entire Bhutan Duar), with a right to settle the Lhotshampas. For the next six and half a decade, cash-starved Bhutan Durbar was provided with their cash requirements by the Bhutanese Agent, which he extracted from the new settlers. It was a case of classical exploitation. The settlers had no tenancy rights. Their settlements were haphazard and huddled around bamboo huts after clearing the dense tropical forests.

There were no means of communication and transportation. They had neither education nor any facilities for health. They had no civil rights and they were exposed to the exploitation and brutalities of the durbar functionaries. Dissent was suppressed with a heavy hand so that the settlers did not deny demands made on them. There were instances when an alleged difficult tenant could be sewn alive in a raw leather sack and thrown away in the turbulent river to meet his watery grave (Dhakal, 1994). In this atmosphere of stark suppression, there was no way a resistance could be organized against the durbar brutalities. The settlers had a limited choice either to comply with all sorts of demands on them or leave Bhutan for good. But all the available alternative destinations to the Nepalese in the first half of 20th century had almost the same features. Thus, bulk of them stayed put on the slippery Bhutanese Duars.

Bhutan could not remain untouched by the fast changing political scenario all around neighboring countries. China had invaded Tibet in the north. The British had withdrawn from India, leaving behind two successor States of Indian Union and Pakistan. The two Himalayan kingdoms on the western border of Bhutan, Sikkim and Nepal, were under the spell of anti-feudal agitation, rooting for the installation of popular governments. Needless to add that the Sikkim State Congress and the Nepali Congress - both spearheading the populist movements in Sikkim and Nepal respectively - were predominantly Nepali fora. Thus, in the very first year of the third Druk Gyalpo's reign (1952-72), one finds the ripples of the Lhotshampas "cogitation in the form of Bhutan State Congress". The agitation programme on the part of the Bhutan State Congress was ill-timed, because of the fact that in a universally illiterate, isolated and an extremely despotic regime, a popular agitation for civil and political rights, abolition of landed estates, responsible government, were premature. No doubt, the movement was suppressed with an iron hand and all types of political agitation were banned on the soil of Bhutan for the time to come. Naturally, the leaders of the Bhutan State Congress kept away from Bhutan and lived in exile till the Royal pardon was granted to them in the 1960's.

Events forced the third Wangchuk ruler to review the Bhutanese approach to the Lhotshampas from a cold tolerance to reluctant acceptance in the Dukpa State structure. For the first time, a Bhutan Citizenship Act, 1958 was enacted, which provided with a status to the Lhostshampas. Their language was recognized and it soon began to be taught in the primary schools. They were permitted to build their shrines and teach Sanskrit, the language of their scriptures. Moreover, the State adopted a conscious ethnic policy of assimilating the Lhotshampas in the Dukpa fold by encouraging inter-ethnic marriage by granting first Rs.5000 and then increasing it to Rs.10,000 as incentives. Furthermore, the Lhotshampas were encouraged to participate in the proceedings of the Tsongdu (national legislative body); they were sent abroad on scholarship for higher studies; were appointed as the bureaucrats; were accorded membership to the Royal Advisory Council, the council of ministers, when such dispensations were introduced in 1970's.

The Lhotshampas proved a much-needed labour force when Bhutan decided to undertake planned development through its Five Year Plan in 1962. J.B. Pradhan, the Commissioner of Southern Bhutan, was entrusted by the Durbar to provide manual labourers and ration required for their consumption on the construction sites. Road transport, buildings for schools, rural dispensaries, administrative and public offices, hydel projects, electric installations and a host of developmental activities were undertaken on a big way.

Erstwhile insignificant sleepy border settlements such as Samchi, Penden, Phuntshilling, Geylegphu, Samdrung Jongkhar etc. turned into border townships with the thriving commercial activities. These settlements also turned to house the infant industrial establishments such as fruit preservation, liquor, cement, woodcraft, etc. Needless to add that it was the Lhotshampas who were the only local labour available to handle these demanding accomplishments. The Bhutan Durbar went out of the way to make the Lhotshampas' life as comfortable as possible. Bhutan was plunged into political turmoil in 1964, when the first and only Prime Minister of the country was shot dead at Phuntshilling. The Lhotshampas kept away from the ensuring royal factional conflict. In fact, two decades from 1962 to 1982 or say 1985 were the hay day of Lhotshampas in Bhutan. Reluctantly in the beginning, but slowy and steadily they developed a sense of assertion, and by the late Seventies, the Lhotshampas found their feet planted on the ground and began to voice their opinions. To the utter surprise of the Bhutanese ruler, the democratic fever caught up in Sikkim and the 334-year old Namgyal rule came to an end in 1975.This was the movement almost entirely organized by the Nepalese with support from the Indian democratic forces.

Land Tenure and Feudal Social Structure

The Bhutanese commoners could be divided into two: the farmers and the serfs, which were further divided into a number of local variations. Further more, various districts had different land tenure practices. For example, Tashigang dzokhang paid taxes to the king. There were regions, which paid taxes to the queen mother, queen, king's sisters, royal uncles, crown prince and other relatives. There were aristocratic families with free land grants, dependent peasants, and hundred of serfs. The important monasteries had their estates for their maintenance. Then, there were tracts of land, which paid taxes directly to the State treasury. The southern Bhutan was in charge of the Dorji family, who depended on the Nepali *thikedars* for revenue collection. Further more, the incarnate lamas with estates were special charge of the king. For example, Tulku Gangtey, a constant companion to the second Druk-Gyalpo, had died in 1931. His estate in Bumthang valley lapsed to the royal household because of the delayed discovery of his incarnation.

All the households in a village were subjected to an obligatory labour tax (chunidon or woola) to the State, which could be allotted for a number of assignments decided by local level functionaries. There could be three types of households in a Dukpa village: *trelpa* (liable to pay taxes), *Zurpa* (splinter household not yet liable to pay taxes) and *Suma* (the households paying taxes to the nobility, e.g. royal family). There were two types of grain taxes: *wangyon* (levy for blessings) and *thojab* (grain tax on land out put). There were numerous other taxes to be paid such as textile tax, butter tax, etc. A typical tax payer would pay annually the following items to the state functionaries: 462 kg of paddy, 28 kg butter, 120 pairs of wooden shingles, besides textiles, baskets, paddy straw, mustard, dry chillies, dry sliced pumpkins, bark for the paper and ash for the field. They had to till the land for the monasteries and local officials in varying man -days without payment. On an average, a Bhutanese farmer spent half of his time working for the State without an express benefit to himself.

There were royal, aristocratic and even monastic herdsmen, and slaves grazing cattle. These herdsmen had to provide butter, calf, wool, hide, and meat and yak tails in taxes. Though there were regional variations, but in effect, there were two types of slaves: *drabas*, who worked for their masters in lieu of land granted to them for their up-keep and *zaba*, who worked only for sake of food and cloth. *Suma* were privileged serfs, who paid taxes in kinds to the aristocracy and ran errand for them. There were other types of slaves as well. It was an extremely violent, unequal and exploitative system in which commoners had a hard time. No wonder, many of them turned to the monasteries for a life of clergy.

In such a situation, one may surmise the welcome waiting for the members of the mission (Bangchen) sent to levy fines/ penalty to the defaulting peasants. There existed a number of officials at district level, who consumed bulk of revenue paid in kind. For example, there existed till1960s in every *dzong* the post of a fodder master, a chief of stable, a cattle master, a meat master, a gate collector, a senior store master, a chamberlain, a chief attendant, a guest master, a fort governor and so on. All these functionaries had an impressive array of staff under them to help them perform their official duties. Evidently, any tax reform intended to alleviate the sufferings of the peasantry equally demanded an administrative reform.

The Lhotshampas were subjected to a classical tenancy pattern. As the southern foothills were assigned to the Dorji family since 1890s to develop the region through the migrant Nepalese labour, these newly settled tenants did not require to pay taxes in kind. However, they were also not free from the labour tax.

The Dorjis collected taxes from the heads of the families through their contractual officials in cash on the basis of cultivated land, number of cattle, fruit trees, and other considerations. Even Dorjis did not transmit the collected taxes regularly to the king. However, they were supposed to provide cash requirements of the ruler and his establishment as and when required.

Stimuli for Ethnic Conflict and Strategy to tackle it

We have enumerated elsewhere the steps initiated by the Dukpa establishment to contain the alleged demographic invasion of the Lhotshampas (Sinha, 2002a). These may be recounted as (i) the Bhutan Citizenship Act, 1985. (ii) the Green Belt Policy, and (iii) the Population Census, 1988.These steps had created so much upheaval among the Lhotshampas that they failed to comprehend the situation initially in the absence a tradition of an acknowledged dissent.

By June 1990, students, teachers, bureaucrats, village headmen and even *chimes* (the members of the Tshongdu) - all felt so much suffocated that they began to attack the State properties such as, schools, offices, factories, workshops, electric installations and even loyal state functionaries. They spontaneously organized common people, agitators, students, teachers and all the sundry elements under the banner of the Bhutan Peoples' Party in June 1990. The police and the army of the Royal Government of Bhutan were equally determined to suppress the dissent. As their homes and settlements were no more safe shelters against the organized State terror, the dissident Lhotshampas fled from Bhutan first to India and then to Nepal. The refugee exodus significantly picked up after the demonstration at Samchi in September 1990. And within two years, their number swelled to about a hundred thousand (70,000 in the UNHCR run refugee camps in Nepal and the rest scattered in India).

The Royal Government of Bhutan decided to reverse its ethnic policy of assimilating the Lhotshampas within the Dukpa fold. The earlier efforts to find commonality between the Dukpas and the Lhotshampas were discarded. Teaching of Nepali and Sanskrit was stopped. Monetary awards to the couples engaged in inter-ethnic marriages were discontinued. State holidays on significant Nepali festivals were given up altogether or were reduced to the bare minimum. For example,

Dasai holiday, which used to be five days in a year, has been reduced to one day. Three day long Diwali holiday has been done away with and so is the fate of the festival of Holi.

Ten rounds of talks between the delegates of the RGB and the RGN (the Royal Government of Nepal) were held alternately in the two royal capitals at Kathmandu and Thimphu respectively for about a decade. After initial bickering and impasse, the two sides agreed to verify the identities of the refugee family lineage, and as on the individuals, as demanded by the RGB. By December 2001, the Joint Verification Team had checked the papers of 12,374 refugees from 1,960 families at Damak, Eastern Nepal and found that almost all of them wanted to go back to their respective lands in Bhutan from where they were allegedly evicted. However, the RGB is silently and stealthily re-settling the shifting cultivators and alleged land less Dukpas from the 'north' on the land left behind by the Lhotshampa refugees. This development was first mildly disclaimed and then grudgingly accepted on the plea that even the RGB had limited land for its land less farmers from the 'north', who had to be settled in the 'south'.

The RGB has adopted a four pronged strategy to tackle the international out cry in favour of the suppressed Lhotshampas: (i) expanding and consolidating their hold on the Nation, (ii) facade of talks and verifications of the refugees in the UNHCR camps, (iii) building pressure on the remaining Lhotshampas in Bhutan and (iv) using the presence of the ULFA/NDFB insurgents in Bhutan to stall the refugee return and resettlement (Sinha, 2002). The RGB has been negotiating with the ULFA/NDFB insurgents to leave Bhutan peacefully and willingly. The Indian rebels, flushed out of Bangladesh and India have taken sanctuary in the thinly populated and poorly defended eastern Bhutanese districts. At one time, the rebels had as many as 32 camps in Bhutan. When the RGB threatened to expel the unwelcome guests, the ULFA had even threatened to blast away the Thimphu palace of the His Majesty, the King. There are unconfirmed reports that some of the State functionaries were even provided with the inducement by the ULFA. The rebels used a two-pronged strategy vis-a-vis the RGB: they use threat and inducement. They pay very handsome price to the villagers for the commodities they procure from them so they do not turn hostile to the rebels.

It is said that an agreement was reached between the rebels and the RGB that the former would disband four of the nine camps by December 2001. In case the agreement was not honoured, the RGB might use armed forces to evict the unwanted guests. The Government of India as well has been pressing the RGB to jointly flush the rebels out of Bhutan. The RGB has been avoiding confrontation with the rebels as well as seeking armed support from India in this context. The insurgents are located in the districts, which are predominantly settled by the Lhotshampas. Anticipating a potential linkage between the two, the RGB advised the Lhotshampas to vacate their settlements and shift to a safer site preferably in the 'north'. The Lhotshampas saw it differently. They felt that the RGB was using the opportunity to displace them from the fertile and well-developed agricultural fields to the barren 'north'.

Such a situation was reported from thickly populated Bhanthar sub-division of Samdruk Jongkhar district, the southeastern part of Bhutan. The Lhotshampas of Bhantar were advised to shift to the safer places in the 'north'. Or they could remain in situ at their own risk, as the RGB was not in a position to provide them with security against the imagined onslaught of the rebels. The residents saw through the game played by the establishment. They reasoned among themselves and realized that the land hungry Dukpa functionaries were behind the eviction conspiracy. They felt that once they would leave their land, they would have no control on the affairs and only alternative left to them would to join their brethren in the refugee camps. And all the promise of alternative land would vanish in the thin air. Incidentally, the settlers' dilemma was resolved by the rebels, who advised the harassed farmers to stay put unmolested and promised to see to it that the former do not suffer because of the presence of the latter.

The Triangle - ULFA/NDFB, Ngolop and The DRUK Establishment

The Royal Government of Bhutan frequently alleges that the Lhotshampa refugees from their camps in Nepal terrorize the Dukpa subjects inside south-western Bhutan and even the Dukpas travelling in northern West Bengal (*Kuensel*, 17(6:5). The RGB has also been raising an issue of the Lhotshampa involvement in the movement for the Greater Nepal in the Eastern Himalayan region (Dixit, 2002). Apparently, the bogey of the Nepali design on the eastern Himalayan foothills was raised as a propaganda, and thus, no body took it seriously. However, a vague warning was issued on the part of Lhotshampa refugees (Dhaka and C Strawn, 1994) way back in 1994:

> "The future of the Greater Nepal scenario is uncertain, but several factors could shape existing tensions into a violent reality. The Nepali Bhutanese really have not developed their external links, not even with Darjeeling and Sikkim. Out side the region, there are other terrorist groups, and of course China, which the Nepalis could approach for links. Needless to say, this would create a virtual war, and Nepal would probably resettle the refugees in Nepal rather risk an all out war with India. If all the conditions are there - if the violence seems the only option for the refugees, Nepal and Darjeeling - India could face a frighteningly serious terrorist movement; a disturbance on a Himalayan scale. This plan might have its supporters, and there are plenty of people. . . . Possibly militants in Assam and Darjeeling, people who fought for themselves and achieved little, would support this kind of action for their own gain . . . this is probably something that (New) Delhi can't, and shouldn't, take lightly."

The presence of the Indian rebels in Bhutan is simply intriguing, to say the least. It appears that a segment of the RGB was hand in glove with the ULFA/NDFB as a counter foil against the Lhotshampa refugees (Gopalakrishna.R and J Saikia: 2001:73-74). The presence of the Indian rebels on the Bhutanese soil would provide a counter balance against the possible support to the Lhotshampas from the Indian and the Nepalese democratic forces. But the story is taking a sinister turn now. In case the so-called Ngolop (the anti-national in Dzongkha, which means Lhotshampa refugees) and the ULFA/NDFB co-ordinate their anti-State actions, one wonders whether the RGB has bargained for such an eventuality? One may take even an indulgent view that India with her decade-old experience of counter insurgency may face the situation some way or other, but how will the poorly-manned, ill-equipped and inexperienced RGB forces fare in the confrontation? Bhutan by its own admission is undergoing a phase of Low Intensity Conflict (LIC)[1]. It is maintaining its armed presence on the entire southern Bhutan from Samchi in the west to Bhanthar in the east. Its limited human and material resources are over-stretched and in spite of all the bravado it is finding it hard to maintain a semblance of presence within the region.

Jaideep Saikia reports on a possible ULFA-RGB coalition in terms of a temporary gain in logistics and maneuverings (Saikia, 2001). The Indian Press reported that ULFA was desperately trying to gain the status in the Unrepresented Nations Peoples' Organization (UNPO). So much so that it is claimed to invite two European human rights activists on 7 April, 2002, on its raising day at their clandestine camp at Marshala in Bhutan (*The Telegraph*, 2002). Marshala ULFA camp is one of the five left-over camps ideally located on the most strategic vantage point and shortest route between their Bhutanese haven and their Bangladesh sanctuary. Its location on the riverine and marshy char land of Manas and Brahmputra rivers and Manas wildlife sanctuary suits an easy human trafficking across the three countries. This is the area, which is the abode of the poorest of the poor and the most neglected part of the SAARC region.

The above scenario invites our attention to a shared destiny of the SAARC countries. Is it not ironic that professedly anti-national elements have clandestinely been defying the national barriers for their anti-national activities and the "States", which are recognized representatives of the people, are so helpless to do anything positive? National priorities, ideologies, ethos, ego and vanity - all are all right to the extent that they contribute to the well being of the citizens. It looks that every thing is happening, but for that SAARC was envisioned as a regional answer to the common ailment of our region, but its charter and noble objectives remain largely unattended. It is a fact that some the founding leaders could see the limits of the SAARC agenda.[2] But should the future generation be a captive of the past helplessness? In a recent academic conclave on the -comprehensive security of South Asia a noted Nepalese scholar, M.P. Lohani, rightly identified the urgent agenda for the regional security: "The common threats (for the Region) include ethnic crisis, national and transnational terrorism, religious fundamentalism, atmospheric pollution, poverty trans-border migration and re-definition of State sovereignty in accordance with the burgeoning trend of supra-nationalism." (Lohani, 2001).

French diplomat Thierry Mathou has identified three 'circles' of the Bhutanese foreign police since 1961: the Indian circle, the regional circle and the multilateral circle (Mathou, 1994). He also found its diplomatic policy steady, cautious and remarkably stable. The Bhutanese elite realized the existential reality of South Asia much earlier than most of its partners among the SAARC countries. In the words of its former foreign minister: "India, by virtue of its size and technological achievements, has a pre-eminent role in the region. The smaller South Asian countries have to live with this reality." However, it is not clear how deep is the Indian factor in the on-going ethnic conflict in Bhutan. As per the past practice there must have been consultation between the two. But the, view that the Indian advice would prevail in all the cases is to expect too much. However, one must hasten to add that there is an impression that Indian silence on ethnic conflict in Bhutan is too eloquent to be ignored. Is India alienating Nepal at the cost of Bhutan?

Unfortunately, this is the impression among a section of the Indian intelligentsia. It is a fact that the entire Himalayan region from Kashmir in the west to the Northeast Indian States in the east has turned into a zone of conflict. Besides India, the two Himalayan kingdoms are embroiled in the worst type of conflicts not experienced by them in the past. In such a situation, Indian experience to handle inter-state issues should have been handy to the smaller neighbours. But it appears that India turned out to be a prisoner of her own priority. In the words of former Indian Foreign Secretary, J.N. Dixit: "India seems to be imprisoned in a jacket of assertiveness and excessively narrow Indo centric considerations. The argument that India should be generous with its smaller neighbours put forward by some analysts is not a relevant point. Generosity smacks of a certain incipient big brotherly hegemonic attitude. A co-operative and accommodating approach towards Nepal is of utmost and vital interest to India in political, geo-strategic and economic terms. Good Indo-Nepalese relations have ramifications for our relations with other neighbours in the South Asian Association for regional co-operation as well as China. This is the empirical reality to which our Nepal policy should respond."(Dixit, 2002).

Conclusion

To conclude the discourse, till 1980's, Bhutan was a model State in South Asian region with its favourable land-man ratio. Its king had an image of being a benevolent ruler, who encouraged integration of the Lhootshampas in its body politic. So much so that it was considered an ideal locale for holding 'Peace Talk' between the Government of Sri Lanka and the Liberation Tigers of Tamil Elam (LTTE). at Thimphu in 1985. Since then much water has flown in Torsha and Raidak rivers. Bhutan has joined the sister nations of the South Asia with its own form of ethnic conflict. We have tried to acquaint the readers with the ethnic scenario and the feudal social structure of Bhutan, which bred ethnic hostility. Secondly, we have traced out the stimuli for the conflict and strategy adopted by the Drukpa State to cope with the ethnic flare up. Thirdly, we have tried to caution the concerned citizen of the SAARC nations about the pitfall of the Bhutanese situation, in which there is a possibility of the linkage between the Lhotshampa refugees and the Indian rebels hold-up in south-eastern Bhutan. God forbid, if it happens, considering the resources in terms of manpower, its limited experience in handling the violent, ethnic conflicts and materials available to it, the RGB will simply can't manage the emergent scenario. It will further aggravate already existing explosive ethnic situation. As a concerned student of the Northeastern Indian ethnic scenario, one apprehends an ominous development, fraught with serious consequences for the region.

NOTES

1. Essentially, Low Intensity Conflict (LIC) is armed conflict for political purposes, shot of a direct combat between the regular armed forces. Such conflicts are asymetrical, ambiguous, and unconventional, and very often develop into war of attrition. LIC is largely a Third World phenomenon and poses a serious and long -term threat to nation building exercises and regional peace and security. LIC subsumes guerrilla wars, civil wars, insurgency, separatist movements, insurrections, communal violence, terrorism etc. There

is little evidence of LIC declining. On the contrary, LIC is on the rise because it is more cost effective, especially in the short term, than conventional war and because it carries less risk of escalation. Cold war had a restraining influence on the eruption and spread of Lie. Its subsidence has realistic and cost effective solution to many groups pursuing different political, ideological and territorial goals. Heightened aspirations of the people, improved means of communication, and easy availability of light weight sophisticated weapons have ensured that various ethnic, racial and religious issues turn into uncompromising demands for self-determination and political independence. All these factors make LIC both desirable and possible. (Mishra. O P: 2002).

2. "India is big in size and that means that the proportion of our problems and difficulties are also gigantic. We don't want to take on more problems. Our policy is not to interfere in the affairs of others. But ours is a troubled region. Most of our countries are multi-racial and multi-religious. It would be idle to pretend that we are not affected but what happens elsewhere." - Inaugural Address of Indira Gandhi, The Prime Minister of India, At the SAARC meeting of Foreign Ministers in New Delhi on August 1, 1983, in V Grover ed. UNO, NAM, NIEO, SAARC and India's Foreign Policy, New Delhi, 1992.

REFERENCES

Dhakal, D N S: 1994: BHUTAN: A Movement in Exile, Nirala Publication Jaipur.

Dixit, J.N., 2002: "Borderline Friendship". *The Telegraph*, April 5.

Gopalkrishna, R and J Saikia: 2001 Development Challenge in India: Assam in 21st Century. Omsons Publications, New Delhi.

Lohani, M P: 2001 "Nepal" in Comprehensive Security for South Asia. edt. by Delhi Policy Group. DPC, India Habitat, New Delhi.

Kuensel News Bulletin, The Royal Government of Bhutan, Thimphu.

Mathou. T: 1994: "The Growth of Diplomacy in Bhutan, 1961-1991: Opportunities and Challenges" in Bhutan: Aspects of Culture and Development, ed. by Aris. M and. M. Hun, Kiscadale Asia Series, No.5, U K.

Mishra, O P: 2001 "Intensity Conflict and the Challenge of Forced Displacement in Northeast India", Draft paper in the seminar on Low Intensity Conflict in Eastern India. Department of International Relations, Jadavpur University, Kolkata.

Saikia, Jaideep: 2001 Contour. Sagittarius Print. Guwahati.

Sinha, A .C., 1998 Bhutan: Ethnic Identity and National Dilemma, Reliance Publishing CO, New Delhi.

Sinha, A.C., 2002a "Dialogue Between Deaf and Dumb: The Lhotshampa Refugees and their Predicament" in Dimensions of Displaced People in North-East India. C J Thomas (ed.), Regency Publications, New Delhi.

Sinha, A. C., 2002b "Terrorism and Low Intensity Conflict in Bhutan seminar on Terrorism and Low Intensity Conflict In Eastern India, Department of International Relations, Jadavpur University, Kolkata.

The Telegraph, 2002: (a daily newspaper), Kolkata & Guwahati, 7 April.

7

Bhutan and India: Partners in Progress

—PARTHA S. GHOSH

It is better to have milk and cheese many times than beef just once.

—a traditional Bhutanese adage

I

Introduction

Bhutan presents a dilemma to researchers. Although significant strides have been made during the last half a decade to democratize the country's political institutions the Bhutanese society still remains by and large closed. Free and open-ended discussions with its people on matters of their society and politics are at best restricted. There is no free press, nor a free electronic media. The government virtually controls the only weekly newspaper the country has, the *Kuensel*, which is published from Thimpu. But such a situation prevails in many other countries too. Therefore, Bhutan's case is not so unique that way. The real dilemma is actually of a different kind. For example, it raises the fundamental question in one's mind whether is it true that human development is possible only through democratic governance, or whether non-democratic systems can as well do the job. Closely related is the question whether monarchical systems could ever provide the necessary environment for people's participation in governance and pave the way for democracy. The dynasty of the Tudors in England (1485-1603) is still remembered for its 'benevolence' though it supplied a bunch of so-called 'dictators'. In school textbooks their period is called 'the age of benevolent dictatorship', although the phrase is a contradiction in terms. Can the Bhutanese monarchy, in the similar vein, be characterized as 'people's monarchy'?[1]

There is yet another dilemma. This pertains to some general theories about India's relations with its neighbours. It has been argued that India's foreign policy interests can be served best if the entire region was democratic. Logically, based on the theory that democracies do not fight (though still untested empirically), it is emphasized that it should be the goal of India's foreign policy to aid and encourage democratic movements in the neighbourhood, for in them lie India's long-tern security and development interests. But the Indo-Bhutan relations throw all these theories in the wind. Not only have Indian democracy and Bhutanese monarchy coexisted peacefully, they have also provided a brilliant example of bilateral cooperation in economic and strategic matters. The existence of China as Bhutan's immediate neighbour, with whom India has a relationship of suspicion, has not come in the way of this relationship, as has largely been the case in respect of Nepal-India relations. Both Bhutan and India appreciate each other's political and strategic compulsions and accommodate each other's sensitivities to the extent possible resulting in what we may designate as one of the most successful experiments in bilateral cooperation between two neighbours.[2]

It is against this background that the Indo-Bhutan relations are to be studied. In this paper an effort has been made to analyze the scope of further cooperation between the two countries with particular reference to India's northeastern region, which is geographically close to Bhutan. Much of the developmental and security problems of both Bhutan and India's Northeast are so intricately intertwined that one cannot be studied without reference to the other. The paper has been divided into four parts, the first providing an introductory, the second dealing with the economic aspects, the third with the politico-strategic dimensions, and the fourth with a general discussion in way of drawing some conclusions and developing an overall perspective.

II

Economic Cooperation

India has been playing a significant role in Bhutan's economic development. It financed almost entirely Bhutan's first two Five Year Plans (1961-71). Although Bhutan began to receive development assistance from the UN agencies and third countries since the 1970's, India remained its main aid partner. In 1974, India decided to set up the Penden Cement Project and the Chukha Hydroelectric Project in Bhutan. The Penden Cement Plant, set up at a cost of about Rs. 159 milllion with an installed capacity of 300 tonnes per day, commenced production in 1981. Besides meeting its domestic needs, Bhutan started exporting about 60,000 metric tonnes of cement each year to the neighbouring Indian States - Assam, Sikkim and West Bengal. During the Fiscal Year 2000-2001, the Penden Cement Authority Ltd. (PCAL) contributed Nu. 127.695 million to the State revenue, which was higher by 11.4 per cent compared to the previous year. This was 2.7 per cent of the total national revenue, ranking fifth as the national revenue earner.[3]

India set up the Chukha Hydroelectric Project at a cost of about Rs. 2,460 million, 60 per cent of which was a grant while the rest a loan. The project was commissioned in 1986, and since then it has increased its generation capacity. Bhutan is an important exporter of electricity to India today. In 1997 it earned Rs. 1,405 million by selling electricity generated by the Chukha Hydroelectric Plant. It may be noted that electricity continues to be the major source of revenue for the Bhutan government. In the Fiscal Year 2000-2001, it accounted for 44.6 per cent of the total revenue, which was 6 per cent more than the previous year's record. In absolute terms, it was Nu. 2086.734 million. Of this, the Chukha Hydro Power Corporation (CHPC) itself accounted for Nu.1818.510 million, about 38.9 per cent of the total government revenue.

India and Bhutan took many other steps as well to expand their mutually beneficial cooperation in the sphere of economic development. In 1990 they decided to develop the Tala Hydroelectric and Wangchu Reservoir Scheme, popularly known as Chukha II and Chukha III. On 4 January 1993 they signed a memorandum of understanding for the development of the Sankosh Multipurpose Project. This project would irrigate about half a million hectares of land in West Bengal (see Tables 1 and 2).[4]

Table 1

Hydroelectric Projects under the Eighth Five-Year Plan (1996-2001)

Project	River	Installed Ultimate Capacity	Estimated Cost (in million Nu.)
Tala	Wangchu	1,020 MW	15,500
Bunakha	Wangchu	180 MW	9,000
Wangchu	Wangchu	900 MW	12,000
Sankosh	Sankosh	4,060 MW	—
Kurichu	Kurichu	45 MW	3,100
Basochu	Basochu	60.8 MW	—

Source: Anasua Basu Ray Chaudhury, *Energy Crisis and Subregional Cooperation in South Asia* (Colombo: Regional Center for Strategic Studies, 2000), p. 20.

India has also been assisting Bhutan in the construction of Kurichu power project, Bunakha reservoir project and in setting up the Dungsum Cement Plant. The implementation of these development projects will further strengthen the relations between the two countries. For the Eighth Five-Year Plan (1998-2002) of Bhutan India made, in February 1997, a financial contribution of Rs. 9 billion along with an additional Rs. 4 billion in development subsidies. The nine billion rupees, of which four billion would be budgetary grant and five billion would be project-tied assistance, would be utilized in the sectors of power, industry, communication, education, culture, judiciary, health and agriculture.

Table 2

Status of Electricity Supply in India

State	Unit cost of power supply (in Re. 1/ kWh, 94-95)	Average consumer tariff (in Re. 1/ kWh, 94-95)	T&D Losses (%)
Arunachal Pradesh	—	—	42.0
Assam	2.84	1.59	22.4
Manipur	—	—	23.9
Meghalaya	1.67	0.99	17.9
Mizoram	—	—	31.9
Nagaland	—	—	33.5
West Bengal	1.88	1.46	16.0

Source: *Energy Data Directory and Yearbook 1996,* TERI, New Delhi, 1996/97. As cited in Anasua Basu Ray Chaudhury, *Energy Crisis and Subregional Cooperation in South Asia* (Colombo: Regional Center for Strategic Studies, 2000), p. 34.

Trade Relations

India has been helping Bhutan in promoting the latter's foreign trade. Earlier, Bhutan's trade was almost entirely with India. In the second half of the 1970's Bhutan desired to develop trade relations with third countries as well, to which India agreed. In March 1978 India allowed Bhutan to export its goods to countries other than India. Being a land-locked country and because of other geographical reasons Bhutan's trade with other countries had to be conducted through the Indian territory. In 1983 India and Bhutan signed a trade agreement, which provided not only free trade between the two countries but also transit facilities to Bhutan for the conduct of its trade with third countries. The agreement was renewed in 1990. In February 1995 the two countries extended the period of agreement from five to 10 years. India is still the largest trading partner of Bhutan and it accounts for about 75 per cent of the total foreign trade of the country. Though, traditionally Bhutan has a trade deficit with India, in recent years it has gone down.

The trade between India and Bhutan has been growing steadily over the years owing to the growing Bhutanese economy, which has registered an average growth of 6.7 per cent. Bhutan exports to India not only primary commodities such as coal, dolomite and gypsum but also industrial and manufactured products like calcium carbide, cement, hydroelectric power, plywood, particle board and processed fruits and juices. Indo-Bhutanese trade is closely linked with the relations of both the countries with Bangladesh. In the 1980's India and Bangladesh signed an MOU to facilitate the transfer of goods between Bhutan and Bangladesh through India, by rail and road. This was followed by a Bangladesh-Bhutan trade protocol and an agreement on economic and technical cooperation. The 30-year treaty between India and Bangladesh signed in December 1996 has been contributing to the further expansion of trade between Bangladesh and Bhutan through Indian territory. The overall idea falls within the scheme of sub-regional cooperation consisting of Bangladesh, Bhutan, India and Nepal. The idea was mooted by Bangladesh at the SAARC Foreign Ministers' Conference held in December 1996 in New Delhi, which received support from the Maldives and Sri Lanka also.[5] Of late, Bhutan has been showing interests to join the World Trade Organization (WTO).

Tourism and Communication Development

Traditionally, Bhutan is skeptical about cultural influences from outside. It is on account of this that although it has allowed tourists to come to the country, it has not gone whole hog to encourage them indiscriminately as many such small, poor but otherwise beautiful countries have done. Of late there is, however, a tendency to open up a bit more, which would naturally encourage tourism. It participated in a big way in the Expo 2000 held in Hanover, Germany, where its pavilion was placed among the top five exhibit sites. Bhutan joined the Federation of the International Football Association (FIFA) and participated in the Sydney Olympics.[6]

In May 2002, in a Thimpu seminar jointly sponsored by the SAARC Chamber of Commerce and Industry (SCCI), the Association of Bhutanese Tour Operators (ABTO), the Bhutan

Chamber of Commerce and Industry (BCCI) and the Ministry of Trade and Industry of the Government of Bhutan, the Prime Minister of Bhutan, Lyonpo Khandu Wangchuk, said: 'We are guilty of overlooking the immense potential of intra-regional tourism. SAARC should take a very realistic approach in identifying impediments to intra-regional travel as well as travels from outside to our region and propose ways and means of overcoming them.' Reciprocating the same sentiments, Padma Jyoti, the SCCI president, emphasized: 'Whenever we say tourism we think of Europeans, Americans or Japanese. We did not give enough attention to our own people and market. It is now time to rejuvenate the huge potential market in our own region.' Some of the obstacles to be tackled were harmonization and standardization of customs and immigration forms and simplification of road transport formalities.[7]

Against this background, one may visualize a larger role for the Bhutanese airlines, the Druk Air, in contributing to the sub-regional tourism and overall economic cooperation. There is an idea being floated these days that the Guwahati airport can emerge as an international airport having direct flights to Bangkok—Paro-Guwahati-Bangkok. If the idea materializes it would not only change the character of Guwahati from one of India's backwaters to an international tourist and passenger junction but also boost trade and tourism. Bhutan also would take advantage of this opening up. If simultaneously the road links (many of which are on the drawing boards now) were also made operational, a real growth quadrangle would be possible.

III

Security Dimensions

There are primarily two aspects of the security relationship between India and Bhutan. One pertains to the use of Bhutanese soil by the insurgency groups operating in India's Northeast, and the other to Bhutan's location between two Asian giants, China and India, which have a relationship of suspicion and anxiety. So far as the first is concerned, the problem has assumed somewhat serious proportions after

1996. In that year, after the Bangladesh government flushed out from its soil the United Liberation Front of Asom (ULFA), the National Democratic Front of Bodoland (NDFB) and the Bodoland Liberation Tiger Force (BLTF), the latter moved to Bhutan from where they continued with their anti-India activities. They built their headquarters in Gubanagand near the Assam border and established as many as 33 camps with 15 to 500 militants in each within a 600 km long arc from near Phuntsholing in the west to the Arunachal Pradesh border beyond Samdruk Jongkhar in the east.[8] They moved freely within the country and purchased their daily needs from the villagers at much higher prices creating a vested interest in the countryside in their continued presence. The threat thus posed to the security of both India and Bhutan became obvious. But the problem was how to deal with the situation. Bhutanese army was not big enough to face the challenge militarily yet Bhutan could not allow the Indian army either to have a free hand there for both nationalistic reasons as well as provoking the insurgents further. Still, Bhutan is cooperating with India, to the extent possible, in dealing with the situation.

Given Bhutan's limitations as a small country and its own vulnerabilities in terms of potential Nepalese insurgency emanating from the displaced southern Bhutan Nepalese it is careful not to go whole hog in doing whatever India wants it to. Still, by balancing all the pros and cons of the situation it has been able to deal with the problem which helps India yet does not provoke the insurgents in collaboration with the Nepalese Maoists and other anti-Bhutan militant factions to make things even more difficult for Bhutan. Sometimes there were difficulties arising out of personal greed of concerned officials. For example, in July 2000 two junior employees of the Bhutanese Foreign Ministry were accused of transferring funds to the ULFA militants. This led to protest in Assam and tended to cause tensions in Indo-Bhutan relations. The government of Bhutan, however, took prompt action. The accused were duly tried and sentenced in accordance with the country's National Security Act.[9]

The policy of the Bhutanese government has been three-fold dialogue with the militants to persuade them to leave

Bhutan peacefully, plugging their supplies including ration, and implementation of the National Security Act. Since 1998 Bhutan has entered into direct negotiations with the militants, sometimes even at the royal and ministerial levels. All these efforts have yielded results and in the first half of 2002 four ULFA camps were wound up. Negotiations continued for the closure of the remaining. In July 2002, the Bhutanese National Assembly reiterated its call to the ULFA to withdraw in a peaceful manner or face military action.[10] Following signals from the Bhutanese authorities, a joint Indo-Bhutan army operation was also mooted. According to newspaper reports, the Defence Ministry of India agreed to provide two para-commando units from the western sector to launch the operation.[11] During the visit of India's External Affairs Minister Yashwant Sinha's visit to Thimpu in August 2002 the possibilities of further cooperation in this regard were discussed.[12] For Bhutan it is a delicate tight rope walking involving diplomatic as well as political skills so as not to endanger its own security yet at the same time not annoying India either. It is probably not difficult for the Bhutanese security forces to see to it that all the insurgent camps were evacuated overnight. But highhanded tactics might result in all kinds of unholy alliances between the Nepalese militants and the Assamese militants to the detriment of security not only of Bhutan and India but also Nepal.

In respect of China both Bhutan and India have coordinated their policies aimed at keeping China at bay yet trying to develop friendly relations bilaterally wherever possible. In mid-1999 an official Chinese delegation visited Bhutan, which resolved some of the outstanding border issues between the two countries. China also indicated, for the first time, its interest in providing economic assistance to Bhutan.[13] In November 2000 the 14th round of Sino-Bhutanese border talks were held in Beijing at the ministerial level. The talks were continued during the visit of Bhutan's Foreign Secretary, Dasho Ugyen Tshering, to China in July 2001 following which the 15th round of annual border talks was held in Thimpu in November 2001. The three sectors, which were discussed, were Doglam, Sinchulumba, and Dramana. Although no diplomatic move was afoot to establish formal diplomatic relations between the two countries the relations went apace smoothly. In April 2001, the vice-premier of China received in Beijing a cultural delegation from Bhutan led by the Dorje Lopen (the second highest-ranking Buddhist leader).[14]

Since the Sino-Indian relations are on an even keel these days, notwithstanding some traditional suspicions about each other's intentions, there is less likelihood of the China factor coming in the way of Indo-Bhutan friendship. In any case, unlike Nepal, it is the fear of China that has drawn Bhutan closer to India. Although the respective dreams of China and India about their perceived spheres of interests continue to overlap, thereby making their relationship the relationship of 'protracted conflict,'[15] it can be assumed that the economic compulsions of both the nations in this age of globalization would not allow those dreams to lead them into a military confrontation. As such, the Indo-Bhutan relationship would also have less tension on that count.

IV

Conclusion

All political and economic indicators show that the Bhutan-India relations are stable and friendly. The occasional irritations that we notice, particularly in respect of dealing with the insurgent groups operating from Bhutan, are common between any two friendly neighbours anywhere in the world. What is most important is that both the nations appreciate each other's security and political compulsions and try to accommodate each other's sensitivities by some mutual give and take. It is a slow but steady strategy in line with the Bhutanese traditional proverb that we have used as the bowsprit for this paper. India's Northeast can nothing but gain from the situation.

NOTES

1. For a discussion on this contradiction see Partha S. Ghosh, 'Bhutan: Ethnicity, Democracy and Nation-Building,' In: John M. Richardson, Jr. and S.W.R. de A. Samarasinghe (eds.), *Democratisation in South Asia: The First Fifty Years* (Kandy: International Centre for Ethnic Studies, 1998), pp. 213-35. For the recent trends towards democratisation of political

institutions, see The Royal Government of Bhutan, *Window on Bhutan 2002: Druk Yul or the Land of the Thunder Dragon* (New Delhi: The Royal Bhutanese Embassy, 2002), pp. 8-12.

2. For a brief discussion on the evolution of this partnership, through trials and tribulations, see Partha S. Ghosh, *Cooperation and Conflict in South Asia* (New Delhi: Manohar, 1989), pp. 136-53.
3. Royal Government of Bhutan, Ministry of Finance, Department of Revenue, *National Revenue Report 2000-2001* (Thimpu, n.d.), pp. 12-13.
4. *Ibid.*, pp. 10-12.
5. Bhabani Sen Gupta, *Bhutan: Towards a Grass-root Participatory Polity* (New Delhi: Konark, 1996), pp. 143-44.
6. Thierry Mathou, 'Bhutan in 2000: Challenges Ahead,' *Asian Survey* (Berkeley), 41(1), January-February 2001, p. 134.
7. *Kuensel* (Thimpu), 18 May 2002, p. 3.
8. A.C. Sinha, *Himalayan Kingdom: Tradition, Transition and Transformation* (New Delhi: Indus, 2001), p. 247.
9. Mathou, *Bhutan in 2000*, pp. 133-34.
10. Wasbir Hussain, 'Ominous Signs in the Northeast,' *The Hindu* (New Delhi), 9 September 2002.
11. *Asian Age* (New Delhi), 25 June 2002.
12. *The Hindu* (New Delhi), 6 August 2002.
13. Leo Rose, 'Nepal and Bhutan in 1999: Some Progress,' *Asian Survey* (Berkeley), 40(1), January-February 2000, p. 193.
14. Thierry Mathou, 'Bhutan in 2001: At the Crossroad,' *Asian Survey* (Berkeley), 42(1), January-February 2002, 196.
15. John W. Garver, *Protracted Conflict: Sino-Indian Rivalry in the Twentieth Century* (Washington, D.C.: University of Washington Press, 2001).

SECTION III

INDO-BANGLADESH RELATIONS - IMPLICATIONS FOR NORTHEASTERN REGION

8

Bangladesh and Northeast: Facing Migration, Ending Rhetoric, Embracing a Realistic Strategy for Change

—SANJOY HAZARIKA

For centuries, India's Northeast - hemmed in on three sides by international land borders with Tibet/China, Bhutan, Myanmar and Bangladesh and connected to the rest of the country by a narrow land corridor known as the Chicken's Neck - has been a frontier land for settlers. Its people are a rich and diverse group of communities, ranging from the Khasis who are said to be descendants of migrants from Kampuchea and still speak a form of Mon-Khmer to the Khamtis, who moved more recently (in the 18th century) from the Burma-China border to Arunachal Pradesh near the Chinese border.

There are currently seven States, the largest among them (in terms of population) being Assam with a population of about 25 million. The other States are Arunachal Pradesh, Nagaland, Manipur, Mizoram; Tripura and Meghalaya. According to one account, there are not less than 350 distinct communities in the region, making administration an extremely complex task with different competing groups seeking to establish their political and social control over land, resources and asserting demands for preferential treatment.

The region is home to about 35 million people with a mix of religious and linguistic groupings: Assam is dominated by the Hindus and the Assamese speakers in the Brahmaputra Valley although in many areas the Bengali-speaking Muslims and the Hindus also are dominant; the States of Meghalaya, Nagaland and Mizoram have large Christian populations of various denominations, while nature worshippers (the Donyi Polo faith) is prevalent in Arunachal Pradesh. Tripura is largely Hindu with Buddhist and Christian communities among the tribes people.

The situation has been further complicated by several insurgencies in different states espousing a variety of causes: in one case, of the Bodos, perhaps the oldest plains community of the region, one militant faction seeks independence from India; the other seeks a separate state carved out of Assam within the Indian Union. There are insurgencies in Manipur and Tripura as well as Assam while Nagaland, which is home to one of the oldest insurgencies in Asia, has seen a shaky ceasefire over the past year and a half between the main militant group and the Government of India although negotiations to settle Naga demands have not really taken off.

It is the relationship between the Northeast, especially Assam, and Bangladesh that is the focus of this paper. A cursory look at the map and at Bangladesh's statistics will tell part of the story for it is perhaps one of the more defining conditions behind the situation. In the area, which now constitutes Bangladesh, the population has doubled between 1961 to 1991 from 55.2 million to 111.46 million. The latest population is about 120 million and population density is computed at about 800 persons per square kilometer compared to 285 for Assam.

Bangladesh, one of the poorest nations on earth, has the highest population density in the world. The pressure on land is acute and both demographers and political scientists say that it is losing substantial numbers of its population in migrations to India and other parts of the subcontinent. Part of the reason for this movement is economic deprivation as well as environmental disasters. One study by the Jehangirnagar University assesses the number of displacees by floods in Bangladesh's sprawling floodplains at 18 to 19 million people annually. Most of these people move to the neighbouring areas but it would not be implausible to regard this as another source of cross-border migration.

Indeed, since the late 1970s, India's Northeast has been troubled by agitations, often student-led, against "illegal immigrants" from Bangladesh. Over the years, this has become a major political issue with different groups vying with each other in taking advantage of the religious, linguistic, ethnic and political factors that have emerged as a result.

This is not a new issue - the question of illegal migration, or migration caused by economic and environmental factors from East Pakistan and now Bangladesh - has been of concern to the region since the 1950s. It was perceived as a "threat" (although at that time, these were part of one British dominion and not fragmented by Partition) even earlier.

"Without fuss, without tumult, without undue trouble to the district revenue staffs, a population which must amount to over half a million has transplanted itself . . . during the past 25 years. It looks like a marvel of administrative organization on the part of Government but it is nothing of the sort: the only thing that I can compare it to is the mass movement of a huge body of ants." Those were the remarks of the Census Commissioner for Assam in 1921 speaking of the movement of peasants from the Mymensingh district of East Bengal into the Assam Valley.

In the 1930s and 1940s, the influx was resisted in Assam and the Congress Party led political campaigns against the settlers. The inflow was largely an organized one in those years, encouraged by the Muslim League Government of Premier Sir Mohammad Saadulla of Assam. The League wanted a change in the religious demography of the State to help Pakistan establish a claim over the resource-rich province. The migrants were predominantly farmers and landless peasants from the bordering districts of East Bengal, especially Mymensingh. In fact, Sir Mohammed boasted in a communication to Liaquat Ali Khan, then the number two figure in the League after M.A. Jinnah, that the inflow of the peasantry from East Bengal had quadrupled the Muslim population in the four lower districts of Assam in 25 years.

The Congress Party in the State opposed the settlement policy and was supported by Mahatma Gandhi. Yet, the Assamese position irked the national Congress leaders such as Jawaharlal Nehru and Vallabhhai Patel because they felt it was holding up the process of independence. But Assam stood firm, resisting being slotted with Muslim-majority Bengal in the Cabinet Mission's proposals of 1946 to divide some provinces into Groups and Sections. The result was that Assam remained with India.

The concerns fuelled by the movements of those days continue to trouble Assamese minds today. Since the 1970s, these worries have spilled over into confrontations between "settlers" and "locals" as pressure on land and other resources has grown. Conflicts and clashes have become increasingly common.

The issue of settlement and migration has been sensitive, as we have seen earlier, and it remains perhaps the most contentious and politically explosive question in the state, one that is still unresolved. Memories are still fresh of the 1979-to-1985 student-led agitation against "foreigners" that left a trail of social and economic devastation, riots and religious clashes as relations between many social groups, including religious, ethnic and linguistic communities, deteriorated and erupted. In 1983, at least 3,000 persons (some regard this as a conservative estimate and believe that 5,000 is more accurate) were killed in clashes and attacks, largely on immigrant settlers and their descendants although other ethnic groups also battled each other in the Brahmaputra valley.

In the killing fields of Nellie, Goreswar and Gohpur, all of which I covered as a correspondent for the New York Times, I found not just overwhelming human tragedy but came face to face with my own inadequacy in understanding the factors that fuelled this absolute hatred by one group for the other. It is in this search to find answers that I have spent time in the Northeast, Bangladesh and elsewhere, trying to understand the complexities of community, ethnicity, religious and political affiliations, and seeking ways in which these complex weave can be unravelled and some measure of calm and dignity be restored to the groups. One also seeks the development of sensible policies and politics, which are capable of implementation, to be brought to bear on the situation.

The Potential for Violence Remains Large

What fuels these concerns is not just a broad perception that people are still coming across the borders but a fear that the influx is substantial enough to change the demographic shape of Assam and the Northeast as well as its political and religious/social/linguistic equations. At the core is the worry that power will go out of the hands of the Axomiyas in the coming century just as surely as large tracts of land went out of their hands during this century.

Comparative data show a substantial growth in the Muslim population of Assam, which demographers believe, is not a result of natural birth rate but that additional numbers have come from migration. Significantly, over the past decades, the Hindu population of Bangladesh has been one to study for it shows the remarkable characteristic of virtually not growing at all!

In the area that constitutes today's Bangladesh, the Hindu population has grown by barely two millions in 40 years from 9.2 million in 1951 to 11.1 million in 1991. The percentage of the Hindus has dropped from 22 percent of the total population in 1951 to 18.5 percent in 1961, 13.5 percent in 1974, 12.1 percent in 1981 and 10.5 percent in 1991. If one takes a "Hindu rate of growth" of even two percent per year, the Hindu population of Bangladesh today should be 60 per cent higher than what it is today (I am taking 1961 as the bench mark and not 1951 because refugee flows and adjustments after Partition continued in the 1950s).

This means that there are about six-to-seven million Hindus who are "missing" from that period. If you take the cutoff point as 1971, you would still get about five million Hindus. And the perception of India as a homeland for the Hindus in neighbouring countries cannot be ruled out:

substantial portions of this population have moved to India, to Assam, West Bengal and Tripura especially.

It is certainly nobody's argument that only one religious community is moving. Large numbers of people from both communities are on the move. The reason for my focussing on religious figures is not, I must assert, out of any bias. I am simply going by the fact that people tend to lie about everything when it comes to reporting to the Government: whether it is their income, their age, their work and even the language they speak. But few people lie about their religion. This is as good an indicator as any to assess demographic data.

There are varying estimates for the number of illegal Bangladeshis that are in this country. The Godbole Report on Border Management, which was submitted to the Government of India last year and has not been made public, says that 15 million or 1.5 crore Bangladeshis are in India. Some of us are asked to appear before this panel to give our views and share our experiences. I tend to err on the side of caution — my figure would still be in the region of 10-to-12 million Bangladeshis in all.

Take the case of Assam, on the other side of the border. In 1971, the number of the Hindus in this State was 10.6 million. The number of the Muslims was 3.59 million. In 1991 (there was no census in Assam in 1981 because of the student agitation), the respective figures rose to 15.04 million for the Hindus and 6.73 million for the Muslims. The Hindu share in the population went down from 72.51 percent in 1971 to 67.13 percent while the Muslim ratio rose from 24.56 percent to 28.43 percent in the same period. The Hindu population grew at 41.79 percent in 20 years. The Muslim growth rate was 77.42 percent or decade-wise 38.7 percent. The Muslim growth rate for the rest of India is about 3 1 percent for 1971-to-1981 and for the following decade.

There are relevant figures from the districts bordering Bangladesh: in 1971 Assam had two Muslim-majority districts, Dhubri and Hailakandi. In 1991 that number had doubled to include Goalpara and Barpeta and figures from three more districts showed that these too were close to reporting Muslim majorities (Morigaon, Nagaon, Karimganj). A former Census Deputy Director for Assam, J.C. Bhuyan argues that with natural growth rate the Muslim population of Assam should have grown from 3.59 million in 1971 to 5.2 million in 1991 instead to 6.7 million. Mr. Bhuyan says that the balance of 1.5 million is illegal settlers.

Bangladeshi scholars view this phenomenon of movement both as a survival strategy and an outcome of environmental crisis, particularly displacement in the floodplains, "In fact, one finds the number of people crossing over to India increasing during periods of environmental disasters," says Dr. Imtiaz Ahmed of Dhaka University. He estimates that 1.72 million people crossed illegally into India between 1961-71, another half a million for 1971-81 and not less than 600,000 crossed over into Assam alone between 1981-91.

It should also be noted here that Indian census data place the number of immigrants at 1.5 million for 1961-71 but the 1981 figures say that not less than four million people resident in India at the time gave their birthplace as Bangladesh. One is inclined to believe that the figure is actually higher but such residents are reluctant to talk about their antecedents during an official exercise should they face legal and political complications such as threat of ouster, dispossession and intimidation.

No Figures for Migration were Published in the 1991 Census

Bangladesh officially denies the outflow, saying that its citizens go to places such as the Middle East and South East Asia for work and not to a neighbouring and impoverished, if not equally poor, nation. But Bangladeshi officials (privately), journalists and scholars (openly) have accepted this reality and are prepared to discuss it. Indeed some of us have been actively engaged with Bangladeshi scholars, former officials and others as well as their Indian counterparts in trying to tackle the rigid mindsets on either side of the border, which are perhaps some of the real stumbling blocks to cooperation and mutual development.

Laws, which have been invented to deal with these problems, have been total failures. Thus first the Prevention of Infiltration from Pakistan Scheme, launched by the Central Government in the 1960s, collapsed in Assam when an influential lobby of Muslim legislators threatened to revolt against the then Chief Minister B.P. Chaliha, and reduce his government to a minority. The PIP programme was curbed, and eventually, quietly died. In 1983, Parliament passed the Illegal Migrants (Determination by Tribunal) Act, which is hardly functional. Only two out of 18 such tribunals are doing any work.

Between 1986 to 1994, a total of 280,791 cases were referred to the tribunals for trial. Of this, 8,477 were found to be illegal and 1,461 were ordered expelled. There are reasons for the low convictions as well as the low rate of complaints: One, much of the evidence turned up by the police, especially witness accounts, is flimsy and cannot stand the test of judicial scrutiny. Two, a complainant has to file a fee of Rs.10 for each complaint he or she wishes to register against a supposed illegal settler and has to live within the jurisdiction of the police station where the "settler" is located.

These disincentives were built into the law at the behest of the Congress regime of the then Prime Minister Indira Gandhi. Under the Act, the complainant must prove that a person said to be an illegal migrant is in fact so. This is very opposite of all anti-foreigner legislation across the world, where the onus of proof is on the accused.

One should remember that mere figures do not reflect the scale of public alienation and bitterness that is involved in this issue. Conflict situations continue to exist in different parts of the State. We have referred to the tragic and terrible massacres of 1983. The complexity of the situation can be viewed by assessing the divisions within the settler community on religious lines although the core issue remains land and its control. Thus in 1992, the riots that spread from the destruction of the Babri Masjid at Ayodhya, included clashes in the district of Morigaon, Assam. The clashing parties were settlers, Bengali-speaking Muslim and Hindu and the struggle was by the former to oust the latter from farmlands. Thus, with time, both the social and political factors as well as clear-cut lines of demarcation tend to be merged in the issue of land.

The land question has become especially important because the eroding might of the rivers in Bangladesh and especially the Brahmaputra in Assam displace people in the floodplains or char areas. Erosion has meant that people are constantly on the move in places such as the Bangladeshi district of Kurigram, which borders Dhubri. One has come across villagers in and around the port of Chilmari who have had to move their homes as often as five times in a year. The riverine areas have always been a port of entry and a place of settlement for the influx into the region. But these days the influx is putting pressure even on old migrants and new routes are being fashioned to other parts of the Northeast.

India has put up barbed wire fences on parts of the international boundary between the two countries much to Bangladesh's consternation and annoyance. The fences are designed to keep "Bangladeshis" out but ranging over only a portion of the border, they are truly symbolic assertions of New Delhi's political response to the problem - which is understandable but which, as one's personal experience shows, does little to curb the influx.

For migration is the way of the world, it is the history of our earth. People, like water, always find their own levels, their ways of getting to where they want to go.

Rhetoric is feeble in the face of this reality; it cannot stand in the face of logic.

And in Assam today, no less a person than the Sabhapoti, the president of the respected and powerful Asom Sahitya Sabha, has declared that the immigrants must be assimilated into the Assamese society. This is as controversial a declaration as that by the students of the 1980s, which sought to oust every "foreigner" living in Assam. There is, therefore, now, a clear division in the discourse within Assam of what is to be done with regard to illegal migration and settlement.

One approach remains that harking back to the 1970s and 1980s: of detecting and deporting the "alien." The other is to detect and disenfranchise them at least temporarily as was done by the Election Commission in 1999 during a revision of electoral rolls in the state. (The revision turned up 320,000 persons of "doubtful origin" or in the language of the

Commission, people who could not prove that they were Indian. Virtually all of them were Bengali speakers and a large number were Muslim). A third option is the assimilation concept outlined by Dr. Homen Borgohain, which reverses the very concept of ouster, which was the core of the Assam movement and turns it into inclusive politics.

The rationale behind this needs to be explored further. Some reasons, from the perspective of this writer, are given briefly here:

1. The size of the population is clearly too large to push out: it would entail massive manpower deployment and extensive precautions to prevent a sectarian/communal backlash or conflict on grounds of alleged discrimination.
2. The law and order enforcement agencies have little time and give little importance to tackling migration; their role is in battling "insurgency" or extremists of one hue or the other and maintaining a semblance of normalcy.
3. Assimilation as a political and cultural policy, as enunciated in the 1950s, could ensure that in terms of language, Assamese will remain dominant in the Brahmaputra Valley. Yet, this is not without its pitfalls, one is speaking here of groups that will be asked to chose the language of their settled land over their natural language. This does not necessarily mean that there is ethnic cementing or territorial/nationalistic loyalty as a result. This needs to be understood clearly; for assimilation has unexpected pitfalls as well as hurdles which are visible even from a short distance. The policy of the 1950s created much bitterness among the hill people of the then state of Assam, leading to breakaway movements, which resulted in Meghalaya and Mizoram while Aruanchal Pradesh was carved out of the North East Frontier Agency, where the Assam Legislature's writ did not run. The alienation of the Bodos is partly attributable to this as well as a deliberate distancing and underdevelopment of their region by the Assamese political elite. This has resulted in much bitterness and now the effort to create a Bodo Territorial Council. Emotions drive politics in the region. Rhetoric pushes policies. Logic is lost, the mid is confused, policies are knee-jerk reactions to temporary

crisis. The people suffer and the circle of despondency and bitterness moves inexorably.

4. On the basis of language, perhaps, it is thought that political efforts can be channelized to ensure that local groups do not become a minority in their own land. Thus, with the Muslim Bengali-speaking settlers as allies, some may be thinking of Constitutional reservations for the State for its "local, Assamese-speaking" communities, which then would form a near-majority, as well as the non-Assamese tribal and backward caste groups, barring the immigrant settlers.
5. The Government of India is clearly not viewing this issue as a priority or taking an overall perspective in terms of employment, development, security and preservation of cultural uniqueness. While there are voices, which support the concept of Work Permits for new migrants (i.e. those who come after an arrangement on this is worked out with Bangladesh and this is still in the realm of future possibility!), others see it as a lever that could encourage Islamic militancy in the region. The Central Government is also concerned that it should not be seen as selling out "local" interests in the region and pandering to what this National Democratic Alliance in New Delhi speaks of as "pseudo-secularism."

Thus, rhetoric remains a sharp political tool that can result in conflict and greater anger. It is therefore important to be realistic and embrace a workable strategy for change and progress.

One of the first elements of such a new approach must be the acknowledgement that Bangladesh is a major trading partner of India, especially its East and Northeast. The illegal trade is at least two times the scale of the "formal" trade. And the biggest single illegal export of India to Bangladesh is not cloth or minerals or finished metal products. It is cattle - nearly two million of them every year.

The Northeast and Bangladesh share 1,956 kilometers of border, of which Assam has 350 kilometers, Meghalaya has 400, Mizoram has another 350 and Tripura has the 'biggest segment - 856. Therefore, it stands to reason that although much of our discussion here has been centred round Assam, a strategy involving better economic relations with Bangladesh must include other States of the Northeast.

In fact, statistics from a few years back show that it is Meghalaya and not Assam or Tripura, which took the lion's share of trade with Bangladesh because its main exports were of coal and limestone. According to Gurudas Das, Meghalaya had 83.04 percent of the NER's exports to Bangladesh in 1996-97 or the equivalent of Rs.8.6 crore. Tripura's share was less than one percent and Assam took up the balance.

The NER is a rich fruit-growing and vegetable-producing region. It is landlocked and hence must necessarily import many consumer goods, including foodstuff and durables from the "mainland", which makes little economic sense. It would be cheaper to important goods through Tripura, from the railhead at Akhaura in Bangladesh, just a few kilometers from Agartala. Similarly, other exit/entry points such as Dawki/ Tamabil in Meghalaya and Dhubri/Satrasal in lower Assam should be encouraged. So should Sutarkandi and Steamerghat (also known as Karimganj ferry ghat) in Karimganj.

The Indian Government should consider commercial flights to Dhaka and Sylhet from Guwahati, which already has an international flight to Bangkok every week. This would be a natural and logical extension of South Block's strategy to 'Look East'. Looking East cannot ignore the other neighbours at your doorstep with which communities along the borders have had historic and trading links.

There is thus a great opportunity for fruit and vegetable produce, including processed foods, to be marketed directly to Bangladesh from the Northeast, provided there is quality control and the quantities are large enough to make economic sense.

Das highlights one additional aspect in his paper: NER-Bangladesh trade has a firm basis in "their differences in natural endowments." ("Trade between Northeastern Region and Bangladesh" presented at Conference in Guwahati, February 2001: India's North East and Bangladesh, Problems and Opportunities).

Thus Bangladesh's need for minerals is supplied to an extent by the Northeast. Similarly, its need for vegetables and fruits can also be met, in part, by the NER.

A third point for cooperation should be asserted: tourism

Bangladesh sends half a million bona fide tourists to India every year. There are 70,000-80,000 students officially in schools, colleges and universities from there in this country. Lakhs come for medical treatment, others for pilgrimages. But the Northeast attracts few if any of these genuine visitors. We seem to draw only the resourceful poor who migrate in search of livelihoods!

Why can't the Northeast be aggressively marketed as a safe tourist getaway for the middle class in Bangladesh, who had hard currency to spend and a limitation on where to go for recreation and holidays? The NER is right next door to Bangladesh. Aggressive marketing has to be done by the State governments (another reason for greater autonomy!) as well as by the Centre. Each State must set up Tourist Boards that looks at resources and opportunities for marketing within the country and outside.

Our tourist brochures (mostly badly produced) laud our friendly people, our wonderful environs, great culture, beautiful hills and great rivers - but we draw nearly zero percent of all tourist arrivals in the country. Time to remedy that. Don't look too far East or West. Look south to our immediate neighbour, Bangaldesh. If 5,000 Bangladeshis spending an average of 500 dollars in each visit, the Northeast for a minimum of seven days, going to Shillong/Cherrapunji, Kaziranga and tea country, Arunachal Pradesh and Mizoram, then the States will get a total of not less than 17.5 million dollars between them (or 875 million rupees) or sneeze at, especially if the States are in such pathetic financial straits.

These are some of the specific strategies that can benefit the region, in the short and the long-term. We can look at also what strategies cannot work because of the nature of society and systems.

Thus, the Indian State and the State administrations are too feeble to take the kind of swift, decisive action that many seek. People talk glibly as they have for decades of deportation of the lakhs of Bangladeshis who are here. Let us stop deluding ourselves. The issue of deportation, which agitators did not understand then and perhaps do not do so even now, is that the concept presupposes one fact: that the other side/country accepts them as their own nationals who have crossed an international border illegally. But Bangladesh officially denies that its people leave. Some of us are working at the unofficial Track II level to persuade Dhaka to understand our concerns and acknowledge the reality. As I have said semi-official groups, academics and media persons are recognizing this fact. But it is a slow and difficult process that involves sensitivities on that side as well.

Let us look at the years of the agitation and let us consider the tangible results: a heightened public perception of the problem in the Northeast but also across India (this is 'a very big Plus); the formation of a regional party and government yet, there has been failure to tackle the very problem that brought this party and government to power and resulted in greater disappointment and failed hopes, greater discontent and resentment against the political system and its representatives. This led to the decisive and popular rejection of the Asom Gana Parishad and the Bharatiya Janata Party in Assembly elections in Assam.

It is time to think logically and with our heads. For far too long we have thought with hearts, with emotions. Feelings are important but issues need to be considered with reason and clarity if we are not to walk on the same that we have walked for more than 20 years — with what effect? What results? Do we plan to spend another few decades, using precious time and energy not to speak of resources, trying to identify the problem? If AASU and the AGP had spent a little more time on research instead of rhetoric, they would have been more credible in their approach to the problem, spent less money and used their energy in far more productive ways.

The reality that migration will continue to take place must be recognized. The push and pull factors will see to that. According to one estimate, the area that can be cultivated is dwindling in Bangladesh and the population growth will reduce by half the amount of cropland available per capita by 2025. One Bangladeshi academic has described the outward movement as a "survival strategy".

The pressure on land is growing on Assam too with the population increase on a cultivable land base that is not more than 70-to-100 kilometers wide at the maximum (the Assam Valley), large parts which are regularly flooded by high water during the summer.

There are a series of steps that can be taken unilaterally by the Central Government and others that should be worked out in consultation and cooperation with Bangladesh. Essentially these are steps aimed at regulating legal work-related migration and discouraging illegal migration for settlement or for work. These suggestions will not end the problem of illegal movements but they can encourage inflows and develop a regulatory/monitoring mechanism, which simply does not exist today. It will also serve as a symbol that Governments mean business instead of promising solutions, which cannot be implemented, such as, mass deportations and detections. We must work to put a regulatory mechanism in place. We are already many years late. We cannot continue to wait much longer, otherwise more conflicts will begin and the creeping radicalization of our borderlands will open up a new security front that we can ill-afford. The latter has begun to happen in a small way, with the involvement of outside agencies and political groups, which espouse a radical Islam especially in Bangladesh and see the Northeast as a lebensraum.

We must push and lobby political parties to put this issue of illegal migration and demographic change on their platforms and agendas. There is no reason, even from a different perspective, why the Congress, the CPI-M, the Samajwadi Party and the Janata Dal cannot approach this issue especially when it affects the Northeast so critically. Why should the BJP and the AGP only show they have policies on migration? The recent elections in Scandanavia should be an eye opener: a party came to power on a single issue - the problem of migration. For too long, migration has been under the carpet, under the table. Let it be on the political table and remain there. Each political party must be asked to state its position on the issue, whether they agree with it or not. They must use the skills and knowledge of demographers and others to understand the scale of the problem and what is to be done about it.

At the top of the agenda must be the setting up of a National Immigration Commission, on the lines of a similar Constitutional body in the United States. This must be empowered to take a detailed look at all the laws that exist and suggest measure to develop ways of tackling the problems. One is suggesting that the failure and ineffectiveness of various laws such as the Foreigners Act, Citizenship Act, IMDT etc. be reviewed by special teams - new plans considered such as a Migration Law, a National Refugee Law and Work Permits as well as Identity Cards. This body must house the best informed minds and persons in the country on the issue of citizenship, migrants and refugees and must be bound to a year-long schedule to finalize a list of "do-able", time-bound steps that can change conditions. The following steps can come in the wake of this Commission's work or at least the top three issues can be tackled side by side with that of the Commission's work. At the moment, we do not know how many refugees are in India or how many migrants - we have no laws to tackle them! We have only ad hoc, ineffective measures to deal with infiltration and illegal settlement which leads to trafficking in women and children as well as drug smuggling and use of gangs for trans-border shipment of illegal arms and contraband.

That all Indian nationals are issued Identity Cards, based on a process started during the tenure of T.N. Seshan as Chief Election Commissioner. This system should be made mandatory throughout the country. At the same time, without fail, border patrolling must continue, detection and deportation at the border must continue without let up for Government must continue to send a clear and unequivocal signal that illegal movement is to be discouraged sternly. The former BSF Director General, Prakash Singh, has suggested that there should be different coloured ID cards so that Indian nationals, immigrant workers can be immediately identified by their ID colour. One would also add the computerized number listings as another safeguard. We had the technical know how to make this possible.

The question arises: what is to be done about "illegal settlers" who have come over prior to the promulgation of the ID card regime? Consideration should be given to the following — that a temporary amnesty be announced for those who have come to India post -1971 till say 1991, saying that if they acknowledge their illegal status, they would be allowed to stay for one year to wind up their affairs and then re-apply to return under a Work Permit scheme which is explained later. This would help identify at least a segment of the population. Another suggestion was made as recently as yesterday by no less a person than K.P.S. Gill, former Punjab Director General of Police and a officer of the IPS Assam cadre with vast experience in this state. This is a bold and sensible idea: that everyone who has come since 1971 should be given citizenship because they are virtually that anyway. Mr. Gill's point was very specific: we need to increase the number of stakeholders in this country, in this region. Many of the settlers do not regard India or Assam as their land; they are easily preyed upon by groups inimical to India and the region. To prevent a greater radicalization of the communities, he suggested that they should be made stakeholders. I think, it is a very practical suggestion that must be considered very seriously.

In addition, we must throw rhetoric out of the window. If the amount of hot air that has been blown about in the past 26 years with regard to illegal migration had been translated to reality, then no migrant would be stand on this soil. But this has not happened. If anything, their numbers have increased! We have been loud on lungpower, pathetic on logic and a considered, reasoned approach to a critical problem. Something has clearly been wrong with our thinking and working if, in 26 years, we can only push about less than 1,500 aliens and that too after declaring there are crores, if not lakhs of illegals!

For too long we have been listening to voices declaiming: Detect and Deport! Or National security imperilled; or that "crores of Bangladeshis are coming over. Of course, there is a problem. That is why you are here, why I am here, why many follow this issue and advocate ways of tackling it. One is not underplaying the gravity of the situation. But we have been talking of the problem for the last 22 years. What have we done to tackle it?

The previous State Government first declared when it first came to power that it would oust the migrants. That did not happen for reasons cited above. The Congress Government of Hiteswar Saikia was disinterested although he made a faux pas as far as figures were concerned and hastily withdrew his remarks. The AGP in its second incarnation made a compromise with the immigrant groups, realizing it had to forge a coalition of interests if it was to gain power and then to stay in office. Electoral exigencies again played the critical role in changing policy. Rhetoric was tamed by those who created this very discourse, this very rhetoric! The defeat of the AGP does not mean that the issue of migration is rejected. It is that people were fed up with a Government that had failed to deliver on a single thing; they were weary of rhetoric. They know that a Bangladeshi is not just a Bangladeshi: he is a Bangladeshi, a Bengali speaker and a Muslim. We have multiple identities. We are not just part of a religious civilization as one false prophet, Samuel Huntington, would have us believe: we are workers, writers, singers, farmers and dreamers. We must be wary of abrupt delineations and categorizations: all Bangladeshis are out to overwhelm us! There is an Islamic conspiracy against the Northeast! We see an ISI hand everywhere just as we saw a CIA hand everywhere earlier. We need false demons to feed our inability to deal with our own inner turmoil and incapacities.

Rhetoric cannot replace reality. Rhetoric is dangerous; it is an enemy of openness, of dialogue, of cooperation. It generates bitterness and confrontation. We have had enough of it in the Northeast.

Let me come back to the policy changes, which can be implemented once all cards are in place, then the Government must, through an act of Parliament, reserve seats for the local people of the State. This has been done to a limited extent in Sikkim with regard to the Bhutia Lepchas. Why not in Assam? And take the basis of this as those individuals and communities, which have lived in a common geographical area for the past 40 years, matched with language and ethnic groupings. Such reservations can be for the next 25 years in the proportion of 60 percent of seats for such "local groups" and 40 percent in the open, general category. Constitutional safeguards for Assam were mentioned 16 years ago in the Assam Accord that ended the student agitation. But they have not been specified and detailed.

The Government should announce a Work Permit quota system for those willing to come from Bangladesh (and extend this to Myanmar) and work in Assam and the Northeast as well as other parts of India on work permits. These Work Permits should be issued to about 25,000 persons for the first year, rising gradually to a maximum of 75,000 for Assam. Similar quotas need to be fixed for other States, depending on their needs. The permits can be issued at the border district level on either side after prior consultations of the district officials. Thus, Bangladeshis who would want to work officially in India would need to apply to the relevant border district in their country with their full particulars. Once the quota for that district has been achieved (or they can be allowed to enter in groups before the quota is complete), the lists are made over to Indian authorities who can call for employers who are prepared to employ them in three specific labour-intensive occupations: construction; fishing and river related-activities; agricultural operations. The employer will be made responsible for the well-being and the non-disappearance of his/her employees under the work permit scheme.

The scheme will be applicable to specific parts of the Northeast where labour shortages are high. The permit will not be issued to individuals but to groups of not less than 20 persons. The permit will carry the photo identity of the workers as well as the name and address of their employer. Other details, such as, validity of the permit (usually for one year extendable to two years) and the nearest police station to which they will have to report every six months.

Under modalities worked out by their respective governments, they will have the ability to repatriate rupee funds to Bangladesh.

Local police who know the areas better than a national force like the Border Security Force be given greater responsibility for detecting and blocking border crossings.

Local communities, through panchayats, village councils, district councils etc., to be involved in this process enabling better local self-governance and greater local responsibility.

The building of fences to stop: those which exist may continue to function but better patrolling and greater responsibility given to local police and the Work Permit scheme be seen as fresh security and political approaches to the problem.

No migrant worker will have the right to vote. That right will rest exclusively with Indian nationals as defined by the Identity Card process.

These policy prescriptions will certainly not stop the influx. They may curb it and result in a set of incentives and disincentives that will reward the legal migrant and discourage, if not actively punish, the illegal settler. They cannot work in isolation but as part of a larger strategy that seeks to improve the economic conditions in migrant-producing and receiving regions. For the best strategy, and often the most economic in tackling migration, lies in improving the living conditions in the region of the migrant, that is Bangladesh. Already conditions are improving there. The growth rate in Assam this year is much lower than previous years —18 percent — indicating either a poor head count or a reduction in migrants.

We must push hard for the giant infrastructure projects, which will generate employment and improve livelihoods on either side of the border. These have been detailed to a degree earlier. But there is little harm in their brief recounting.

Border trade must be encouraged and made easier (pineapples, oranges, ginger, cotton and areca nut from Meghalaya; tea and cooking oil and fuel from Assam; in turn, fish and chilli from Bangladesh); Bangladesh can export natural gas to Assam and other parts of India; the river routes should be thrown open to transport; access to the Chittagong Port should be made possible through a railway line connecting

Agartala through Akhaura in Bangladesh— this would greatly reduce freight costs as normally sent through Calcutta or the Siliguri land corridor. It would reduce transport time, it would help develop the local economies and give access to quality goods from the region to an international seaport and airport.

It is in understanding each other in changing mindsets and accepting economic growth as the key to change that long-term, flexible strategies of mutual growth and benefit can be evolved. But to tackle the demographic crisis, we must accept that control mechanisms are called for and a new road map that charts the path to change is needed.

This is one person's vision of this road map, of the way forward. There are other views, other visions. But let us seek a road that maps prosperity for all, for without collaboration and cooperation, we will find ourselves hemmed in not by physical boundaries by our own prejudices and lack of realistic vision.

There is an African saying:

The earth plays music for those who want to listen. But there are few who hear.

9

Ethnicity and Security in Assam: A Plea for Greater Indo-Bangladesh Partnership

—SAMIR KUMAR DAS

India and Bangladesh being 'kin States'[1] to each other share many a commonality. Bangladesh being predominantly composed of the Bengalis has her obvious cultural and ethnic affinities with the Bengalis of eastern and northeastern India. The imagined reunification of two Bengals has been one of the favourite themes of the contemporary Bengali literature. The huge land border that supposedly separates the two countries remains fuzzy at some places becoming a subject of albeit mild dispute between the two countries, and to say the least, the hugeness and the tricky terrain especially during monsoons often make it virtually ungovernable. Besides, geographically they also form part of the greater Indo-Gangetic delta that has a long history of peasant migration. It is only with the establishment of two sovereign States (India and East Pakistan-turned-Bangladesh) that the hitherto free and unfettered peasant migration has been rendered illegal and overt social interactions amongst the Bengalis of both sides have become infrequent. Being 'kin States' to each other, India and Bangladesh also face many problems, which at times are perceived as threats to each other's national security. Their common past history and ethnic and territorial continuities are now seen to have become more of a liability than an asset. For, these commonalties seem to have posed a challenge to those symbols of a country's nationhood that any modern state seeks hard to secure and protect. Sometimes the cultural, ethnic, territorial and historic continuities have turned out to be a symbolic threat to the nationhood of both these countries. Our argument hence is grounded in the old English proverb that familiarity breeds contempt.

This paper focuses more on those commonalties that pose a threat to national security than those that do not and argues that bilateralism as the term is conventionally understood will not be able to address the threats, let alone taking care of them. We see the establishment and maintenance of a partnership regime between India and Bangladesh as a pre-condition of the resolution of our mutual security problems and threats emanating from the commonalties. It takes at least two to be involved in a partnership but it is not a simple bilateral relation. Accordingly, the paper is divided into two relatively different yet closely inter-connected parts. The first part draws our attention to at least two major threats born out of the commonalties that Northeast in general and contemporary Assam in particular have been facing. It also points out how these threats amount to a symbolic assault on a country's national security. The second part shows how the bilateral framework that the two States are following while conducting their inter-relations and promising to resolve these problems is inadequate in addressing them. India's principled opposition to multilateralism in order to resolve essentially bilateral problems is by now pretty well known. But we argue that the conventional bilateral framework may not be the panacea for the unusual problems that the two neighbours have been facing right from their birth as separate and sovereign nations. Hence the second part also outlines the framework of a future partnership regime between India and Bangladesh as a step towards resolving these problems and threats.

Viewed in this light, the paper has some limitations: One, it proposes to view the threats from the Indian perspective as telescoped in Assam, one of the constituent States of the

Indian Union. Assam being a bordering State has been facing threats, which in some quarters are described as 'an Indian problem'.[2] Indian nation according to them is put on trial in Assam. But how far the case of Assam is potent enough to influence the threat perspective of the Indian State is a question that is beyond the purview of the present paper. Jaideep Saikia known to be close to the official security circles in Assam in one of his recently written papers has actually written about the South Block's inexplicable apathy towards the security problems of the Northeast.[3] In fact, we argue that notwithstanding the threats faced by the people of Assam, the Indian State including the consecutive Governments of Assam remain oblivious to them. It only shows that there is no one single Indian perspective and that it is to say the least terribly ruptured and fragmented. Even if an analysis of the Bangladeshi perspectives is necessary to carry forth our arguments to their logical conclusions this paper for obvious limitations of space, does not elaborately delve into it. Two, the paper as we have said, underlines only the ethnic, territorial and historic continuities between the two countries. It should not give us the impression that the continuities are confined only to these three inter-related sectors of social life. The economic and political complementarities are nevertheless significant, but are beyond the scope of this paper. We are only interested in discovering the security problems insofar as they arise out of the ethnic, territorial and historical continuities between the two countries under review. Three, our outline of the proposed partnership regime is very sketchy. The purpose of this paper is to initiate a debate rather than providing any definitive answer to the problems mentioned here.

Securing/Building the Nation

While it is true that territorial and ethnic continuities are an inseparable part of our common past history, we were called upon to adjust ourselves to the new realities unleashed by an otherwise rapid process of de-colonization of the subcontinent. The transition was by no means easy and requires little bit of an elaborate discussion.

It will be tautological to say that our national security was contingent on securing our nationhood against external threats. While security preparations are necessarily directed against an external power or maybe a coalition of them, seldom is the question of what it is that is, or is sought to be secured asked in either the official circles or the conventional writings on national security in India. In recent years, however, there has emerged some kind of sensitivity towards the internal sources of threat to the country's security. But in both the official and the conventional circles, these threats are predominantly, if not exclusively, seen as being masterminded and sponsored by foreign powers. Thus, internal sources of threat are always considered to be secondary to the external ones.[4] That these preparations are directed at securing the 'Indian nation' is too taken for granted to be doubted, let alone be re-examined. 'Indian nation' according to this possesses an 'absolute value' that not only informs the entire gamut of our security preparations but place them above any kind of critical scrutiny. Our argument is that the nation that the Indian State sought to protect and secure was, or is, in some fundamental senses divergent from the one that we were ethnically, territorially and historically endowed with. In that sense, nation building in post-colonial India involved a journey against our historical heritage. Strange yet true, our security thinking and preparations also mark a departure from our historical past, our cultural and ethnic lineages and most importantly, our inherited notions of territoriality. While securing and protecting the nation, the Indian State seemed to have brought as it were a new and hitherto unknown Indian nation into existence. Securing nation in that sense forms an inseparable part of greater nation-building exercise.

For all these departures bore and albeit in most cases continue to bear the mark of the Indian State. One, never before in Indian history, was the idea of Indian nation supposed to be 'Indian' in the sense of being confined only to the presently demarcated territory of the Indian State. Today the State's territoriality becomes one of the key determinants of Indian nationhood. Any modern State seeks to build its nationhood by seeking to contain it within its territorial borders. Any modern nation is necessarily a territorially bounded body. Borders in other words, serve as a means of capturing and securing the essence of nationhood.

They secure its essence first of all, by not allowing the nation to merge and subsequently melt into the vast ocean of humanity that lies outside it and also by preventing the foreigners from surreptitiously slipping into the national body and thereby robbing it of its essential particularity.

Territorial demarcation in the Indo-East Pakistan/ Bangladesh context hence involved a combination of two complementary historical processes. It first of all means that an otherwise ethnically and culturally continuous social space was getting vivisected into two independent and sovereign States, separated by a nearly impenetrable border. It brought the hitherto existent cultural exchanges and interactions to an abrupt halt and had made us believe as if these had historically never existed. Thus the imperative of drawing clearly delineated and demarcated territorial borders led us to invent their existence from time immemorial. The fictive history was only complementary to the process of delineation and demarcation of territorial borders. The fictive history is premised on the erasure of the historical reality of everyday exchanges and transactions amongst a culturally continuous and territorially contiguous body of people.[5] As a result, we seem to believe that such exchanges and transactions never had taken place. As Tibet came to the grip of China, India, East Pakistan/Bangladesh and Burma/Myanmar were born as separate and independent States, and Northeast as a region linked with India through an extremely vulnerable Siliguri Corridor – described as 'chicken neck' in strategic circles [6], took its shape as a distinct entity. It was de-colonization that was responsible for the birth of this region as a distinct entity. Takeshi Fujii traces the history of the birth of Indo-Burmese border. Many tribes of the then NEFA, as he informs us, continued to pay tributes to the Tibetan Chieftains even after the Independence of India. The important task that the newly born Indian State was faced with was to turn them away from the fold of foreign authorities towards its own administration of New Delhi.[7] Even such uncertainties and indeterminacies mark the process of delineating and demarcating the inter-State borders within the Indian Union. The Assam-Nagaland border is perhaps one of the most hotly debated borders drawn on what is believed to be a culturally continuous plane. Joyshankar Hazarika, for example, shows how both the international (external) and inter-State (internal) borders of post-colonial India militate against many traditional and indigenous 'habits' and 'practices' of the ethnic communities living in the Northeastern region. The dispute between Assam and Nagaland over territorial borders took place at a time when the modern State had felt it expedient to draw the border in a neat and precise manner literally by drawing a line on the ground. Such neat and precise division went against the traditional Naga 'habit' of raiding the villages of the contiguous plains and foothills and settling in those places, thereby constantly expanding the area under their control. The British encouraged a policy of extending tea plantation beyond the revenue line for commercial gains and chose to pay taxes to the Naga Chiefs. Similarly, the British policy of leaving the 'frontier tribes' of erstwhile North East Frontier Agency (NEFA) (presently Arunachal Pradesh) largely un-administered and unaffected by its rule is the source of contentious claims of India and China over large tracts of territory in the region.[8]

The second historical process that is also implicit in the delineation and demarcation of borders is the establishment of cultural particularity of those who live within the borders and organize them as a nation. Benedict Anderson also emphasizes that any national imagining is necessarily 'particularistic' and can never be universal to the point of encompassing the entire universe.[9] While universality is the antithesis of nationhood, borders are instrumental in investing it with its particularity. It is through the instrumentality of borders that the State brings the nation into existence, secures and protects it and most importantly, marks it off from what it considers to be its other. More than anything else, the Indians and the Bangladeshis are marked off from each other by the presence of an international border – howsoever porous and practically indefensible that is. In many ways, the Bengalis of both sides are the same and culturally indistinguishable. Once Bangladesh was formed on the basis of language, she faced the apparently intractable problem of differentiating the Bengalis of Bangladesh from those of West Bengal, or for that matter, India. While asserting the cultural particularity of the Bengalis of Bangladesh, the Bangladeshis seem to have emphasized their Bangladeshi rather than the generic Bengali identity. The essence of Bangladeshi identity lies not so much in the generic Bengali identity that otherwise is likely to unite both of them – primarily the Bengali Hindus and the Bengali Muslims but in privileging their composite linguistic and religious character. The Bengalis of Bangladesh are primarily Muslim and the quest for their Bengali identity was never the one for pure linguistic identity. It was rather a quest for their specifically Bengali Muslim identity as distinguished from the identity of their Hindu counterparts that informed their struggles. In a recently written paper, Prof. Sabyasachi Bhattacharya traces the history of this quest to the 1920s when the Bengali Muslims for the first time felt the necessity of cultivating what was known as 'Musalmani Bangla' and the quest according to him, has been more or less consistent since then. The process acquired a fillip since 1971 when Bangladesh became independent.[10] The case interestingly shows how the necessity of constructing a cultural identity that would respect their ethnic and cultural difference was more deeply felt only after Bangladesh was born as a separate state and the boundaries were reorganized between the nations. Cultural differentiation in this example was a consequent and not an antecedent of territorial demarcation. I have shown elsewhere how the imperative of asserting the cultural particularity of the nationals living within the bounded territory and normalizing its newly established borders was felt as soon as the post-colonial states were formed in the wake of Partition of the subcontinent and their territorial borders were reorganized.[11] In other words, as soon as the territorial borders are demarcated and the modern sovereign States are formed, there is no going back and social life has to come to terms with the new reality of States and the territorially bounded peoples that they are supposed to enclose and represent. Joya Chatterjee, while speaking on the Radcliffe Line and Bengal's border landscape, describes it as 'evolution of new ways of life'.[12]

Two, the Indian nation in colonial times did not have the obligation of being governable by the State in order to qualify as a nation. In fact, the anti-colonial struggles at times were so strong and intense that some sections of the people turned out to be highly obstinate and completely ungovernable to their colonial masters. Now of course the situation is different. The nation has to be governable in order to be regarded as a nation. The ethnic elements that refuse to be governed by the post-colonial State are instantly stigmatized by it as 'anti-national' and hence deserve stern punitive action. 'Anti-national' and 'anti-State' in India have for all practical purposes become interchangeable words. Governability today is another key determinant of Indian nationhood. Governability in short sets forth the limits within which ethnic communities of the Northeast are entitled to assert their identities and voice their demands. What is interesting to note in this connection is that governability as a condition of political articulation does not completely rule out the political role of ethnic communities. It only means that they are required to operate within the parameters set forth by the imperative of governability. We know that the national body that is regarded as governable is also a body of loyal citizens. Citizenship more than anything else is the expression of an individual's willingness to be governed by the authority of the State. It is the acquiescence to the authority of the State that gives credence to her identity as a citizen and overrides all other identities. We may note at least two major kinds of ethnic movements in Northeastern India that emphasize the citizenship identity of those who are involved in them.

Continuous population flows from outside India have made the issue of citizenship highly problematic. This is not so much in the commonly understood sense of identifying the Indian citizens in an otherwise physically and culturally contiguous region, like, South Asia, but in the fundamental sense that citizenship in a country such as India serves as a role-sign for the assertion of various ethnic identities. In this context, it may be instructive to find out the changes that ethnic assertion in different parts of eastern and northeastern India brings about in the very notion of citizenship. Assuming that the issue of citizenship is based on an elemental distinction between citizens and foreigners or aliens, one notices two complementary types of citizenship movements in eastern and northeastern India. On the one hand, there are movements that centre on a community's yearning to be different from foreigners or aliens as a means of retaining its linguistic and cultural identity. The spate of anti-foreigners' agitation targeted mainly against the Bangladeshis and the Nepalis that shook various parts of the Northeast in the 1980s may serve as a case in point. The Assam movement (1979-85) that was successful in bringing various cross-sections of the people of Assam into its fold was essentially an anti-foreigners movement. It harped on the three popular demands of detecting, disenfranchising and deporting the foreigners migrating to and settled in Assam. Viewed in this light, it was out and out a movement that aimed at asserting the rights of citizens vis-à-vis the foreigners. While at one level it was true, at another, it was also a movement that looked upon Indian citizenship as a means of preserving the language and culture of the Assamese as a community. For, it was by way of raising their demands against the foreigners that they thought of preserving their identity as Assamese supposedly under the threat of losing their identity and culture as a result of almost unlimited influx of foreigners from across the international borders. Their identity as Indian citizens in this example is considered to be instrumental in preserving their identity as the Assamese. Sometimes, the citizenship identity of the Assamese is so much blown out of proportions that their specifically particularistic identity is lost sight of and conveniently forgotten.[13] Unless the subtext of the Assamese identity is properly taken care of and recognized, our understanding of the Assam movement is bound to be partial and one-sided. On the other hand, we may refer to those movements that are marked by a community's aspiration for being recognized as an empowered body of citizens in the form of a separate political unit, such as statehood. The Gorkhaland movement in the Darjeeling Hills of West Bengal that culminated in the establishment of Darjeeling Gorkha Hill Council (DGHC) illustrates the point. By way of designating them as 'Gorkhas' as distinguished from the Nepalis, they in fact seek to emphasize their Indian identity. They no longer prefer to be classified as the Nepalis – literally people from Nepal. As a sequel to it, they also tried to point out that 'Gorkhali' is a language presumably distinct from the Nepalese. Many linguists have questioned the veracity of such a thesis. But the point is that even these apparently academic questions exceed their academic innocuousness and acquire political overtones in times of crisis when a community is bent on proving its point and establishing its separate political identity. The classical theory of citizenship hardly admits of any differences on lines of religion, race, caste, sex and place of birth. But it has become difficult – if not impossible, in the northeast of the country to separate the issue from the question of a collective identity of an ethnic community that predicates on the legal reality of citizenship and impels a redefinition. Citizenship in a region like the northeast is by and large a vacuous site that gives the particular communities reasonable freedom to enact their respective ethnic identities within it.

Three, our independence has resulted in a transformation of colonial subjects into legally free and rights-bearing citizens, thanks to our Constitution and other ancillary legal instruments. Much of our anti-colonial awakening was directed at securing the democratic rights for the Indian people. Nationalism was regarded as a means of securing these rights. It was by way of positioning the hitherto unequal and hierarchically placed Indians within the national body that their social and ethnic differences were sought to be leveled-off and obliterated. Our march to freedom and equality was ordained through the nationalist road. Nationalism in a country like India served as a great leveler for, never before in Indian history, were the people organized or sought to be organized as free and equal legal personalities.[14] Colonial State hardly gave us the right to freedom and equality. Indeed, it will be more accurate to say that it ruled by way of establishing the principle of difference, a principle that says that the colonial masters and their subjects can never be equal and that the subjects being subjects deserve to be ruled by the colonial masters. John Stuart Mill, one of the staunchest proponents of representative democracy, made a case against it when he had argued that the colonized are too 'uncivilized' to stake their claim to it.[15] Besides, the colonial state also introduced many other kinds of division amongst the colonized people. Indeed, these divisions are so intense that they also make India ineligible for being considered as a single and cohesive nation. Much of the intellectual justification of the colonial rule came from him. It was only with the attainment of Independence and coming into force of the Constitution that the noble egalitarian objective of the nationalist project could be actualized. Notwithstanding the fact that the colonial State was an extension of the metropolitan power that witnessed the European Enlightenment and with it, the celebration of the twin value of freedom and equality, it remained an anathema to the powerful intellectual movement of the 17th and 18th century Europe. Colonial State in India therefore was a negation of whatever the metropolitan state of Great Britain stood for in the eyes of British citizens. The rights are inalienable now and the post-colonial state is expected to ensure and guarantee them and most importantly, not to encroach on them excepting on certain legally stipulated conditions. Right to freedom and equality of the citizens is the third most important determinant of post-colonial Indian nationhood and today Indian nationhood is inconceivable without free and equal Indian citizens. In sum, in all these departures the post-colonial State plays an indispensable role in articulating and elaborating the nationalist discourse. The nationalist discourse in post-colonial India invariably bears the State's seal of approval.

The Threats

We have already said that since India and Bangladesh share many commonalties, they also face many problems. In this section, we may restrict our attention to an analysis of the problems that have the potential of being translated into formidable threats to India's national security. Bangladesh is reportedly facing similar but not exactly the same problems that also pose a threat to her security. As we do not propose to approach the problem from the Bangladeshi side, we refrain from adding a Bangladeshi angle to the paper though of course we strongly feel that such an angle is only complementary to the plea for greater Indo-Bangladesh partnership. For purposes of convenience, we focus our attention on only two of such threats: immigration and insurgency. It will be wrong to treat them as absolutely separate or for that matter, completely separable threats. But they are important in the sense that they emanate from the same historic, territorial and ethnic continuities mentioned above.

That immigration has been one of the most nagging problems – perhaps the most nagging problem of the northeast in general and Assam in particular is too obvious to be exaggerated. We have already made a reference to the continuing anti-foreigner frenzy visible albeit in its most prominent form in the northeast since the late 1970s. It is true that hair-splitting estimates concerning the exact nature and magnitude of the demographic challenge as well as the debates over the appropriate methodology for ascertaining, quantifying and fathoming it have marked the academic scene of the northeast during the last few years. We do not propose to create a new controversy by providing still another estimate about the number of illegal immigrants presently settled in Assam. The figures have been the subject of an intense political debate in Assam. All the estimates that were done in course of the Assam movement (1979-1985) kept the number of illegal settlers somewhere between eight lakhs and 4.5 millions, while the actual number of them deported during this period was incomparably lower than even the lowest of these estimates.[16] The point is that very little attention is paid to the question of how the problem of continuing immigration from across the borders has assumed alarming proportions in recent years so much so that it is believed to have posed a formidable threat to the country's security.

Researches intermittently conducted on the problem of immigration in the Brahmaputra valley point to some alarming trends. First, the migrants no longer come in any haphazard and sporadic manner. They do not pour in from wherever they can. Nor do they settle in wherever they see vacant land in Assam, which earlier was the case. In most cases, the immigrants enter Assam from some well-known points of entry in an organized and planned manner. They usually take the help of their local contacts – sometimes people of their own villages settled in Assam or even Indian brokers or middlemen who make money by way of getting them transported to their places of destination. It seems that there exists a well-knit network thorough which migration takes place. The role of the early settlers coming from the same village or district of Bangladesh is important in getting the latecomers settled and economically rehabilitated. In most cases, it works as a chain. They do not come like the classical economic migrants who leave their places more out of necessity and destitution and who are not certain about their destination. The push factor seems to be more important than the pull in their case. Although the rate of immigration is believed to have dropped in recent years, thanks to rising anti-foreigner crescendo all over the Northeast and greater governmental vigilance over them and improved border patrolling etc., much of today's immigration is organized and planned and therefore defies any easy detection. They know exactly the points thorough which the immigrants are supposed to enter, the places where the transport will be made available to them, the places where they are going to be settled and most importantly, how they will be provided with papers like, ration cards and voter identity cards. Since the entire process works as a chain, the likelihood of their detection and punishment by the guest-state is either low or non-existent. By the time their presence starts being felt in the polity and economy, they are pretty well settled and it is impossible to single them out and detect them. While the presence of operatives, middlemen and brokers establishing a network though which immigration takes place and continues unabated can hardly be doubted, their connection with what Hiranya Kumar Bhattacharyya calls, 'Muslim conspiracy' of transforming the demographic composition of Assam is not all too apparent.[17] He has described in somewhat greater detail the modus operandi of these brokers and middlemen who always try to integrate the immigrants into the ever-wider networks of the early settlers. It is the systematic and organized nature that has made immigration particularly alarming in recent years.

Secondly, the settlement pattern of the immigrants suggests that they do not settle themselves wherever they can. Rather, they seek the assistance of the early settlers. Since the early settlers act as a conduit, the new batches of immigrants seem to flock in those areas where their brethren are already in substantial numbers. The demographic pattern of the Brahmaputra valley thus has undergone a distinctive change in recent years. The valley is known for the presence of some very conspicuous immigrant pockets and there is reason to believe that these immigrant pockets are swelling in terms of the percentage of population living there. The extraordinary growth of population in pockets known to have a very high concentration of immigrants is disproportionately greater than the average growth rate of population in Assam. Two factors continuously work against any neat and precise estimate of the district-wise composition of population in Assam. The cracking and splitting of districts especially since the early 1980s do not allow us to compare the population trends in any simple manner. Moreover, since no census operation could be held in Assam in 1981, population data usually come in the bloc of twenty years. However, if one chooses to break up the entire bloc in order to obtain the average for the decade - whether of 1971-81 or of 1981-91, certain interesting facts stare at one's face. Most of the districts – though not all, that have during either of these two decades recorded a growth rate higher than that of 1961-71 are believed to be immigrant-infested pockets of the state. Table 1 below gives us some idea of the population trends in these districts.

Table takes only those districts into consideration where the percentage of population growth during 1971-81/1981-91 has been greater than that of the previous decade. Not all cases of unusual increase can be attributed to the influx of population from across the borders. For example, the increase in some of the upper Assam districts like, Jorhat may have been due to the displacement of population caused by the devastating rounds of annual floods in the adjoining districts of Majuli and Dhemaji.[18] Cachar and Hailakandi though outside the Brahmaputra valley are a favourite destination of the immigrants primarily because of their ethnic proximity with the local population. N.C. Hills has a substantial percentage of tribal population and of late there is believed to have been a perceptible immigration of the tribals from the neighbouring States. But the districts of lower Assam mentioned above are widely taken to contain many immigrant pockets. The ethnic divide between the immigrants and the natives shows signs of coinciding with a certain territorial segregation in the state of Assam. The hitherto noticed cheek-by-jowl settlement of the immigrants and the natives might have its pitfalls, but it certainly gave both these groups an opportunity to know each other and interact. This has led a number of social scientists to express satisfaction with the process of social assimilation that takes place between them. In a sense this was true.

Table 1

District-wise Population Trends (in Percentage) in Assam

Sl.No	District	1961-71	1971-91	1971-81/1981-91
1	Kokrajhar	8.12	22.48	11.24
2	Kamrup	1.07	26.92	13.46
3	Darrang	1.51	12.39	6.19
4	Sonitpur	-8.2	29.52	29.52
5	Morigoan	0.38	13.39	6.69
6	Nagaon	3.08	12.27	6.13
7	Golaghat	4.81	27.27	13.63
8	Jorhat	6.7	15.63	7.81
9	Sibsagar	-3.89	12.29	9.64
10	Tinsukia	4.9	16.01	8.00
11	N.C.Hills	3.05	58.3	29.15
12	Hailakandi	-3.62	22.93	11.16
13	Cachar	1.36	22.63	11.81

Source: ***Statistical Handbook: Assam*** (Guwahati: Directorate of Economics and Statistics, Government of Assam1996), pp. 18-19.

Let us take the example of the people living in the Char (embankment) areas. Some of the recent studies conducted on them point to their growing assimilation. According to a report prepared by Assam's Char Unnayan Nigam in 1997, an estimated 21 lakh people live in as many as 2089 Char villages. Muslims constitute an overwhelming majority (about 18 lakhs) amongst them. Most of their forefathers came to Assam in the late-19th century and have become in the words of Dr Rezaul Karim, "an inseparable part of the Assamese nation".[19] They have adopted Assamese as their mother tongue and even sided with the Assamese in the language movements of 1960 and 1972. But with the change in the demographic settlement pattern, occasions of interaction between them are few and far between. Since they are territorially segregated, social interactions between them are becoming highly improbable. As the immigrants mostly Muslims live in ghetto-like settlements and in the process reduce the natives to a minority in the immediate neighbourhood, they cannot be expected to 'accept Assamese cultural icons and institutions so easily'.[20] Hiranya Kumar Bhattacharyya refers to a survey conducted by Sudhakar Rao on the settlement pattern in the district of Marigaon known for its high concentration of immigrants. According to him, during the early 1980s when the Assam movement was at its peak, as many as 25 villages of the district were 'totally de-Hinduized'. Rao analyzed the case of 74 other villages, which were 'exclusively Hindu villages until 1983' but which were in the process of 'being taken over by the Muslim immigrants'.[21] It only shows that the immigrants settle in the form of ever-widening concentric circles engulfing in the process larger and larger geographical areas. The rate of immigration exceeds that of assimilation. In fact, if Udayon Misra's words were to be believed, it was the other way round. The inclusion of 'the neo-Assamese Muslims' (in an obvious reference to the immigrants who have returned Assamese as their mother tongue in the consecutive census operations) has led to the 'transformation of the Assamese identity'.

Regarding the majority of the Assamese language, there seems little doubt because the number of neo-Assamese will keep on increasing. But while the future of the Assamese speaker is ensured, the future content and course of Assamese language and literature is bound to change along with the expansion of the cultural determinants of the Assamese society. While the large majority of the neo-Assamese Muslims are today in the process of being integrated with the Assamese community whose cultural determinants are largely Hindu, yet further imbalance in the demographic structure in favour of immigrant Muslims may result in the rise of pan-Islamic positioning.[22]

Thus to conclude, the particular settlement pattern and the waning of social intercourse between the immigrants and the natives are what make the present-day immigration particularly threatening.

Thirdly, the immigrant pockets seem also to turn fast into hotbeds of fundamentalism and insurgency. It is true that fundamentalism has never been altogether alien to the political practice of the immigrant Muslims. Yet, its present-day version is remarkably different from its earlier versions. One, there is reason to think that the newly ascendant Islamic fundamentalism has acquired an organized and militant character. Security agencies in India reportedly have the information that as many as 15 different militant Islamic organizations are operating in the state of which 3 (viz. Muslim Liberation Tigers of Assam or MULTA, Muslim Liberation Army or MLA – formerly known as the Muslim United Liberation Front of Assam or MULFA and Islamic Liberation Army of Assam or ILAA) are quite strong. Many of them are acting at the behest of such foreign espionage agencies as Inter-Services Intelligence (ISI) and ultra-fundamentalist bodies as Islamic Chhatra Shibir and Jamiat-I-Islami of Bangladesh. Formerly their activities were restricted to the multi-ethnic areas of the Brahmaputra valley (like, Nagaon and Marigaon) where Muslims have always been in sizeable numbers. But now their activities have spread out to the vast areas of Barpeta, Goalpara and Dhubri and even to such far-off areas as Cachar of the Barak valley.[23] While their activities are engulfing the ever-newer areas, they are also undergoing a certain militarization. The roots of fundamentalist militancy among the immigrant Muslims may be traced back to days of the large-scale anti-Muslim pogroms in the Brahmaputra valley organized during the tumultuous days of 1983. One may recall that the Muslim section of the AASU-leadership comprising such persons as Nurul Hussain and Nekibur Zaman was so deeply hurt at this that it severed all its connection with the organization for turning itself into a mouthpiece of the chauvinist Hindus and thereby sacrificing its secular character. A Muslim Volunteers' Force was raised in Assam as a vanguard for protecting the Muslims against the attacks from the Hindus. It's stated objectives are:

> ...to impart training in the Muslims for self-defence, to form 'death squads' to enroll people and training them for protecting the people belonging to the Muslim community in buses, trains and in public places, to take suitable measures against those who by virtue of their power and high ranks are condemning the Muslims, torturing and killing them, to take counter-measures then and there, to take steps for restoring Muslim interests wherever they are in jeopardy, to extend help to Muslims who are in dire straits, to convert Assam into the Waterloo of RSS (Rashtriya Swyamsevak Sangh) and to take a constant vigil on government employees and to inform the authorities about their misdeeds.[24]

Even Saiyad Azad Madani, widely appreciated for his moderate views, called upon the Muslims to get united against the Asom Gana Parishad, a proclaimed successor to the forces loyal to the erstwhile Assam movement and to take up arms whenever necessary:

> Religion has not prevented the Muslims from fighting the enemies. If someone comes to attack you, then try to make him understand with sympathy; but if someone does not understand, then be engaged in a formal battle against him.[25]

He also in the same public meeting held at Doboka exhorted upon them to train themselves in karate and kung fu in self-defence and to spend three/four hours at the minimum in a day for arms training. The Muslims, he added, should remember that Asom Gana Parishad had killed 'thousands of their brothers' in earlier years. Muslim fundamentalism has so far made it a point to see the Indian state as the ultimate saviour and the protector of their interests. But now it seems that the fundamentalists no longer show the patience of keeping faith in the State. Their faith has of late been severely eroded with the effect that they either fall prey to foreign forces or feel the necessity of standing on their own and resolving their problems without resorting to the Indian State or both. That the Muslim faith has considerably eroded in recent years is evident from the fact that *Kalam* by its own admission is the spokesman of the Muslims, accused Hiteswar Saikia, then Chief Minister of Assam, of falling a 'victim to the Hindutva-wadi game-plan.'[26] The more this feeling gets entrenched, the less they are likely to approach the State for the ventilation of their grievances.

As we have pointed out, immigration and insurgency as threats to internal security are not altogether unrelated. Immigration in many ways has been responsible for the conflagration of many an insurgency in various parts of Assam. One, the pressure on demography, land, language, culture and economy in general caused by the already high and rising waves of immigrants has led to widespread disgruntlement and at least a section of the autochthonous people to take up arms against them. The immigrants as a result become soft targets everywhere. The consecutive bouts of attacks organized and staged by the Bodo rebels in the predominantly Bodo-inhabited areas on the Muslims as well as the Santhals who came over to Assam to serve as indentured labourers in the plantations of Assam in the 19th century are a case in point. Although the Assam movement (1979-85) has been widely hailed as a 'mass movement' analogous to the one of 1942 organized by Gandhi, a section of its leaders definitely felt the necessity of arms in order to accomplish their objective of detecting, disenfranchising and deporting the illegally settled immigrants. The pogroms of Nellie and Chaulkhowa Chapori in 1983 illustrate the point.[27] Two, initially the immigrants were at the receiving end of all this. For obvious reasons, they meekly gave in to what was meted out to them and had to be the victims of the rage of the so-called sons-of-the-soil. But, the decade of the 1990s has also witnessed a certain organization and militancy on the part of the immigrants not only in Assam but also in other parts of the northeast particularly Tripura. The Tribal Cobra Force on the one hand, and Amra Bangali and the Bengali Tigers' Force on the other, serve as the representative organizations of the Santhals and the Bengalis respectively. Three, of course there are some insurgent organizations that have a perspective larger than merely defending or driving away the immigrants. Now it appears that the United Liberation Front of Assam for example, is not opposed to the immigrants *per se* - especially those who came from East Pakistan. In an otherwise longish pamphlet entitled 'Asombasi Purbabangeeya Janagoshthiloi ULFA Ahvan' (ULFA's call to the groups from East Bengal living in Assam), ULFA redefines the concept of 'the Assamese' (Asomiya) as 'a people of all communities, the mixture of people who are determined to work for all-round progress of Assam'. Thus the scope of the concept no longer remains restricted only to those who speak the Assamese language as their mother tongue. Obviously, the immigrants from Bangladesh being the largest group of immigrants are 'an indispensable part' of them[28]. However, according to Sanjoy Hazarika, within one year from the publication of this pamphlet Anup Chetiya – one of ULFA's top leaders issued another statement in which anyone migrating to Assam after 1971 was straightaway branded as a 'foreigner' and most importantly as a potential deportee. A similar statement of Arabinda Rajkhowa released to the press in late-2001 is reflective of ULFA's continuing uneasiness with the question of foreigners. ULFA seems to be caught up in a dilemma: On the one hand, it cannot disregard for long strong Assamese sentiment against the foreigners especially the Bangladeshis. Many of the top leaders of ULFA had actually taken an active part in the anti-foreigners' agitation (1979-1985). On the other hand, they cannot afford to alienate Bangladesh for some strategic reasons described below. For ULFA, it is really tight roping insofar as the question of foreigners is concerned.

Insurgency poses a threat to the country's internal security insofar as it acquires an external dimension and involves a foreign country like Bangladesh. It is through the external linkage that insurgency refuses to remain a purely internal phenomenon, that is to say, an unmediated engagement between the Indian state and the insurgents. Bangladesh's role in fomenting and abetting insurgency in Assam has already received some attention especially in the strategic circles. Her role is believed to range from providing safe hideouts to the militants when they are on the run to directly extending diplomatic and military support to them. As the army was called in to tackle the ULFA insurgency in the 1990s, many of the ULFA cadres took refuge in Bangladesh and established temporary camps from which they could organize and conduct their operations. It is widely believed that as soon as the Awami League came to power, those camps were forced to shut down at the instance of the Government of India. It was during this time that ULFA decided to shift its operational base from Bangladesh to Bhutan. That Bangladesh serves as a conduit in the supply of arms and ammunition to the militants of the northeast has been brought home in some of the recently written papers.[29] Jaideep Saikia argues that the support extended to the insurgents by the Bangladeshi Government is both overt and active to the point of providing insurgent leaders taking refuge in Bangladesh with armed bodyguards.[30] We do not have any independent way of either confirming or disputing his database. The problem with Saikia's analysis is that he has a privileged access to certain kinds of information, which we cannot simply verify. His information is bound to have very limited value to methodologically sensitive students of social science for we cannot use them without proper verification. But given that an organization is engaged in an insurgent battle against a state apparatus that is disproportionately stronger than it, it is extremely unlikely that it will not seek help from the neighbouring countries.[31]But the problem arises when it subordinates its revolutionary ideology to the operational requirements of strengthening the organization by seeking help from others. It is at this time that the organization starts acting at the behest of a foreign country and surrenders its autonomy to the latter and a foreign country hijacks its agenda. There is reason to believe that ULFA was sensitive to this danger at least up to a point. As Sanjoy Hazarika informs us, when ULFA turned down the directive of the Pakistani authorities to 'disrupt communications and economic targets such as oil, pipeline and gas fields, create chaos and pave the way for a general uprising against the government', it had thought that 'major attack on government property would alienate us form the people and they would turn against us'.[32] The shift in its stance on the question of immigrants from Bangladesh in 1992 noted above is often explained in terms of the organization's need for securing safe hideouts in a foreign country at a time when the Indian security forces have successfully turned the pressure on it. Jaideep Saikia has accused ULFA of having taken the turnaround at the instance of its operational requirement of finding out a safe haven in a foreign territory from which it can mastermind and organize all its activities but escape the security dragnet. The insurgents, as Saikia argues, have scant respect for strong Assamese sentiments against alarmingly high rate of immigration from across the borders threatening their language and culture. Thus in Saikia's words, the dream of a 'Swadhin Asom' (Independent Assam) may soon turn into a nightmare of a 'Brihat Bangla' (Greater Bengal), were ULFA to continue its hobnobbing with external espionage agencies.[33]

From Bilateralism to Partnership

India's declared policy towards her neighbours has been one of bilateralism. According to this policy, the problems of immigration and insurgency need to be resolved within a bilateral framework in which the concerned countries only have the freedom of resolving the problems that affect them. Bilateralism is a policy that is intended to be an antidote to foreign power interference in the South Asian region. The rationale is: Insofar as the foreign power interference is effectively preempted, the countries of the region will enjoy their relative freedom in conducting their relations with others. In fact this policy was developed in the Cold War era when the fear of superpower interference loomed large in the South Asian region. It was apprehended that any attempt at solving the region's problems in a multilateral manner would only pave the way to growing superpower interference. Viewed in this light, the success of bilateralism depends on the fulfillment of at least three important conditions: One, more than India preferring it, the neighbours in the region also have to agree to resolve the problems in the way India wants to. Bilateralism as a framework of conflict resolution has to be acceptable to the concerned parties. This is possible when the parties left to themselves feel that their interests are best served if they keep their interrelations confined to themselves instead of referring to the third parties. Bilateralism in order to be effective has to facilitate the fulfillment of a country's national interests. The promise of quid pro quo of bilateralism has to be sufficiently high in order to encourage the parties to chart out a bilateral path. Or else, India must be strong enough to make others conduct their affairs bilaterally. Forcible bilateralism is an anathema to its very spirit. Two, its success also depends on the mutual credibility of the parties involved in bilateral relations. A party should have a reasonably high faith in the other so much so that they can address their mutual problems and solve them together. Both national interests and credibility are equally important for the success of bilateralism. It is to be noted in this connection that these conditions are not unrelated to each other. For instance, the faith and credibility can grow only when the bilateral framework begins to deliver the goods in the form of fulfilling at least partially, one's national interests. Three, the problems have to be of mutual nature so much so that both can look upon each other for their resolution. If one faces the problems and the other does not, there is no reason why the other should at all bother, let alone try to resolve them. The point is that if any of the parties gains by way of not resolving the problem or keeping them alive or even by aggravating them, bilateral framework is bound to fail. If its perceived national interest lies in sending the immigrants and receiving them or masterminding and sponsoring insurgencies or even fighting them, neither immigration nor insurgency can serve as a binding force that can bring the contending parties together within a bilateral framework.

Preliminary investigations suggest that the contending parties have an interest in not solving the problems of immigration and insurgencies in the northeast in general and Assam in particular. Bangladesh's 'Alice-in-Wonderland' policy of denying the presence of any Bangladeshi immigrant in Assam or anywhere in India may not have been inspired by the search for a lebensraum where she can dump her excess population though of course the argument has been made by a section of Bangladeshi intellectuals.[34] We have absolutely no independent evidence to suggest that Bangladesh has been doing all this at the instance of Inter-Services Intelligence of Pakistan, though of course such an accusation has often been made by columnists like, Jaideep Saikia. The point is simple: Bangladesh does not have to suffer when people migrate in numbers from out of the country and take refuge in a foreign country. In simple terms, Bangladesh does not have any reason whatsoever to recognize it as a problem. Unless Bangladesh has to suffer in some way, she is not going to recognize immigration to India as a problem. While India has been accused in some circles of having fanned and instigated the Chakma insurgency in the Chittagong Hill Tracts (CHT), the presence of the ULFA and Bodo rebels in Bangladesh can hardly be denied. As the peace process has been initiated in CHT, Bangladesh has hardly any reason to accuse India any longer. Of course, the newly started process of repatriation of the Chakmas has by no accounts been free of troubles and hiccups. But it is beyond any doubt that the erstwhile insurgency has lost much of its steam in recent years. Viewed in that sense, India seems to have lost her strategic edge over Bangladesh with the weakening of the Chakma insurgency. Unless the stakes are high, no party will feel encouraged either to recognize them as problems or to settle them bilaterally. In the scenario marked by a highly sentimental and emotionally charged diplomacy, India did not have anything to claim in exchange of the Farakka Treaty. [35] The point is not that India should not have signed the Treaty. As an upper riparian, India probably was under a moral (and maybe legal) obligation to share the Ganga water with Bangladesh. The point is simple: India did not seem to have gained anything in return.

Current researches on the problems of immigration and insurgency in Assam seem to suggest that the political elites have a vested interest in not solving them, of keeping them alive and in some cases, of aiding and aggravating them. The elites' linkage with the immigrants is most blatant when the latter are used as vote banks in the electoral politics where numbers matter more than anything else. The AGP that came to power in 1985 as a sequel to the prolonged Assam movement conveniently forgot to implement the Assam Accord – thanks to its own political compulsions once it had come to power.[36] AGP's attempt at wooing the immigrants especially in the Brahmaputra Valley paid rich dividends in the elections of 1996.[37] Other parties are no better. We have decided to refer to AGP for it is the only party in Assam that is the product of an intense anti-foreigners agitation. Ajai Sahni and Jacob

George have very cogently brought home the nexus between the insurgents and the politicians at the helm of power:

> ...we find that the usual presumption of a clear opposition of interests between government (and its officials and various agencies) and the militants is often unjustified. Indeed, complex, collusive arrangements between various political groupings, administrators and officials, on the one hand, and different militant factions, on the other, are more the norm than the exception. Some of these 'collusive arrangements', in fact, are often institutionalised by various secret or public 'peace agreements' that are forged from time to time between government negotiators and extremist factions.[38]

They view the relationship between AGP and ULFA especially during the late-1980s in the same manner. In short, neither India nor Bangladesh feels sufficiently charged to see them as problems that are in urgent need of being resolved through bilateral means.

It is in this context that I make a plea for partnership. Partnership of course is a bilateral relationship. But not all kinds of bilateral relations can be called partnership. In the case of partnership, the perceived short-term national interests do not necessarily guide the parties while setting the ball rolling. Rather they are required to agree on an agenda that can bear fruit only in the long term and the short-term obligations need to be fulfilled without any visible or immediate quid pro quo. The partnership first of all implies a commitment to a common agenda that is set on a long-term basis and the antecedent obligations are not only of short-term nature but are unlikely to bear any immediate fruit. Thus instituting a joint patrolling and border-surveillance mechanism along the Assam-Bangladesh border may apparently serve nobody's interests. But it may be instituted provided both the parties agree to be partners and agree to meet the obligations without an eye on the immediate gains. We can describe it as the take-off stage of a partnership. Secondly, how do the countries make the crucial take-off? One can do it precisely by making the stake of the other high in the interrelations. Thus the best way to stop immigration from the Bangladeshi side is to offer to Bangladesh some kind of an incentive. The idea of issuing work permits to the immigrants, according to which they will have to register themselves as Bangladeshis before they enter the Indian territory and will be allowed to stay in India for a fixed period of time, in that sense, is very interesting. Their departure may be ensured if the accountability is thrust on them on a group basis. The members of the group will remain responsible for each other.[39] Thirdly, once the short-term regime of obligations can be founded, the long-term gains will start being felt. A peaceful northeast or for that matter an equally peaceful CHT will be beneficial to both Bangladesh and India respectively. Once the take-off is made, the returns of the fulfillment of short-term obligations will consolidate them.

But for partnership to crystallize, the nation-States are required to move a long away from the traditional notions of security and territorial integrity.[40] The states of course do not have to cease to be states in order to accomplish this objective. But how long do we have to wait for the States of the region to realize the importance of partnership?

NOTES

[All translations from original Assamese/Bengali sources are mine. I am thankful to Sanjoy Hazarika, B. G. Verghese, Walter Fernandez and Partha Ghosh for their valuable comments on an earlier draft of this paper. SKD]

1. Rajat Ganguly has used the concept of 'kin state' in the South Asian context. See, Rajat Ganguly, *Kin State Intervention in Ethnic Conflicts: Lessons from South Asia* (New Delhi: Sage, 1998)
2. Mahesh Joshi, *Assam: The Indian Conflict* (New Delhi: Prachi Publishers, 1981).
3. Jaideep Saikia, 'Terrorism sans Frontiers: ULFA digs deeper into Bhutan' (2002, mimeo.).
4. I have elsewhere reviewed the so-called 'Foreign Hand Theory'. See, Samir Kumar Das, 'National Security in the Age of Globalization: A Study of the State's Responses to Ethnic Insurgencies in Assam'. In: Gurnam Singh (ed.), *Ethan-*

Nationalism and the Emerging World (Dis)Order (New Delhi: Kanishka, 2002).

5. Nowhere is this more eloquently shown than in Ranabir Samaddar's book though of course in the slightly different context of West Bengal. See, Ranabir Samaddar, *The Marginal Nation: Transborder Migration from Bangladesh to West Bengal* (New Delhi: Sage, 1999).
6. For an understanding of the strategic importance of this corridor, see, Pinaki Bhattacharya, 'The Shiliguri Corridor: Question Mark on Security'. *Faultlines*, 10 January, 2002, pp. 107-23.
7. Takeshi Fujii, 'Mirrors of the Colonial State: The Frontier Areas between North East India and Burma'. In: Mushirul Hasan and Nariaki Nakazato (eds.), *The Unfinished Agenda: Nation-Building in South Asia* (New Delhi: Manohar, 2001), pp. 197-246. Prof. B. K. Roy Burman in one of his recent addresses recounted his experience of meeting a chieftain in 1975 in an Indian village along the Indo-Burma (now Myanmar) border who had proudly confessed of receiving periodic tributes from people living across the border. B. K. Roy Burman, 'Dialogical Approach to State Security with special reference to NE India' (mimeo.)
8. Joyshankar Hazarika, *Geopolitics of North East India* (New Delhi: Gyan, 1996), pp. 108-39.
9. Benedict Anderson, *Imagined Communities: Reflections on the Origin and Spread of Nationalism* (London: Verso, 1991), p. 6.
10. Sabyasachi Bhattacharya, 'Identities in Indian History' (2002, mimeo.)
11. See, Samir Kumar Das, 'Extraordinary Partition and Its Impact on Militant Ethnic Politics in Assam'. In: Girin Phukon (ed.), *Ethnicity and Polity in South Asia* (New Delhi: South Asian, 2002), pp. 208-28.
12. Joya Chatterjee, 'The Fashioning of a Frontier: The Radcliffe Line and Bengal's Border Landscape 1947-52', *Modern Asian Studies*, 1999 33(1): 185-242.
13. Dipankar Gupta for one does not seem to be sensitive to the open nature of the citizenship. He describes it as one that was 'contained within the prevailing constructs of the nation-state'. See, Dipankar Gupta, *Political Sociology in India* (Hyderabad: Orient Longman, 1991), p.21. This view does not take into account the highly instrumentalist and contingent nature of the citizenship identity in India.

14. Rajeev Bhargava, 'Democratic Vision of a New Republic: India 1950'. In: Francine Frankel, Zoya Hasan and Balveer Arora (eds.), *Transforming India: Social and Political Dynamics* (New Delhi: Oxford University Press, 2000), pp. 26-59.
15. John Stuart Mill, *On Liberty, Representative Government and the Subjection of Women*, intro. by M.G. Fawcett (London: Oxford University Press, 1861), Chap. XVIII, 'The Government of Dependencies'.
16. I have presented the figures of actual deportees in a tabular form in Samir Kumar Das, *Regionalism in Power: A Study of Asom Gana Parishad (1985-1990)*, (New Delhi: Omsons, 1997), pp. 164-65.
17. See, Hiranya Kumar Bhattacharyya, *The Silent Invasion: Assam versus Infiltration* (Guwahati: Spectrum, 2001), pp. 122-8.
18. Studies have been conducted under the auspices of O.K.D. Institute of Social Change and Development, Guwahati in order to survey the impact of these floods on the population composition of some of the upper Assam districts. The reports are available for private circulation.
19. Rezaul Karim, '*Asomar Jatiya Jeewan Aru Char-Chaporir Musalman*' (in Assamese) in *Asom Sahitya Sabha Patrika*, 56(2), February 2001, p. 29.
20. Udayon Misra, 'Immigration and Identity Transformation in Assam' in *Economic and Political Weekly*, 34(21), 22 May, 1999: 1264-71.
21. Quoted in Hiranya Kumar Bhattacharyya, *op. cit.*, p. 125.
22. Udayon Misra, *The Transformation of Assamese Identity: A Historical Survey*, H.K. Barpujari Endowment Lecture - 4, (Shillong: North East India History Association, 2001), p. 82.
23. Dileep Chandan, 'Assam: Closing Ranks', *Sunday*, 11-7 May, 1997, pp. 59-60.
24. *Saptahik Neelachal* (in Assamese), 20 July, 1983.
25. *Agradoot* (in Assamese), 25 February 1990.
26. A.H. Imran, '*Anuprabesh: Sharanyantrer Neel Naksha*' (in Bengali) in *Kalam* (Calcutta), August, 1992.
27. For an analysis of the forced displacement of population in northeastern India, see, Monirul Hussain, 'State, Identity and Internal Displacement in Northeastern India', *Economic and Political Weekly*, 35(51), December 2000.

28. The pamphlet has been reproduced verbatim in *Budhbar*, 24 June 1992

29. See, Anindita Dasgupta, 'Small Arms Proliferation in India's North-East: A Case Study of Assam', *Economic and Political Weekly*, 6 January, 2001: 59-65. See also, Binalakshmi Nepram, 'Society under Siege: The Proliferation of Small Arms and Narcotics in India's Northeast' (mimeo.).

30. See, Jaideep Saikia, *Contours* (Guwahati: Sagittarius, 2001).

31. I have described it as a 'deal'. See, Samir Kumar Das, 'National security and Ethnic Conflicts in India: A View from the Northeast'. In: Arun Banerjee (ed.), *Security Issues in South Asia: Domestic and External Sources of Threats to Security* (Calcutta: Minerva, 1998), pp. 115-16.

32. Sunil Nath, ULFA's one-time Publicity Secretary quoted in Sanjoy Hazarika, *Strangers of the Mist: Tales of War and Peace from India's Northeast* (New Delhi: Viking, 1994), p. 174.

33. Jaideep Saikia, *Contours*, *op. cit.*, p. 19. For an understanding of ULFA's connection with the fundamentalist forces of Bangladesh and Pakistan, see, Subir Bhaumik, 'Bangladesh: The Second Front of Islamic Terror' (2002, mimeo.)

34. See, Sadeq Khan, 'The Question of Lebensraum' in Holiday (Dhaka), 18 October, 1991. Also, Abdul Momin, 'Lebensraum for Bangladesh?', *Holiday* (Dhaka), 22 November, 1991.

35. Shri Swarup Gupta, one of India's negotiators with Bangladesh has made the point in his address to the Symposium on 'The Problem of Chitmahals (Indian enclaves encircled by Bangladeshi territory) and Adverse Possessions' organized by the Centre for Development Studies (CDA) in collaboration with Oxfam Trust (*Violence Mitigation and Amelioration Project*) on 14 and 15 September, 2001 at the Academy of Fine Arts, Calcutta.

36. For an appraisal of the performance of AGP from the standpoint of the Assam Accord, see, Debo Prasad Baruah, '*Asom Cuktir Dah Bacar*' (in Assamese) in *Ancalikatar Dastabej* (Guwahati: Lawyers', 1998). See also, Debo Prasad Baruah, 'The Assam Accord and its Aftermath', *Peace Initiatives* (New Delhi), 4 (1-2), January-April, 1998: 12-18.

37. For a thorough discussion of the party's evolving stand on the question of immigrants, see, Samir Kumar Das, *Regionalism in Power*, *op. cit.*

38. Ajai Sahni and Jacob George, 'Security and Development in India's Northeast: An Alternative Perspective', *Faultlines* (New Delhi), Vol. 4, p. 54.

39. Sanjoy Hazarika has worked out the details of such a system. See, Sanjoy Hazarika, *Rites of Passage: Border Crossings, Imagined Homelands, India's East and Bangladesh* (New Delhi: Penguin, 2000), p. 261-68.

40. B.G. Verghese for example makes such a plea. See, B.G. Verghese, *India's Northeast Resurgent: Ethnicity, Insurgency, Governance, Development* (New Delhi: Konark, 1996), p. 377.

10

Partnership in Indo-Bangladesh Economic Development: The Case of Jaintia Hills in Meghalaya

—L.S. GASSAH

The Jaintia Hills district of Meghalaya was inaugurated on 22 February, 1972. On 16 November, 1869 A. Eden, Secretary to the Government of Bengal issued a notification to the effect of declaring the whole of Jaintia Hills as a Subdivision, then known as the Jowai subdivision, with its headquarters at Jowai. The subdivision then included under its jurisdiction the whole of the Jaintia Hills and it continued to be so even after India's independence till 1971. Before the new district for Jaintia Hills came into being, a separate District Council under the provision of the Sixth Schedule to the Constitution of India was created for Jaintia Hills on December 1, 1964 but became operative only from 1 February, 1966 after its bifurcation from the then United Khasi-Jantia Hills Autonomous District Council.

The district, which lies to the eastern part of the State of Meghalaya, covers a land area of approximately 3900 square kilometres. The northern part of the district is a highland area covered almost from one end to another with rolling hillocks, small bushes in between and towards the easternmost and southern parts are covered with thick forests. The southern portion has a highly irregular feature. As it recedes further towards the south and moves closer to the border of Bangladesh, the sudden drops and depressions become more prominent till they abruptly end in sheer precipices. It is in these precipitous slopes that a large number of different horticultural crops are grown - the most prominent ones are oranges, betel nuts, betel-leaves, and fruits of different varieties.

The estimated population of Jaintia Hills is about 3 lakhs, according to the figures of the year 2000. The district is predominantly inhabited by the Jaintias who belong to the Scheduled Tribe category. "JAINTIA" is a generic term, which covers the Pnars or Syntengs and other sub-groups such as, the Mikirs (Karbis), the Biates, the Bhois and the Wars.

The Jaintias are among those tribes who lived under the traditional formations of the hills until the area was integrated into the British Indian colonial State, although their economy had already been linked with the markets in the bordering plains of the Sylhet district (now in Bangladesh). The Jaintias living in the hills portion of the old Jaintia kingdom practised slash and burn method of shifting cultivation, although this practice cannot be said to be so prominent as compared to other hill tribes of Northeast India. The agricultural economy of the Jaintias is far more advanced. They were terraced-builders even before the coming of the British. They had also used small irrigation canals for bringing water to their fields and had more lands under wet-rice cultivation. Unlike other hill tribes in Northeast India, the Jaintias had been using the plough drawn by bullocks long before the British came to their hills.[1] A.J.M. Mills also confirmed that cultivation had greatly extended in the hills portion of the Jaintia Hills and chiefly confined to the villages where rice was grown. Ploughs were used in some places.[2] Another source stated that paddy had long been found in the low lands in parts of Jaintia and Bhoi, the only places where the plough was found.[3] This suggests the knowledge of the use of plough by the Jaintias at a much earlier period and the influence of its use by their neighbours in the plains, especially that of the Sylhet plains.

The Jaintia kingdom was one of the oldest kingdoms in Northeast India. It was ruled by many *Syiems* (kings) or Rajas till 1835 A.D. The kingdom extended over both the hills and plain areas. In 1835, the British annexed the southern plain territory of the kingdom, known as 'Jaintia parganas'. The Jaintia *Syiem* having declined at the time of the annexation of his territories in the plains to retain the hills portion, knowing fully well his power and status over these areas, they lapsed to the British East India Company's government and were placed under the administration of the Political Agent at Cherrapunji. The British Political Agent took over the administration of the hill areas on March 15 in 1835. In the same year, the British abolished the office of the Jaintia *Syiem* but retained the offices of the other traditional chiefs like the *Doloi, Pator* and village headman. These traditional chiefs were allowed to continue functioning during the British rule and they continue till today aiding and assisting the District Council in running the district and village administration pertaining to the welfare of the people.

When the British first took possession of the Jaintia Hills (hills portion), no change was made in the indigenous revenue system, which consisted simply of the payment of a he-goat once a year from each *Elaka* (administrative unit) of a *Doloi;* the *Syiem* or Raja deriving the greater portion of his income from the plains. The country remained un-taxed by the British until the year 1860, when a house tax was imposed, whereupon the Jaintias broke into rebellion. The rebellion was put down after stiff resistance. In 1862, the Jaintias again rebelled, this time owing to the imposition of the income tax, and later the stamp tax. The outbreak was not completely put down till 1863.

The British rule accelerated the process of extraneous domination through the markets that had emerged as the sensitive pressure points in tribal economy. The colonial restructuring of the socio-economic institutions in the hills of the area under study, was intended to serve the British interests by ensuring the regular flow of income not only from the Jaintia Hills but also from the neighbouring areas, especially that of the Khasi and the Garo Hills. But the trade relationship between the hills and plains had at times been adversely affected by the retaliatory challenges of the Jaintias to the British imperialism. The British thought of the people of the Khasi and Jaintia Hills as troublesome marauders upon the plains of Sylhet, where they were much dreaded. It was reported that their ravages between 1780 and 1790 were specially mentioned as severe. A line of forts was kept under the hills to check these incursions.[4] However, in spite of those frontier troubles between the people of the hills and the plains, the British period stands out as the most crucial phase in the socio-economic transition of the Jaintia society, and the development in the post-independent era could not be in exclusion of the colonial hangover as change and continuity co-exist as a historical process.[5]

The Jaintia economy depended much on the markets along the foothills. The increasing dependence on these markets in later years was particularly due to the absence of professional social groups of artisans and craftsmen, which stood in the way of effective social formation. It was reported that in the hill districts there were considerable differences in extent to which the tribesmen engaged in trade. In most cases the people used the simple form of barter, the exports consisting chiefly of cotton, wax, ivory and forest produce, and the imports of rice, salt, dried fish and cloths.[6] But in the Khasi and Jaintia Hills, there was a much more active commerce, and the trade in the commodities like limestone, iron ore, wax, ivory and forest produce was kept by the people almost entirely in their own hands. Many of them were adventurous merchants, traveling as far as Dacca, or even Calcutta, during the cold season.[7] In particular, the Jaintia traders were very adventurous in extending their areas of trading as far as Calcutta, Udalgiri and Bhutan.[8]

Jaintia Hills is endowed with rich mineral resources. Their presence had a tremendous effect on the changing economic pattern of the society both in the past and at present. But the exploitation and economic utilization of these minerals have been very slow. In many cases, the people have only recently started exploiting and making use of the minerals available, especially that of coal, into commercial enterprise.

As early as 1879, it was reported that coal has been discovered in Jaintia Hills in Amwi, Lakadong, Narpuh, Sutnga and Shyrmang areas. Among these, Lakadong has the most extensive coal beds. The coal fields of Jaintia Hills were computed at that time to expand over 0.394 of a square mile, and the estimated yield of the mineral was about 1,100,000 tons. The coal at Cherrapunji (in Khasi Hills) and Lakadong (Jaintia Hills) is in quality equal to some English coals; as a gas-producing coal it is considered superior to English produce, both as regards to quality and purity of the gas.[9] Another Survey report by La Touche, estimated that the Lakadong coalfield would have contained some 1,164,000 tones of coal.[10] These vast coal reserves are found both in the cretaceous and nummulitic formations. The Census of India in1961 reports that in the Jaintia Hills the largest deposits of nummulitic coal are found at Lakadong and Narpuh and cretaceous coal is found at Wapung or Bapung.

The presence of these vast coal reserves in Jaintia Hills, encouraged the local people themselves in exploiting this mineral even in the past, though it was done in a very primitive way and essentially for their domestic consumption and local supply. For example, the town of Jowai got its supply of coal from the small bed at Jarain, a village about 30 kilometers away to the south. The method employed by the people to mine the coal is said to be rather wasteful. The local people themselves mostly did the mining, and many of them were doing it on a cottage industry basis. Scientific mining machineries have not yet been used to exploit the coal.[11] Even then, it is well known that individuals have embarked on mining and quarrying with the expectations of large profits, which in some instances at least have been realized.[12] The British authorities right from the time of East India Company had realized the abundant reserves of coal in the area and with their farsightedness, soon embarked themselves on commercial exploitation of it. The coalmines of the Khasi and Jaintia Hills were then leased out to Messrs Inglis & Company and others as well, out of which a huge amount of revenue was received annually by the British Government.

Besides coal, limestone of excellent quality is also found in abundance both in the Khasi and Jaintia Hills. The needs and demands of the people in the neighbouring plains were therefore provided and immediately fed through the supply of limestone from the hills. The earlier records indicated that lower Bengal obtained nearly the whole of its lime supply from the Khasi and Jaintia Hills. The lime is known as 'Sylhet Lime', and obtained by quarrying from the beds of stone, which line the base of the mountain along the whole length of the Sylhet boundary. The supply was literally inexhaustible and the wants of Calcutta and of the whole of lower Bengal were met from these Hills for a long period in the past. In the Jaintia Hills, limestone quarries were located in Chunchhora, Lama-pushi, Lithang, Myrli-punji, Nongtalang, Rupnath and Rowai,[13] and other deposits were also found to be more extensive at lakadong, Syndai, Sutnga, Nongkhlieh and near Hari Prang and Lubha.[14] The Jaintias used to work and exploit these lime stones, and also engaged themselves in the trade of this mineral. They therefore practically had the monopoly over the entire supply chain to Bengal. The demand for this mineral was so great from lower Bengal that trade in limestone brought more employment and wealth to the people until the coming of the British. When the British came, they took over the limestone quarries by declaring all of them to be under the exclusive right of the Government and leased them out to their own people. The trade in limestone was placed chiefly in the hands of Messrs. Inglis & Company whose depot was at Chatak on the banks of the Surma river.[15]

In the southern slopes of Jaintia Hills, the War Jaintias are mostly engaged in their economic activities in the cultivation and production of oranges, betel leaf, and betel nut. The plantations begin from the plains and foothills bordering the Sylhet district of Bangladesh and rise to an elevation of about 1500 feet above the sea level. It is upon this small precipitous area of both Khasi and Jaintia Hills that the greater part of Bangladesh and Assam depend for their supply of oranges. The British officials reported that before and after they took over the administration of Jaintia Hills, oranges formed one of the prominent goods exported by the Khasi and the Jaintia people to the people of the plains of Assam and Sylhet. The British Government received annually handsome revenue also from the export of oranges to Sylhet and Assam side. For example, Hunter estimated that in the year 1874-75, the export in oranges alone was worth of Rs. 78,750.[16]

Besides mining and quarrying of coal and limestone and the production of oranges, betel nut, betel leaf and other fruits, the Jaintia people also grew cotton to a limited extent. The Jaintia cotton is of a small round-boiled variety and is said to be the best cotton in the then province of Assam. Cotton was mostly grown on forest clearings or *jhums,* except in the few places where it was mostly grown in the plains.[17] The Jaintias having their own local production of cotton, got themselves engaged in the spinning and dyeing of cotton thread and weaving, especially that of eri silk. Cotton spinning and dyeing can be found at Khyrwang and Nongtung villages, Biate villages, Mynso and Sutnga; eri-worms rearing and silk industry at Khyrwang and Nongtung villages and now at Um-mulong and Moodymmai. In the past and even today (though in a very limited way) the people weaved their own cloths and shawls. This trade, however, did not develop into a commercial enterprise.

Lac and the income derived there from its sale added something to the economy of the people in the northern side of Jaintia Hills. In 1906, the Sub-Divisional Officer, Jaintia Hills, during his tour of the Subdivision was able to make experiments in the growing of cotton and rearing of lac in the Raliang *Elaka.* In a few other *Elakas,* cotton and lac were already grown. The same year (1906) it was reported that there were villages where the inhabitants made very fair profits by growing cotton and rearing lac. These villages were situated in the Bhoi, Mynriang, Langsoh and Nongphyllut circles. A little cotton and lac were also grown in the Nartiang and Raliang *Elakas,* in places occupied by the Mikirs (Karbis)[17]. In the Mynriang Sirdarship, the people cultivated both cotton and lac in addition to their *jhums.* They realized considerable profits from the sales of cotton and lac. The price of these two articles was sufficient to indicate that the people earned a good sum.[18] The villages where cotton and lac were grown, situated in the north of the then Jowai Subdivision. Other industries which the Jaintia people were and still engaging themselves can be found in the smelting of iron ore for manufacturing of ploughshares, hoes, bill-hooks, etc. These are located at Tuber and Biate villages. Apiculture is also predominant in the War villages and pottery industry at Larnai village, where earthen pots were made without the potter's wheel, as is known among the Konyak Nagas. Nowadays, the people have also engaged themselves in horticulture, pisciculture, poultry and farming. The Jaintias are also good stock breeders. They used to rear cattle, driving them either to the Sylhet plains or to the Khasi Hills, and presently to the Mikir (Karbi Anglong) and North Cachar Hills.[19]

Some of the economic activities mentioned above are to be found exclusively prevailing in the northern and northeastern parts of the Jaintia Hills district. The southern part or the War area of the district presents quite a distinctive feature as far as the economic activities of the people are concerned. The people in the War area engaged themselves in agricultural activities and subsist on cultivation of horticultural and cash crops for their livelihood. The cultivable lands in the area are mainly used for the cultivation of cash crops and various kinds of horticultural and plantation crops such as - orange, betel nut and betel leaf, pineapple, banana, jackfruit, black pepper, bay-lea or tezpata, etc. Of these, orange, betel nut and betel leaf are the most important crops grown in large quantity. Rice, though it is the staple food of the people, holds a less exclusive place among the crops cultivated. The reason is due to the non-availability of suitable land for such cultivation as the land is quite rocky and stony in character. But wherever arable lands are available, especially in the foothills along the international boundary with Bangladesh, these are made for wet-rice or rain-fed paddy cultivation. In the War uplands, plots are so small that their produce is very less and not even enough for household consumption. Small irrigation is also practiced to maintain constant water supply to the fields. But unfortunately as those rice fields are mainly situated along the international boundary, troubles always flared up with the people from across the border especially during harvest season. Sometimes, the same thing happened during plucking season of oranges, betel nut and betel leaf.[20]

The Khasi-Jaintia people are believed to be the first to have started trade and commerce with the people of the then East Bengal (now Bangladesh) especially that of Sylhet district in the pre-partition period. It was thus remarked that from the time Sylhet emerged out of the blue water of what is now known as the Bay of Bengal, the people of the Khasi and Jaintia Hills must have been the first to put their feet on it and as things started to grow there, they must have been the first customers of all products of the vast plains of Sylhet. With this background of necessities, trade grew up between the hills and the plains and continues till the modern times.[21]

On the basis of the account of trade relations and commercial dealings between Sylhet and its highland neighbours, two important features were explicitly noticeable in which the Khasi and the Jaintia people contributed to their neighbours living in the southern plains. One is that they were 'the first from the hills to put their feet on the soils of Sylhet' and secondly, they were 'the first customers of all the produces' in the plains of that district. This, therefore, explained and confirmed the extent of trade and the intimate trade relationship between the people of the two different areas. Moreover, trading between them was not a one-sided affair but rather there was an equal exchange of goods and commodities from both sides. Thus, besides trade in coal, limestone and oranges, the natural outlet for the latter being in the plains, there were hosts of things that went to the plains which included big stones (one man drop, for embankments and such other works), *Silbatas* (grinding stones), potatoes, fresh vegetables and fruits, the hot favourites of Sylhetees, the *Satkoras, tezpatas,* timber fuel, *Jarul* timber for boat making and coal. As against these, the Sylhet people produced coarse rice, dry-fish, the hot favourite in every home in the hills. Fish and a lot of other things and at one time, the markets of Sylhet were the base for almost all the consumer's goods that went to at least the southern side of the Khasi and the Jaintia Hills.[22]

Although occasional raids and skirmishes in the frontier took place between the fierce tribes from the hills and the plainsmen, business transactions were however carried on when a peaceful atmosphere prevailed. Jaintiapur, besides being the capital of the old Jaintia kingdom, also served as an entrepot between the hills and the plains, which led to an extensive trade and commercial relationship. Pemberton was of the opinion that a considerable trade in cotton, iron ore, wax, *ivory, paan* (betel-leaf), and clothes was carried on between the plains and the hills, and Jaintiapur, the capital, was the great entrepot in which all commercial dealings were transacted between the inhabitants of the plains and the hills. The articles specified were bartered for salt, tobacco, rice and goats, but the intercourse was much obstructed by injudicious monopolies and heavy transit duties.[23] This led to a serious interruption of trade and commerce for quite sometime. This account gives a clear picture of the trade and commercial dealings transacted between the inhabitants of the Khasi-Jaintia Hills and the plainsmen of Sylhet during the period as far back as 1834.

The chiefs of the hills and their people attached great importance to the establishment of markets as these would surely help them in the exchange of articles. While the markets in the hills were important to the economy of the people in trading of goods among themselves, they also showed a keen interests in the establishment of markets at the foothills and the plains. This would add more avenues for the people from the hills as there were always great demands of their produce from the people of the plains. Bareh mentioned that according to the local tradition, one *Myntri* or Minister, U Iuma Laskor, opened four markets in the hills and five in the plains. Markets in the hills were at Nartiang, Raliang, Sutnga and Shagpung. Those in the plains were at Borkhat, Kulakhat, Iaplem, Mulakor and Jaintiapur. These small market centers exist even now.[24] Of the five markets in the plains, the last three were frequently visited by the War Jaintias in the pre-independence period. Iaplem and Mulakor are also locally called as Ju-plem and Danakor respectively and these are the nearest market centers along the international border with Bangladesh. Till today, the War Jaintia people especially those inhabiting the villages within the Bangladesh territory go to these markets to sell their goods. The articles they bring to these markets for selling are mostly betel leaf, betel nut and oranges; they bring back from these markets other essential commodities like fish, dry fish, eggs, etc. for sale in the border markets (Indian side) especially at Dawki and Muktapur.

The fast development of trade and commerce between the Jaintia people and that of the inhabitants in the plains of Sylhet was possible and encouraging because of the presence of different means and types of communications like bridle paths, navigable rivers up to certain points, and during the British period, they also built roads to connect certain points between the hills and the plains. Though some of these means of communications were in crude form, they served useful purpose in transportation of essential goods and materials to and fro the hills and plains.[25]

As far as bridle path is concerned, an important one was that which connected Jowai, a prominent administrative and market center in the hills, with Jaintiapur in the plains of Sylhet; its length is 30.25 miles. Besides the bridle paths, there were all over the country the Khasi paths, which were generally passable by a mountain man.[26] S.M. Ali also mentioned of the presence of a foot track from Amchoi (in Kholahat) in Nowgong district leading to Jaintiapur. It goes southward through Bar Amni, Bar Rangkhoi, Umpanai, Nartiang, Jowai, Jarain and Muktapur up to Jaintiapur. J.H. Hutton travelled along this track during his visit to Jaintiapur in 1925.[27] Along these bridle paths, the people from the hills walked a long distance carrying their goods on head loads. This is the traditional way of how the hills people transported their produce from one place or market to another.

In the Jaintia Hills, three rivers, Hari or Myntdu, Piyain or Myngngot and Lubha, being navigable, served as important means of communication between the hills and the plains. Goods were transported by means of boats and canoes. Against this background, it may be noted that though the rivers of Jaintia Hills are not very largely used for the purpose of navigation, canoes penetrate for a short distance into the hills from the district of Sylhet. Hari or Myntdu is navigable for canoes carrying from 25 to 30 maunds as far as Borghat; the Lubha is navigable for canoes as far as Lahalein, but is dangerous when the river is swollen in the rains.[28]

Colonial Transformation

Jaintia Hills came under the direct British administration with effect from 15 March, 1835. Before that, the British had come in possession of Sylhet in East Bengal as well as Assam. They left the Jaintias for sometime undisturbed and carried on trade and exports and imports with the hills people which they amassed immense profits. In fact, the British first came into contact with the people of Khasi-Jaintia Hills since 1765 when the East India Company obtained the *Diwani* of the Province of Bengal. The British after their occupation of the Sylhet plains came directly in contact with the Khasis and the Jaintias on the southern frontiers with Sylhet in the later half of the 18th century. Thus the first westerners whom the Khasis and the Jaintias met on their borderlands were the merchants of the East India Company. The contact between them became more frequent, as the interest of the Company gradually increased and expanded in the district of Sylhet, which had a hundred mile of common frontier with the territories of the independent chiefs of the Khasi and the Jaintia Hills.[29] Another earlier contact between the Jaintias and the British took place when the former were attacked by a force under Captain Ellerker in 1774. This was supposed to have been done in retaliation for the aggression by the Jaintia Raja, Chatra Singh, on the inhabitants of the adjacent plains of Sylhet. Such action rendered chastisement necessary on the part of the British to protect the security of their territories and subjects in the plains.[30]

In 1824, a treaty was signed between the British and the Jaintia Raja, Ram Singh II assuring him of his independence and help against the foreign invasion particularly the Burmese. Some trade relations were also stipulated in the treaty. As a result of this treaty, the Jaintia king allowed the British to build a road-link connecting Nowgong with Jaintiapur, the capital, to facilitate communication between the British areas of Assam and Sylhet.[31]

Ram Singh II reigned from 1789 to 1832 and initially had a peaceful relationship with the friendly British until his death. However, after his death, the incident of 1832 in which three British subjects were alleged to have been sacrificed by the Raja of Gobha, a dependent chief of the Jaintias, led to an unfriendly relationship between the British and the Jaintias which ultimately culminated into the incorporation of the Jaintia Hills under the direct British rule in 1835 by treating it as a 'British Area'. In doing so, the British intention was to administratively hasten their control over the area and promote their commercial interest which was in fact one of the primary purposes of the British in India in general and the hill tribes of Northeast India in particular. The Jaintia Hills was not an exception. The British brought it under its direct administration to control the local economy. That the British were concerned about the security of the territories and their subjects in the plains was only to ensure the increased flow of revenue from the hills. They also gradually realized that the Jaintia Hills could be used as raw material producing area and as market for the British goods.

The British interests in Jaintia Hills in particular can be broadly divided into two main categories - Political and Economic. On the economic plane, the British were interested in the exploitation of the rich natural and mineral resources. The presence of rich coal and limestone deposits in Jaintia Hills immediately drew the attention of the British. Besides these, the abundance of iron ore of the best quality and superior quality wood of various kinds adaptable to ship building, and cash crops like cotton, lac and oranges, all this prompted the British to find a way out for their immediate exploitation. And this they did which became the major source of revenue coming from the hills. The British merchants and traders also manipulated trade and commerce. The British were also trying to raise their sources of revenue by imposing different kinds of taxes on the Jaintias. This led to three bloody wars between the British and the Jaintias. Much before these incidents took place and during their initial period of administration over Jaintia Hills, the British even went to the extent of asking the *Dolois* to continue the payment of he-goats every year to the British authorities. Prior to the coming of the British, the *Dolois* from the hills presented annually one he-goat from each of their *Elakas* to the Jaintia kings. These he-goats were actually used by the kings as sacrificial animals during their religious ceremonies performed at Rajbari in Jaintiapur. To the British these animals became a source of revenue as they were auctioned every year. A considerable amount of revenue was realized by the sale of the tribute goats. Besides this, the British undertook various measures to raise their revenue from the house tax, income tax, and stamp tax, the rent on land leased by the Collector of Sylhet, the rent on coal mines, limestone quarries; fines imposed for offences and duties on *hats* in the form of rents and toll tax. Revenue from forests and forest products was also collected by way of leasing the right of tapping the trees.

The British rule had superseded the traditional political isolation of the Jaintia Hills and integrated the area in their colonial empire primarily for the purpose of economic exploitation. In turn, they had reconstructed the socio-economic system of the traditional economy, mainly based on a primitive type of agriculture, into a modern economy. This produced a multi-structural economy, which continued till India's Independence.

In the process of colonial transformation of the country, the Jaintia Hills, like its other neighbours, was also affected. After all, the hills were either annexed or incorporated in the British *raj* not primarily for the hills but for protection of the more yielding plains that were at times ravaged by the predatory tribal raids.[32] In the case of Jaintia Hills, the raids over the plains were too frequent to make the British authorities unattended as such raids are bound to create insecurity to the British subjects and territories in the plains. This, however, did not change the basic policy of the British to make the hill tribals pay for the administration.

Moreover, in the hills, the British could, as they did, exploit the natural resources, extract the raw materials and market their imported goods.[33] This British policy had vitally affected the Jaintia economy and whatever natural resources available in the area had gone into the hands of the British authorities. For example, since the entire Jaintia Hills was declared as

'British Area', the Government of the day, claimed unto itself as the sole proprietor of all the limestone quarries in the area.

The British impact on the economy and the material condition of the Jaintia people was, however, a mixed one. The loss of the most fertile plain territories, known as the 'Jaintia parganas', had dealt a severe blow on the economic life of the Jaintias. They were left with only the larger area of the hilly tracts with the exception of few flat lands for wet rice or rain-fed paddy cultivation. These lands are however poor substitute compared to the ones lost in the Sylhet plains.

The Jaintia uprisings led to the extensive destruction of their economy and it took years for its recovery. However, in spite of the loss of the fertile plain territories and the destruction of the hilly economy due to the Anglo-Jaintia wars, their economy of subsistence subsequently developed under the British administration, into one of surplus. This was possible due to the initiative taken by the British in introducing a number of changes in agriculture and horticultural activities of the Jaintias. They introduced crops and fruits which were earlier unknown and foreign to the land and its people. The initial experiments made on their cultivation however proved successful on a large-scale. Having found that these new crops and fruits were adaptable to the soil and climate of the land, the Jaintias did not lose time to cultivate them in a much larger scale. The British also popularized the cultivation of fruits, vegetables and medicinal herbs of foreign origin. Foreign fruits like pears, plums and peaches were also introduced.[34] Growing of cotton and rearing of lac were also experimented and encouraged. Potato was another important crop introduced by the British in 1830 in these hills. W.J. Allen opined that potato had been the greatest boon that a British ruler had conferred upon the Khasi-Jaintia people.[35] The cultivation of potato in the Khasi and the Jaintia Hills proved to be very successful right from the time it was first introduced and since then till date potato has remained the principal crop and an important item of export. Its yield is also quite spectacular. It has therefore become a great source of income of the people. Other measures were also adopted by the British for the improvement of agriculture and horticulture among the people. These included introduction of rotation of crops, proper drainage of the fields and change of the mode of cultivation. The British therefore brought a tremendous improvement on the agricultural practices and the means of communications for better trade and commerce of the Khasi-Jaintia people.

To consolidate their exploitation of the natural resources available in the area under study, the British established a network of roads that connected the hills with the adjoining plains and the main market centers in the borders along the foothills. The construction of roads to link the area both in the hills and the plains particularly with the sub-divisional headquarters at Jowai was immediately undertaken. One of the British officials responsible for this innovative plan was Henry Hopkinson. He strongly advocated the construction of roads in order to open up the Jaintia Hills country for easy communication and movement throughout the country for proper administrative supervision of the area.[36] Hopkinson pleaded that without roads the British authorities could not do anything; proper supervision would be jeopardized and commerce, the great civilizer, cannot find out the people of the area concerned. He therefore repeatedly impressed upon the authority and the department concerned with these matters to sanction necessary amount of funds for road construction in the Jaintia Hills. During the time when Captain Morton was the Deputy Commissioner in charge of the Khasi and the Jaintia Hills, he prepared a memorandum of the roads chiefly required; one such road would connect Jowai with Jaintiapur covering a distance of 30 miles.[37] W.J. Allen in his report in1858 recommended for the annual repairing of the old road between Sylhet and Assam, which passed through the hills, namely, Jaintiapur and Jowai to Jaggee Chowkey in Nowgong. This was a very useful road to the people of Jaintia Hills as it provided them direct communication with Sylhet and Nowgong. A considerable traffic passed along this road to Sylhet and Nowgong.[38] There has been also a well-maintained motorable road, which connected Shillong with Sylhet through Dawki, one of the main market centers at the foothills of Jaintia Hills since

1933 when this road was declared open by His Excellency, Sir Michael Keane, the then Governor of Assam.[39] This road also linked Shillong with Gauhati. The road by linking Sylhet-Shillong-Gauhati thus became the lifeline of communication for trade and commerce. The economic condition of the Jaintia people was much stable and improved during this period of time due to the facilities that were made available at their disposal.

The presence of the various means of communications, opened up to the Jaintia people in general and the War Jaintias in particular, a better avenue and an encouraging opportunity to venture for more extensive trade and commerce even outside their own territory. The crops produced by the people from the hills were transported in a faster rate to the plains due to better communication facilities coupled with a tremendous demand of the same. Thus their produce found suitable markets in the southern plains. It is important to note that before partition took place, there was free trade and commerce between the hills and the plains, and on this basis, the people of the hills lived a somewhat prosperous life. Hills-plains trade was therefore at the peak of its flourishing height during the British period. Deterioration of trade especially in the border areas started soon after 1947, the reason being the closure and sealing off of the border *hats* which led to the collapse of the booming border trade.

Post-Independence Trends

The transfer of power in 1947 and the change of administration thereafter, had severely hit the economic life of the Khasi-Jaintia people, their relations in trade and commerce with their counterparts in the plains, and caused a set-back in exchange of goods and essential commodities. There was also a setback in marketing facilities after the Partition of the country into India and Pakistan and later on Bangladesh in 1971. One writer was of the opinion that the ultimate halt of the entire trade between the hills and the plains of the Khasi-Jaintia Hills and Sylhet was due to the short-sighted policy of the erstwhile government of Pakistan, the policy which was to starve the neighbouring areas in India, their avowed enemies, of their normal and legitimate facilities.[40] There was therefore a tremendous after-effect on the economic life of the Khasi-Jaintia people due to the closure of the border trade and commerce immediately after 1947. Marketing facilities from both sides of the border were stopped, as the people could not cross over the border. Economic activities came to a standstill. The worst sufferers were those people who lived in the border areas of the Khasi-Jaintia Hills and Sylhet. They were so much dependent on each other and the markets in the border that they did not know what else to do with their produce after the Partition due to the total dislocation of trade and commerce.

At a particular period of time, an agreement was arrived at between the Governments of India and Pakistan to free the people from both sides of the border from trade suffocation. According to this agreement, certain commodities produced in Megalaya were allowed for export to the then East Pakistan. These items were - candles, Indian ware, earthen ware, turmeric, vegetables and fruits of local produce, limestone, ginger, spices, hardwood, detergents, betel leaf, pots, fuel, thatching grass, bamboos, stones, boulders and shingles.[41] But unfortunately, this agreement was purely temporary and a short-lived one. It did not bring any relief to the affected people of both the areas. The only alternative was to find out markets in the uplands, which was very difficult as most of the orchards and fruit plantations are situated in the areas of deep precipices. Direct communication with the market centers in the uplands is almost an impossible task. Due to this difficulty and the lack of other facilities, the local produce such as fruits and other perishable goods worth lakhs of rupees were left to rot in the plantations. The trade of betel nuts, betel-leaf and tezpata, which usually exceed the volume of income yielded by potato is then limited both in production and circulation.[42]

Liberation of Bangladesh: Expectation in Partnership for Development

There was an air of expectation for things to improve, especially in terms of trade and commerce between India and Bangladesh after the liberation of the latter in 1971. The people of the Khasi-Jaintia Hills especially those inhabiting the border area with Bangladesh eagerly expected that better relationship, at least in trade, would prevail between the two countries and this would lead to the reopening of the border markets. There was no doubt an attempt between the two governments to channelise the much-needed trade between the bordering neighbours and allow them to exchange their normal necessities through official routes, but this was short-lived. Therefore, once again it belied the hopes and expectations of the people when the whole border was again sealed off and markets across the international border were closed down. The economic prospects of the people came into a near standstill.

However, the re-opening of a few border *hats* for a brief period between December 1970 and March 1971 seemed to suggest the fact that the people living in both sides of the international border shared the same anxieties and sufferings arising out of the closure of the markets. Thus after a prolonged negotiations in March 1971, a few border *hats* were declared open for transaction in listed articles only. Before the other developments ensued, the maintenance of relations was upset by the Bangladesh affairs bringing with it influx of refugees into the State of Meghalaya.[43]

The influx of refugees from Bangladesh during and after the war of liberation of that country in 1970-71 to Meghalaya was alarming. This state of affairs brought immense suffering on the people living in the border area of the Khasi-Jaintia Hills districts. The influx was much beyond the expectation of the State Government. It put the Government of Meghalaya into a precarious situation, which was far beyond *its* capacity to handle such a sea of human beings within its small territory. But the worst sufferers due to the influx were the people living in the border area with Bangladesh. They suffered a great deal of hardship. The whole economic life of the people was completely disturbed. It was impossible for the people of the area to work in their orchards or to cultivate, plant and harvest as the whole area was swamped with the refugees. The entire economy of the local people had to undergo severe stress and strain owing to this influx of evacuees from Bangladesh. The socio-economic tension accompanied such a heavy influx, more particularly when the economy of the border areas of Meghalaya has been badly disrupted ever since the creation of Pakistan and where even in normal time special border programmes have to be undertaken to rehabilitate the border economy.

Meghalaya was formed as an Autonomous State in 1970 and two years later became a full-fledged State. During these 30 years, much development has taken place. There was improvement in road communications, electricity, water supply and other technological development in agriculture. In many districts of the State, the people have accepted the new improved technology in agriculture and other allied fields and this led to the improvement in the economy of the people to a large extent. As far as Jaintia Hills district is concerned there are however many fields left unattended for better improvement of the economy of the people.

In terms of formal border trade, agreements were signed between India and Bangladesh in order to alleviate the sufferings of the people living near the border areas on both sides. The first Indo-Bangladesh Trade Agreement which was signed on 28 March, 1972, made a specific provision for the border. Article IV of the Agreement reads as follows:

> "In order to meet the day-to-day requirements of the people living within the sixteen kilometer belt of border between West Bengal, Assam, Meghalaya, Tripura and Mizoram on the one hand and Bangladesh on the other and with a view to providing facilities to these people to dispose their goods, border trade shall be allowed in specified commodities in accordance with 'Schedule B' attached to the Agreement."

The salient features for the operation of the border trade were:

(i) entry of the individual trader was to be regulated by the issue of permit by the local authorities on both sides;

(ii) only the specified items in given quantities could be exchanged or purchased;

(iii) border trade would not be subject to the normal export, import and exchange regulations as well as custom formalities, and

(iv) each trade could carry an amount not more than Rs/Taka 100 when crossing the border from either country into the other.

Although border trade between the two countries started in the middle of April 1972, in actual effect, it did not take off the ground because, firstly, it took considerable time to devise instructions for the issue of special permit which was the principal instrument of control and then finalization of measures on routes, check posts, travel and custom documents and common inspection facilities.[44]

However, this expectation in trade partnership did not last long. Only after a six month period, that is, in September 1972, the Government of Bangladesh complained of large-scale smuggling by unscrupulous traders. In October 1972, the then Prime Minister of Bangladesh told the Indian High Commissioner that there were stories that border trade was responsible for large-scale smuggling of jute into India and thus wanted the border trade to be scrapped. During the mid-term trade talks held in early October 1972, the Bangladesh side wanted border trade to be suspended on the ground that meaningful implementation of the provisions of the border trade was not possible unless adequate checks and controls could be established along the entire length of the Indo-Bangladesh border. Accordingly, border trade between the two countries was suspended with effect from October 13, 1972. Though the border trade legally stands cancelled, position was different on the ground and *de facto* border trade in the form of smuggling continued. Most of this illegal trade was in the form of head-loads, which diluted the anti-smuggling drive and seizures made represent only a fraction of what actually moves across the border.[45] The fact remains that in spite of the failure of the formal or legal trade agreement between India and Bangladesh, the need to participate in trade and commerce continues. The border people's perception of their needs and interdependence may not be the same as that of their Governments. The failure of the Governments did not stall their participation, however illegal it might be.

It was in this situation that the two countries agreed to sign the second trade agreement on 5 July, 1973, which came into force from September 28, 1973 to cope with the completion of the outstanding contracts of the previous agreement. Practically, the second agreement was an extension of the previous 'Rupee Trade' as well as the 'Trade in Hard Currency', beneficially called the 'Balance of Trade and Payments Agreement'.

The fact that such agreements were concluded from time to time clearly indicates the interdependence between the two neighbouring countries in terms of trade and commerce. The Northeastern States bordering Bangladesh have frequently requested the Union Government of India not only to revive the trade agreement with Bangladesh but strengthen them so as to enable the State Governments to continue the trans-border trade with a view to bring about an economic revolution in the otherwise insurgency ravaged and under-developed frontier Northeastern region. In most of the requests and proposals put forward by the State Governments of the region, they stressed upon the basic need of continuous diplomatic dialogues with the Government of Bangladesh for opening up of all border points and markets for trading. As far as Meghalaya is concerned, a dozen or more such border markets were in operation with the then East Pakistan or the present Bangladesh before the Partition of the Indian Sub-continent. The same feeling was also expressed by the Government of Bangladesh from time to time in which it also wanted the border trade with India in general and the neighbouring States of Northeast India in particular to be resumed. Bangladesh economy has been severely affected owing to the closure of border trade.

The Indira-Mujib accord was signed in order to revive and facilitate the traditional border trade, particularly between Meghalaya and Bangladesh. The accord was also signed with the good intention of allowing the border trade to continue for the benefit of the concerned people of both sides. The Indira-Mujib accord had allowed eight kilo metres of free-zone all along the border between Meghalaya and Bangladesh to help grow and enhance in the participation of border trade and commerce along the international boundary of the two countries. However, due to the political changes in Bangladesh following the assassination of Sheikh Mujibur Rehman, the subsequent leaders in Bangladesh had flouted the provisions of the accord.

There are of course, as stated earlier, attempts to revive the border trade but it is an on and off situation with so much of frustration on both sides. In these days of liberalization of global trade, neither India nor Bangladesh can play a role of passive onlooker. They have to have a perception of closer participation in trade and commerce to improve the economy of both the neighbouring countries.

What is urgently needed today is the perception on partnership for the overall development of the economy of the areas along the Indo-Bangladesh border. It is obvious that the past economic history of the people living along this international border had to heavily depend on each other in terms of trade and commerce. Realizing the importance of partnership, the affected people of the border areas have demanded some kind of a trade zone. Of late, a ten-kilometer free trade zone on either side is also being demanded. This perception clearly indicates and reflects the psychology as well as the feelings of the people at the grassroots level who are more worried about their means of livelihood rather than the complexities of international politics. All efforts have therefore to be made to sincerely address the problems, and shift the focus from mere cosmetic treatments to seeking holistic solutions to the basic problems and issues at stake.

NOTES

1. Pakem, B.: The Jaintia Tribe of Meghalaya, Seminar Paper on '*Social and Political Institutions of the Hill People of North East India*', Shillong 1977.
2. Mills, A.J.M.: *Report on the Khasi and Jaintia Hills, 1853*, Shillong 1901 (Reprint), p.5.
3. MacCormack, P.Anna: "The Khasis". In: *Ethnic Groups of Mainland South East Asia*, Frank M. Lebar et al. (Eds.), New Haven 1964, p. 108.
4. *Report on the Administration of North East India*, Mittal Publications, Delhi 1984 (Reprint), p.41 (footnote).

5. There is a similarity of the Garo situation and that of the Jaintia Hills. For details, see J.B. Bhattacharjee 'Pattern of Economic Change in Garo Soceity'. In: *Garo Hills: Land and the People*, L.S. Gassah (Ed.), Omsons Publications, New Delhi, p. 196.
6. Bhattacharjee, J.B.: *Ibid.* p.198.
7. *Report on the Administration of North East, op. cit.*, p.29.
8. Gait, Edward: *A History of Assam (1905)*, LBS Publications, Gauhati 1984 (Reprint), pp.358-359.
9. Hunter, W.W.: *A Statistical Account of Assam*, Vol. II (1879), B.R. Publishing Corp., Delhi 1975 (reprint), pp. 232-233.
10. Census of India 1961 (Assam), District Census Handbook, United Khasi and Jaintia Hills, Government of Assam, Gauhati 1965, pp. 6-7.
11. Mills, A.J.M.: *op. cit.*, p.120.
12. Hunter, W.W.: *op. cit.*, pp.233-234.
13. Bareh, Hamlet: "*Major Economic Potentials of the Tribal Region (Khasi-Jaintia Hills*", Seminar paper on 'Development Strategies for North Eastern Region in Historical Perspective', Vol.II, NEHU, Shillong 1980.
14. Hunter, W.W.: *op. cit.*, p.237.
15. *Ibid.*
16. *Report on the Administration of North East India, op. cit.*, p. 18.
17. Government of Eastern Bengal and Assam, Rev. Dept., No.99: Gordon to the Commissioner, Surma Valley and Hill Districts, No.616, Shillong 10 April 1906.
18. *Ibid.*
19. Pakem, B.: *op. cit.*
20. L.S. Gassah: "Effects of Partition on the Border Marketing of Jaintia Hills". In: *Marketing in North-East India,* J.B. Ganguly (Ed.), Omsons Publications, New Delhi, 1984, pp.63-69.
21. A.R. Choudhary: "Sylhet and its Trade with Highland Neighbours", *Souvenir: The Frontier Chamber of Commerce*, Shillong, 1972, p.41.
22. *Ibid.*, p.43.
23. R.B. Pemberton: *Report on the Eastern Frontier of British India*, Gauhati, 1966, p.224.
24. Hamlet Bareh: T*he History and Culture of the Khasi People*, Shillong,1967, p.63.

25. L.S. Gassah: "Trade Routes and Trade Relations between Jaintia Hills and Sylhet District in the Pre-Independence Period", *Proceeding of NEIHA*, Ninth Session, Gauhati, 1988, p. 486.
26. B.C. Allen: *Gazetteer of the Khasi and Jaintia Hills, Garo Hills and Lushai Hills*, Gian Publications, Delhi 1980 (reprint), pp. 90-91.
27. S.M. Ali: *The History of Jaintia*, Dacca, 1954, p.5.
28. B.C. Allen: *op.cit.*, p.91.
29. N.K. Sinha: The History of Bengal, pp.31-33, 39; quoted in Dutta: *Impact of the west on the Khasis and Jaintias*, Cosmo Publications, Delhi, 1982, p.28.
30. R.B. Pemberton: *op.cit.*, p. 210.
31. *Ibid.*, p. 220.
32. The British Policy towards the Garos in respect of economic exploitation is very much similar to that of the Jaintia Hills, for details see J.B. Bhattacharjee, *op.cit.*, p.201.
33. *Ibid.*, see also P.M. Passah: "British Colonial Impact on the Socio-Economic Life of the Khasis-Jaintias before India's Independence", *Seminar paper*, 1985.
34. W.W. Hunter: *op.cit.*, pp. 211-212.
35. Selections from the *Records of the Government* of Bengal, No.XXXIX, Part I Calcutta, 1863, H Hopkinson to the Secretary, Govt. of Bengal, No. 20, 28 Feb. 1862; J.D. Gordon to J.C. Houghton, No. 436, 8th September 1862.
36. L.S. Gassah: *op.cit.*, p.487.
37. Selections from the Records, *op.cit.*
38. W.J. Allen: *Report on the Administration of the Cossyah and Jynteah Hill Territory*, 1858, Calcutta, Govt. Press, Shillong, 1975 (reprint), p.73.
39. L.S.Gassah: *op.cit.*
40. A.R. Choudhary: *op.cit.*, p.43.
41. *Provisional Meghalaya Legislative Assembly Debates*, Vol.II, No. I 22 September 1970, p.52.
42. Hamlet Bareh: *op.cit.*, p.467.
43. Hamlet Bareh: *Meghalaya*, Shillong 1974, pp. 209-210.
44. S.K. Agnihotri: "Border Trade with Bangladesh", *Journal of NEICSSR*, October 1993, (17:2), Shillong, p.30.
45. *Ibid.*, p.31.

11

Indo-Bangladesh Relations and its Implications for Northeast India

—ABU NASAR SAIED AHMED

The post-Cold War world has experienced encouraging thinking on multilateral and regional arrangements basically directed towards ensuring sustainable relationship. The central focus of the new thinking is to handle serious non-military issues, such as, abysmal poverty, decline of national resources and economy, flight of people, governance, violations of human rights, gender discrimination, ethnic and regional conflicts causing untold suffering to mankind, environmental pollution threatening life support system and so on. One kind of threat that had kept the world fully absorbed in the Cold War era is replaced by new kinds, which are basically non-military. Unfortunately, our understanding of these seems to be inadequate. The threats are transnational in character, and therefore, know no national boundary. It is geo-politics that rationalizes the management of the threat and warrants regional or international cooperation among concerned nations.

India's Northeast shares with Bangladesh historical experience, geo-strategic needs and a long international boundary about 1490 km stretch. Some parts of present Bangladesh were within Assam in the colonial period, and consequently, there had been enormous movement of population, economic activities, educational linkages between Northeast India and then East Bengal. Post Independent India witnessed massive exodus of people from East Pakistan as a fall out of the Partition. Later on, migration of people took place in search of better livelihood in Northeast India. The partition of India put its Northeast region in a geo-political predicament as its link with the rest of the country was reduced to a narrow bottleneck of about 20 km strip of land. However, Northeast India used the water route to reach out to other parts of the country through the East Pakistan till the 1965 India-Pakistan war. This river route once said to have contributed to the economic growth of the region.

With the end of the Cold War and changes of positions in the regional and international spheres, the past experience of having regional cooperation in respect of India's Northeast and Bangladesh has provided a clue for a futuristic paradigm for cooperation on a number of issues, which are basically non-military but at the same time are likely to enhance national security of both the neighbours. The theoretical formulation of such an arrangement can be found in the Gujral Doctrine, which can be regarded as the basis of cooperation among the countries of South Asia. Five core principles of the Doctrine which deserve attention are:

- India will not insist on reciprocity on any concession that it might offer in dealing with its smaller neighbours.
- Will not allow its territory to be used against the interests of any other country.
- Will not interfere in the internal affairs of other countries.
- Will respect the territorial integrity and national sovereignty of the States of the region.
- Will adhere to settlement of all disputes through peaceful bilateral negotiation.

The adoption of the doctrine paved the way for the settlement of two important issues with Bangladesh - (a) agreement on sharing the Ganges water and (b) resettlement of the Chakma refugees. Two other agreements with Nepal also were forged - the Mahakali river agreement and direct land route from Nepal to Bangladesh. These developments brightened the prospects of regional cooperation between the Northeast India and Bangladesh.

The current thinking on India-Bangladesh relations concentrates more on economic and environmental issues than on politically contentious issues. The two countries have to a great extent resolved the contentious issues like return and rehabilitation of the Chakma refugees in India and sharing of water of the Ganges. These were low intensity conflicts. Once these are settled, the political atmosphere is likely to become conducive to meaningful dialogue to resolve other outstanding political issues like Northeast rebels getting land and training facilities in Bangladesh, border skirmish between the security forces and systematic attack on the minorities. Another irritating issue, which used to cause tension, was migration of the Bangladeshi nationals to India's Northeast. A recently concluded study shows a declining trend in the migration. The migration can be controlled, if not totally stopped by active security patrolling and border fencing, but other issues like border skirmish, minority problems and sheltering the rebels need greater political consensus and will. It might take longer time to find a solution of these issues. It may be noted that these issues directly affect the geo-political scenario of Northeast India.

Even in the backdrop of these unresolved issues, India and Bangladesh stand on a fair chance of taking up two vitally important matters for mutual benefit. One is environmental protection and the other is trade relations. Northeast India and Bangladesh have been facing environmental problems like land degradation and soil erosion, frequent flood devastating the agricultural fields, deforestation, freshwater scarcity, water and air pollution. A regional management approach is the only solution to these problems. Soil erosion is caused by three factors - water erosion, wind erosion and human activity. It is human activity like *Jhumming*, deforestation, and mining, road construction that lead to soil erosion. A regional approach to proper planning of human activities in the Bangladesh and India can control soil erosion and degradation. Deforestation adversely affects climatic balance, destabilizes soil, and destroys biodiversity. Deforestation in Northeast India has not only affected the ecological balance in the region but also has laid spillover adverse impact on Bangladesh. There are common features relating to human activities in the hilly regions of the Northeast and in the Chittagong Hill Tract affecting the ecological balance. The magnitude of deforestation in the Northeast India and in Bangladesh, and for that matter in entire South Asia leaving only 15 percent of the land area under forest cover presents a gloomy picture. Some of the ecological effects of deforestation have hit hard the peoples of India's Northeast and Bangladesh are:

- Soil erosion and silting up of riverbeds and lakes.
- Decreased river depth leading to flood, riverbank erosion and shifting courses of rivers.
- Decreased cooling effect of the atmosphere.
- Decreased rainfall.
- Increased intensity of cyclones and storms

Deforestation has causeed some grave problems for Bangladesh, and these are:

- Soil erosion in the coastal areas
- Storm surges and cyclone in coastal areas.
- Loosening of soil in the coastal areas and easy intrusion of saline water in the mangrove forest, which eventually destroys the rest of forests and aquatic habitat.

A joint approach to handle forest management will benefit both India's Northeast and Bangladesh.

Bangladesh and India's Northeast are known as lands of rivers. Two major rivers of north, the Brahmaputra and the Barak, pass through Bangladesh to meet the Bay of Bengal. These two rivers provide an enormous scope to revive the time-tested sustainable water transport system. In addition to the large volume of water carried through by the rivers, the water resource in the region consists of three other components - rainfall, water bodies like beels and lakes and ground water. Paradoxically, Northeast India does not have a concrete policy for water management, nor has it formulated an strategy to seek regional cooperation among neighbours for management of water resources. Seasonal fluctuation of rain, lean and dry seasons make some places water-starved, while other areas suffer from flood and consequential devastation. Similarly, while urban areas of the Northeast suffer from inadequacy of water for daily use, the coastal areas of Bangladesh suffer from the adverse affect of saline water. All these, including the control of air pollution, invite regional management involving both India and Bangladesh.

The most vibrant area of cooperation between India and Bangladesh, which is likely to dramatically change the economic scenario of the region, is bilateral trade. While the regional economic trend in South Asia in recent years has been marked by deregulation of industry and liberalization of trade, the impact has not been so far felt in respect to trade relations between Bangladesh and India. Bangladesh began to follow market liberalization approach in the early 1980s and agreed to reduce the list of controlled items of import from 193 to 139 initially and then to 39 only to comply with the principles of free trade. In the case of India, the process of liberalization of market started one decade later. Yet, till now India-Bangladesh economic relations plagued with unremitting growth of huge trade imbalance against Bangladesh. There are a number of issues involved in the whole trade question. Some of these are: New Delhi's reluctance to reduce tariff restrictions on Bangladeshi products, infant industry argument, and illegal or informal trade. Certain steps might ease out the trade imbalance. From the Indian point of view, if Chittagong port facilities were made available to Indian commerce using a transit route through Bangladesh, the imbalance of trade could be mitigated dramatically. From the Bangladeshi point of view, trade reciprocity is the most viable means to improve bilateral trade relations. Legalizing the existing informal trade might profit both the countries. The promotion of SAPTA might be a long-term solution to the entire issue of trade relations. Expansion of India-Bangladesh trade would undoubtedly benefit Northeast India because of its geographic location. This step will act as a facilitator to materialize other long-term proposals like trans-Asian highway and railway.

12

Plight of Minorities in Bangladesh with Special Reference to their Exodus to Northeast India and Related Issues

—BIMAL PRAMANIK

Since the creation of East Pakistan in 1947 the minority communities living there have been subjected to unmitigated terror and torture in various forms quite frequently. Murders, rape, extortion, abduction, grabbing of properties (specially landed properties) from the minority communities were the common features of all these pogroms. The riot of 1950 and the post-martial-law dictatorial torture of 1958 and again the riots of 1962 and 1964, the wartime terror on the minorities of 1965 and the mass killing, rape and arson of 1971, and the continuous torture of the Hindus after the brutal murder of Sheikh Mujib in 1975 coupled with terrible communal flare up of 1990 and 1992 witnessed large scale migration of the Hindu population from Bangladesh to India. As a result of the step-motherly attitude of the government towards them, the minority communities live continuously under a threat of violence making them mentally weak. This has been going on unabated even after Bangladesh became an independent country through a liberation struggle where the Hindus, the Buddhists, the Christians and the Muslims fought together against the Pakistani army.

The primary reason for unleashing a massive terror on the religious and ethnic minority communities after the 8th Parliamentary election of Bangladesh in October 2001 has been attributed to the fact that the minorities vote for the Awami League (AL). Though many of them also vote for the Bangladesh Nationalist Party (BNP), the Jatiyo Party (JP) and other left parties, they are primarily considered as supporters of the AL, and they have been paying the price for this 'offence' since this election. Starting from murder, rape, physical assault, looting of properties, setting fire on houses, eviction from houses, demolition of temples and deities, nothing has been left out from the purview of revenge. Judging from the circumstantial evidence the primary object of the BNP and its allies is to make Bangladesh a monolithic Islamic State like Pakistan by driving out all the minorities from Bangladesh.

The atrocities that have been perpetrated on the minorities (especially on the Hindus) had taken the shape of a festival in some of the areas. Though there has been some difference in the ways and means of torture perpetrated previously, the degree of torture has reached a greater magnitude this time almost everywhere, and the traditional mode of grabbing land, house properties, shops and establishment, in a word, wealth of any kind, has remained the same. The sole reason is not, however, political or economical, but a horrifying design chalked out by certain religious fundamentalist groups to wipe out the Hindus from Bangladesh. It is evident from the pattern of atrocities that ethnic cleansing of the Hindus is the primary goal. The underlying policy is "don't kill them, molest their women" so that they are compelled to leave Bangladesh gradually and slowly out of mental agony in view of the fact there may be adverse international reaction and the India Government and its people may not view it lightly if they are driven out in one go, and the liberal-progressive element in Bangladesh, though very small in number, may try to raise a hue and cry. As time will pass on the liberal and progressive elements in Bangladesh will be weakened gradually and the little power that they have still now will vanish. The fundamentalist forces in Bangladesh have resorted to this policy of 'go-slow' as a consequence of worldwide reaction after the demolition of World Trade Centre (WTC) in New York on 11th September by a terrorist attack which has compelled even General Musharraf of Pakistan to reconsider and review the activities of the ultra religious fundamentalist elements and teachings in the Madrassas in Pakistan.

The government-backed terrorists slogan was "leave this country and flee to India". The torture that has been unleashed on the minority community cannot just be passed off as a communal frenzy. Behind this looms large a well thought out cold-blooded blueprint to drive out the minorities from Bangladesh for good.

It has become a regular and normal feature since the time of election to capture household properties, fisheries and landed properties of the minority Hindu community and to rape their womenfolk. These activities are not considered illegal and are being passed off by the authorities as stray incidents. The grassroots level workers of BNP-JIB alliance think that the minority Hindus should be suppressed since they vote for AL. They have chosen election victory as a most suitable plea to take revenge against the Hindus.[1]

Begum Khaleda Zia, the Prime Minister of Bangladesh said during a nationwide broadcast on 19.10.2001:[2]

> "Bangladesh is a country of communal harmony. Everybody' irrespective of his religion is a Bangladeshi and not just a Muslim, Hindu or a Christian. In this wonderful country of religious harmony we caution the people of our country to be watchful against those people who are trying to create a division' among us by uttering the word 'minority' with a motive"

In response to a demand raised in a recent seminar held in United States of America for the protection of minority in Bangladesh, the Foreign Minister of Bangladesh has observed, "No minority community exists in Bangladesh and as such the complaint of torture on them is redundant."[3]

If this is the perception of the Government, the plight of the minorities in Bangladesh is easily discernable.

The Home Minister Altaf Hossain Choudhury, a retired Air Vice-Marshal said in a press conference held on Dhaka on 15.10.2001:[4]

> "Most of the incidents are stage-managed, and concocted stories, and the reports published in the newspapers are mostly false, and fabricated 80-90% of what has been published in the newspapers are false and baseless since we do not find any conformity between the news reports and the reports submitted by the district administration."

In this press conference were present the Minister of Local Self-Government Abdul Mannan Bhuiyan, Minister of State for Home Affairs. Lutfuzzaman Babur and the Political Secretary of the Prime Minister, Harish Choudhury.

The contents of the report submitted by the Cabinet Committee formed by the government to probe into the matter of minority harassment, clearly bring out the role of the Bangladesh Government on this issue.

> "What has been stated in the 6th meeting of the cabinet committee on the law and order about the alleged harassment of the minority and their migration from Bangladesh has been a matter of surprise to us all. It has been stated that out of nine specifically alleged complaints about the torture and persecution of the minority commu-nity only two have been found partially true; and there, has been no evidence of their leaving the country and migration to India. The cabinet committee has furnished this information after carefully going through the four-tier reports submitted by Ministerial, Parliamentarian, Secretariat and diplomatic level. The obvious question that will creep into the minds of the people, is: Are the reports on the atrocities committed on the minorities that have been published in the newspapers are all false and fabricated? We would like to put this question to the cabinet committee and the government do they mean to say that countries media are all lying?"[5]

After the demolition of the Babri Masjid in December 1992, when there were arson, loot, murder, rape and demolition of about 3000 Hindu temples and deities all over Bangladesh which continued for over a month, the then Prime Minister, Begum Khaleda Zia said on the Floor of the Parliament:

> "Nothing has happened anywhere in Bangladesh, a wonderful communal harmony is reigning in Bangladesh."

As all these utterances of the Prime Minister and the Home Minister though are inhuman and incorrect they are quite inspiring to the communal forces. The local administration has been made to understand that not more than 10 incidents can be admitted out of 100 such incidents. The district administration and the police have precisely done this. Not more than half the incidents of atrocities find any place in the newspapers, and not more than 10 per cent complaints are recorded in the police station. Living under a constant threat of violation this hapless religious minority do not seek any help from the police or newspaper unless they are in an extreme situation. In many cases, they are subjected to police harassment for lodging complaint and face renewed violence of a higher degree by culprits, when administration moves for action. Media also shy away from reporting torture on the minority Hindus lest it affects communal harmony.

This is, of course, nothing new in Bangladesh. During the 1971 freedom struggle, hand in hand with the Pakistan army, the local Bangali Rajakars. Albadars and the members of the so-called Peace Committee created by the Pakistan army, mercilessly killed and raped in thousands. Of innocent yet vibrant people in Bangladesh belonging to the minority communities and they were never brought to book even after Bangladesh became free. In the communal frenzy of 1990 & 1992 nobody had to face any trial not to speak of any punishment for committing heinous crimes. It has become irrelevant to the minority communities to seek justice.

That the Constitution of Bangladesh is meant for the majority people is amply clear from its Preamble with salutation of Allah. In reality this Constitution aims at declaring Bangladesh an Islamic country. With a few exceptions, all the governments since 1975 have pursued a communal agenda just like Pakistan. An atmosphere of anti-Hindu, Buddhist and Christian sentiment is pervading the society barring a handful of intellectuals. The communal face of the government is looming large in Bangladesh and former East Pakistan for the last 50 years. During the Pakistani regime, the Defence of Pakistan Rule (DPR) has been applied to the leaders belonging to the minority communities without exception. During the 1965 war, the Hindus were subjected to DPR indiscriminately, and through the operation of Enemy Property Act, the Hindus might have mistakenly, to be euphemistic, realized that they are nothing but second class citizens of Bangladesh.

Bangladeshi intellectuals very poorly perceived that all communal riots ever taken place were consequences of the divide and rule policy of the British power, and subsequently, the secular intellectuals remained idle and ineffective mostly looking like dwarfs, when blood along the lanes of communal riots created rivers to consolidate the Pakistani rule in East Pakistan. They say that the communal riots of 1992 and 1990 were the fall-out of the demolition of the Babri Masjid in India and a result of the conspiracies hatched by a dictatorial government respectively. This time also, many have put forward the same logic based on political considerations. And they still believe that people of Bangladesh are not at all communal and never were. The major political parties of Bangladesh and their servile obedient intellectuals would hardly admit, I am afraid, that Islamization and communalization of the Bangladeshi society has gone the full circle during the last 50 years. Performing *Haj* regularly using *hejab* (band round the head), wearing caps and keeping beards on gross political considerations are rampant among the important political leaders and this has assumed an immense importance in the communalized politics of Bangladesh.

What has been happening in Bangladesh is the outcome of this sentiment. What the common Muslim population is doing now is grossly soaked in communalism and anti-Hindu sentiment. It has now become a wishful thinking that the wind of communal harmony is blowing in Bangladesh. These are the reasons that the Enemy Property Act survives for decades after decades.

A recent study entitled "An Inquiry into Causes and Consequences of Deprivation of the Hindu Minorities in Bangladesh through the Vested Property Act" has estimated violations of the Hindu's right to property as follows:"[6]

> "Approximately a million Hindu households (40 per cent) have been deprived of over 1.64 million acres of landed property, which is 53 per cent of the land owned by Hindu households. This included 81.7 per cent agricultural land, 10 per cent homestead land, 1.74 per cent garden land, 2.4 per cent ponds, 0.68 per cent fallow land and the rest was 3.4 per cent.
>
> At the time they appropriated the property, approximately 44 per cent were affiliated with the Muslim League, 20 per cent with the BNP, 17 per cent with the Awami League, 5 per cent with the Jatiyo Party and one per cent with the Jamaat-e-Islami. In 1995, 72 and 11 per cent of those who appropriated minority property belonged to the BNP and the AL respectively, while in 1997, an equal number of 44 per cent each from the AL and the right wing parties were involved in appropriating Hindu properties." (See Annexure I for details)
>
> Mr. Abul Barkat, a Professor of Economics in the University of Dhaka has stated in his research survey, "the average amount of dispossession shown in the official record would be 20 per cent less than the actual amount ascertained in the survey. This implies that the total amount of Hindu land disposed of under Enemy Property/ Vested Property Act would be 2.1 million acres. The estimated value of the 2.1 million acres of dispossessed land at current market price would be about Taka 1209600 million (equivalent to 70 per cent of Gross Domestic Product of the Year 2000). On the other hand, according to 1991 population census the total size of the Hindu population was 11.2 million. Assuming the 1961 population share of the Hindu population (18.4 per cent) the absolute size of the Hindu population in 1991 would have been

18.4 million instead of 11.2 million as reported in the census This estimates substantiate the earlier findings regarding the missing Hindu population, "The estimated total missing Hindu population during 1964 to 1991 was 5.3 million i.e. 196296 Hindus are missing every year since 1964. In other words, if out-migration of the Hindu population is caused mainly by communal disharmony resulting from the Enemy/Vested Property Acts, the approximate size of the missing Hindu population would be 538 persons each day, since 1964."[7]

Condition of Ethnic Minorities

The situation of ethnic communities in the greater Mymensingh district is particularly distressing. The persecution of the Garo, Hajong and Koch by the members of the majority community seldom finds a place in the mass media. The Garo community is becoming relatively smaller in size day by day.

According to 1991 population census, there are 64,280 Garo people in Bangladesh. The Garo population increased at an average annual rate of 0.66 per cent during last eighty years (from 1911 to 1991) compared to 1.36 per cent annual growth of population in the greater Mymensingh district and 1.59 per cent in Bangladesh during the corresponding period. The implicit fact is that there has been large-scale migration of the Garo people to India during this period. The main reason behind this 'involuntary displacement' has been the loss of traditional land rights of the people. New settlers from other parts of Mymensingh and Tangail have now occupied most of the land. Large-scale displacement of Garo peasants has reportedly been caused by an ADB-funded rubber plantation project in Modhupur in the early Eighties.

In 1911, there were 32,000 Hajong people in greater Mymensingh district. The number shrunk to 11,540 in 1991. Similarly, the number of Koch people dropped to 16,567 in 1991 from 32,000 in 1911. In 1911, the Hadi community of Mymensingh had a membership of 26,000. They have been completely extinguished. The plight of these ethnic communities and their migration to India has rarely been reported in Bangladesh mass media and has never found a place in the agenda of the political parties and mass organizations.[8] I leave out the Chakma issue since much has been said and written about it. The treaty of friendship, cooperation and peace with Bangladesh came to be signed over the military defeat of Pakistan and exodus of about 10 million people from Bangladesh to India of which 9.3 million were the Hindus, so-called minorities who are nothing but Bangladeshis as Begum Khaleda Zia feels, in the flight. Further, after some dust was settled, when many of the minorities went back to retrieve their own properties, much was by then vested under the Enemy Property Act and by a strange Islamic secular persuasion they came back dispossessed to India again. It shows that Bangladesh fought against Pakistani exploitation and cultural domination but she could hardly keep up her friendly face either to the government or to the people of India. The circle was complete when BAKSAL was formed for a hypothetical land reform and Mujib and his entire pro-liberation leadership was liquidated.

This political behaviour fitted fine in the general framework of the political objective of Bangladesh Republic after the initial euphoria of Mujib period was over. The liberation of Bangladesh from the yoke of Pakistan could not educate enough nor could it have any stable imprint upon the people of Bangladesh to evolve a friendly attitude towards India. The anti-Indian attitude of various political leadership, whether one is from the Muslim League, or from the Awami League or from the BNP remains a common characteristic to shape and influence the complementary relations between the process of minority exodus and demographic expansion of the majority Muslims.

During the last two decades it had been possible to imbibe among the rural masses as well as among a large section of urban middle class a belief that Bengali Muslims have to strengthen the Islamic identity in order to maintain a sovereign entity of Bangladesh. There must be an admixture of Islamic culture and social values with the existing Bengali culture. Consequently, Islamization of Bengali culture is more pronounced among the rich, middle and lower middle class people than it was during the Pakistani rule. Use of Hejab, cap and burkha is evidently on the rise. Islamization in a gigantic scale is being manifest in the style of keeping beard and dresses, cultivation of Arabic language and culture and religious fanaticism. During Mujib's time not only the AL leaders, but also a section of the Muslim League leaders were never seen to use caps and keeping beard or reciting namaj on political ground. Public meeting and functions were never kept in abeyance during the recitation of Namaj. Madrassa education was totally neglected and non-acceptable compared to general education. But now political leaders are seen to accept vigorously Islamization on political ground. One-third of the total student community is passing through Madrassa education, and their role in the society cannot be ignored. As a result, the political leaders are trying to win the support of these masses in a manner acceptable to them.

It is quite impossible that such a large section of Madrassa educated students can be absorbed in the mosques and Madrassas as imam or teachers. Where will they go? They cannot participate in the planning activities of modern age since they more or less unfit and as such suffer from frustrations. This is primarily the cause that they are being attracted strongly to terrorist activities. The modern society cannot accommodate them and they can neither make themselves suitable for the society. Consequently, they hinder the progress of society and try to reorient society according to their needs and ideas. This is being amply manifest in the cruel and destructible religious fundamentalist activities in recent times in the districts of Brahmanberia, Sylhet, Rajshahi, Chittagong etc. The governments, controlled by military and eager to serve the purpose of the fundamentalist forces, also lent support to these people and with the help of these groups and other strongly religious fundamentalists ISI is raising militant cadre and using them in anti-Indian activities.

Madrassa education is the main plank of nurturing this process, which has been strengthened by policies adopted by the Bangladesh Government from time to time. Islam has become the State religion according to its constitution. Thus there always existed a propensity in Bangladesh society to hate the Hindus, Buddhists and Christians, i.e. non-Muslims. The boys and girls get this propensity from their families in the first instance, which get strengthened through religious teachings and Madrassa Education supported by the State. In addition, the ill effects of Islamic fatwa coupled with ultra Islamic militancy of Taliban, Rajakar, Mujahedin and Ladenic varieties have intensified this feeling. With this social situation the claim of the politicians and intellectuals that the Muslims of Bangladesh believe in communal harmony and are protectors of the minority communities is nothing but a wisp in the wind.

The Bangladesh Nationalist Party's (BNP) electoral alliance included the Jamaat-e-Islami, which won 17 seats in the 300-member parliament. The Jamaat, which actively opposed independence from Pakistan in 1971, now has a voice in government for the first time. Its leader, Motiur Rahman Nizami, was appointed agriculture minister, while MP, Ali Ahsan Mohammad Mujahid got the social welfare portfolio. In a developing, mainly agricultural country like Bangladesh, these are powerful positions. While Jamaat is moving cautiously toward its goal of an Islamic state, its elevation to government has encouraged other more extreme Islamic fundamentalist groups and individuals. They range from rabble-rousing cleric Maulana Obaidul Haq to a dozen radical groups often referred to as the Bangladeshi Taliban.[9]

Those who could not fulfil their dream of having the entire East Bengal and Assam in one province in 1905 and entire Bengal as East Pakistan in 1947 were all the more felt devastated after the defeat of 1971. So if the 10 per cent remaining minorities could be thrown out from Bangladesh making her a 100 per cent Muslim country they might have been nourishing a dream of changing the so-called Bill Clinton's 'moderate Islam' into a new brand of Talibanic Islam yet unthinkable and possibly incomparable with the practicing Talibanism of Pakistan. Possibly the Jamaat are enjoying a God-sent opportunity to add new militancy which their classical fundamentalism would not comprehend.

The thinking people of Bangladesh suffers from a "small State" paranoia and very often would bask under a pretentious knowledge of age-old history of India. They are happy having a constructed Islamic telescope to build up a structured history of Bangladesh as a part of the subcontinent in South Asia. Since many aspects of historical processes shall remain alien to such telescopic articulation-knowing history became highly truncated attributing fabricated meaning to such efforts.

When such absurd way of writing history becomes the normal practice of general intellectual exercise for this Bangladeshi scholarship they become that obsessed to present contemporary India as if there is no Muslim population living as an integral part of Indian society. And this shall put them in a disarrayed frame of anti-Indian amounting to anti-Hindu.

One should appreciate that no tangible history of Bangladesh could be so written on a well-founded structure if it does not dare to go beyond another one or two thousand years before 1704 A.D.[10] to evolve the genesis and the path of evolution of a part of greater Bengal which. is described to be present day Bangladesh, just co-incidentally. Therefore, the practicing effort of building Bangladesh history is nothing but a cumulative result of the systematic falsification of history of Bangladesh as propagated and understood in the last quarter of the outgoing century.

After the gruesome killing of Sheikh Mujib in 1975, there has been a rapid change in the socio-political scenario of Bangladesh during the 21-year rule by General Zia, General Ershad and Begum Khaleda Zia that followed. India bashing and Islamization have taken a firm root in the body politic of Bangladesh under these regimes and percolated to the social fabric of the country to a considerable extent.

A section of the Army, the bureaucrats, the intellectuals and well-organized political forces think that support should be lent to the secessionist forces of the Northeastern India, which are waging an armed struggle against the Indian Government and carrying on subversive activities disrupting economic and social fabric of eastern and Northeastern India. This is no longer a secret. Some terrorist organizations including JIB built upon the theory of establishing an Islamic hegemony in this region, the fundamentalist Islamic forces and the ISI have been carrying on their activities to reorient the Bengali society according to their ideas and goals and are pursuing a long-term policy to achieve this by building an Islamic culture through the Madrassas. (See population pattern of this region: Annexure II)

During the last three decades and even now all the major parties of Bangladesh have been very active in making India a scapegoat in their internal politics by manufacturing various anti-Indian issues to reap political advantage. This tendency is more marked in the border region. Consequently, the bonhomie that was established in 1971 through the liberation struggle between India and Bangladesh had gone to the winds long ago; instead an unfriendly relationship has developed. It has been our experience during the past years that small incidents regarding smuggling and minor skirmishes between BSF and BDR have been utilized by some political parties/ quarters to instigate Bangladeshi people against India and build up an anti-India euphoria.

In the past three decades, powerful economic push factors combined with politically and economically motivated pull-factors in India have generated an unending flow of the Muslim infiltrators into the bordering States of India. This process is fast changing the demographic and communal composition of our border population. Here I quote P.M. Sayeed, former Minister of State for Home Affairs, from his speech in Parliament in 1995: "There has been a continuous influx of Bangladeshi nationals into India for a variety of reason, including religious and economic considerations. The demographic composition in the border areas has been altered with new entrants flooding the area and the locals migrating into the interior. Besides, the population that inhabit the Indo-Bangladesh borders, is ethnically, culturally, linguistically and religiously identical. Large-scale infiltration of the Bangladeshi nationals is one of the factors responsible for a steady growth of the Muslim population (almost homogenously) in West Bengal and other border areas."[11]

On the other hand, innumerable economic and political problems have been created in Assam, Tripura, West Bengal and other Northeastern States as a result of the continuous influx from Bangladesh. These problems have also started afflicting the other States of India. The political parties are utilizing this demographic situation coupled with conspiratorial policy adopted by Bangladesh to get political advantage.[12] Since neither the Central nor the State governments have yet been able to take suitable steps to curb this problem, its magnitude is ever increasing. India's secular polity is being threatened. This is fast creating a situation of disbelief between the Muslims and the non-Muslims of the entire region, threatening the communal harmony that exists there.

There is also the other side, which is no less disturbing and no less dangerous. This ceaseless increase in infiltration assumes a new dimension when it slowly and steadily takes a shape of the demographic expansion and its consequent socio-political disturbances that can possibly destabilize the entire Northeastern region. There can be a proxy study of this problem, which now threatens the very political stability of Assam. This 'distress infiltration' can finally turn into enough volcanic to disrupt and bring disintegration of the country. "It is a serious matter. Serious and honest attempts should be made to stop illegal infiltration to the Northeastern States where it is threatening the demography," said former Chief Justice of India Justice A. S. Anand, while hearing a public interest litigation.[13]

Further, it has also created a danger posed by the close nexus between the illegal migrants and the Islamic and other ideologically similar fundamentalist organizations on the one hand, and between the fundamentalists and the Pakistani ISI, on the other.

Since the purpose of my paper is limited to the plight of the minorities and their exodus in general and related issues I leave out from the purview of my paper. The pattern of migration to different States of east and northeastern regions from Bangladesh (a rough estimate) is given below:

It has been suggested that during 1971-81 and 1981-91, West Bengal has accommodated two million outsiders. Actually, this number should be much larger, because, from Bangladesh alone, above 3.9 million Bengali-speaking

Hindus have entered into India (mainly West Bengal) during 1971-81.[14]

It is noteworthy that of the nearly 10 million Hindu refugees leaving East Pakistan for 'India in course of the 1971 liberation struggle, a large number did not return to Bangladesh. Moreover, of those who returned, a big number, failing to recover movable/immovable properties looted/ misappropriated during 1971, came back to India in one or two years. These refugees have not been taken into account by the Bangladesh Census reports in 1974. Their number soars above 2.78 million.[15]

In addition, for the 1981-91 period, Bangladesh Census authorities detect the somewhat unique phenomenon of "missing population", and estimates the number at eight million of which 1.73 million are the Hindus.[16] It is, therefore, entirely plausible that the rest of the eight million, i.e. 6.27 million Muslims, have infiltrated into various parts of India, notably Northeastern Region and West Bengal. The Government of Bangladesh naturally observes silence on this vital issue.

It is, therefore, pertinent to affirm that six million Hindus have left Bangladesh for India during 1971-1991, and not less than six million Bangladeshi Muslims have infiltrated into India during 1981-1991. To this should be added one million standard Muslim Biharis in Bangladesh moving to India.[17] Since the extent of Muslim infiltration during 1971-1981 awaits appraisal, it is fair to conclude that at least 13 to14 million infiltrators/migrants have crossed over from Bangladesh to India from 1971 to 1991.

The large-scale communal riots of 1990 and 1992 and the discriminatory communal role of the Bangladesh Nationalist Party (BNP) Government during 1991-1996 forced the Hindus to migrate from Bangladesh. It was highlighted on a research survey[18] published in 1997, that a large number of minority Hindu people migrated consequent on the operation of the Enemy Property Act. There is no lack of evidence that this process continued even during the Awami League rule. The political advisor of the Prime Minister Sheikh Hasina, Dr S. A. Malek observed: "It is true that the conditions of minority people is deteriorating day by day, but it is really painful to note that more than 500 persons are leaving this country per day."[19] As a result of this large-scale migration about 18 lakhs of Hindus have taken shelter in India as refugees during the period 1991-2000. (See ***Annexure III:*** Percentage of Religion-wise population growth of Bangladesh from 1941-1991).

Conclusion

To conclude my paper I would like to remind the readers as well that unless the Bangladesh's perception of establishing a monolithic Islamic State - contrary to the description by Bill Clinton and the likes as a "Moderate Islamic State"- is properly understood and countered effectively, the sad plight of the minority communities in Bangladesh and their problems will never cease to exist.

NOTES

1. K. G. Mustafa, *Janakanhta*, a Bangla daily, Dhaka, 29.10.2001.
2. *Janakantha* (Bangla Daily), 23.10.2001.
3. *Ibid.*, 1st May, 2002, Dhaka. (Internet edition).
4. *Ibid.*, 18.10.2001.
5. *Prothom Alo*, a daily Bangla newspaper from Dhaka, 23 October, 2001.
6. An inquiry into Causes and Consequences of Deprivation of Hindu Minorities in Bangladesh through Vested Property Act, edited by Abul Barkat, PRIP TRUST, Dhaka, 2000, p.63.
7. *Op. cit.*
8. An essay on Minority Ethnic Communities by Mohiuddin Ahmed published in the Holiday, Annual Number, a weekly news magazine from Dhaka, 1993.
9. *Far Eastern Economic Review*, Issue Cover, dated April 4, 2002.
10. *History of Bangladesh 1704-1971*, 3 volumes (edited by Sirajul Islam, Asiatic Society of Bangladesh, Dhaka, 1992.
11. Unstarred Question No.2635, answered on the 17th, August 1995 at the Lok Sabha.
12. A formidable threat to India Begum Khaleda Zia, the Prime Minister of Bangladesh, stated in 1991, during the "Population

Day" ceremony, that, in the opinion of experts, Bangladesh in its existing conditions had only a capacity to sustain a population of 13 crores of people. Extending this limit would put the country into a larger danger. (*Dainik Sangbad*, a Bangla daily from Dhaka, 6 April 1993.)

It is observed that, during 1981-1991, the IMR per thousand came down from 111.5 to 91, i.e., the death rate of children came down remarkably. During this time too the CDR per thousand came down from 11.5 to 11.0 and CBR from 34.1 to 31.6, although during 1981-1991, the average birth rate was 34.24, and the average death rate was 11.7. It may be observed from the above facts that in real sense the rate of growth of population had never come down. (Bangladesh Population Census 1981 and *Statistical Year Book of Bangladesh 1992*, *Bangladesh Bureau of Statistics*, Government of Bangladesh.)

It may, therefore, be said without any doubt that the rate of growth of population can never be 2.17% in 1993 without an extensive external migration. It can be inferred that migration from Bangladesh is the primary cause of the problem of infiltration suffered by India. Mr. Abu Hossain, an economist, writes that the Growth Rate of Population (GRP) in 1991 is 2.7, which is equal to the GRP of 1961. Hence, it is a fact that the GRP never had fallen during the last thirty years. (Abu Ahmed (Economist), *Dainik Sambad*, 10 April 1993.)

The uncontrolled and unharnessed growth of population in Bangladesh is, therefore, not only a matter of grave concern for that country but also for India. This problem will pose a formidable threat to India, especially for the Northeast India in future if we do not become adequately aware of it.

13. *The Sentinel*, 22nd September 1999.
14. Bimal Pramanik, "Interface of Migration and Inter-Religious Community Relations in Bangladesh and Eastern India", a paper presented at a Workshop organized by the Bharat Bangladesh Maitri Samiti (BBMS) in Calcutta on 12 May 1990. This paper makes an extensive use of Census reports of Pakistan and Bangladesh.
15. *Ibid.*
16. Mohiuddin Ahmed, "The Missing Population", Holiday, Weekly, Dhaka, 7 January 1994.

17. For details, see *The Telegraph*, English daily. Calcutta, 26 September 1994.
18. Dr Abul Barkat *et. al*. "Political Economy of the Vested Property Act in Rural Bangladesh", *Association for Land Reform and Development (ALRD)*, Dhaka, 1997.
19. *Prothom Alo,* Dhaka, 26th December 1999.

ANNEXURE I

Table 1

Distribution of the beneficiaries by their past (at the time of occupying property) and present political affiliation (1995 and 1997 studies)

Political affiliation	Past (at the time of occupying property)	1995 study	1997 study
Muslim League (ML)	43.8	1.2	1.9
Awami League (AL)	16.8	11.1	44.2
Bangladesh Nationalist Party	19.7	71.6	31.7
Jatiyo Party (JP)	4.8	4.9	5.8
Jamaat-e-Islami (JI)	1.0	3.7	4.8
Other Parties	2.4	1.2	1.0
Affiliation difficult to ascertain	11.5	6.2	10.6

ANNEXURE II

Table 2

Population of West Bengal, Assam and Bangladesh 1991

Total Population	196,807,279	%
Hindus	77,076,159	39.16
Muslims	116,304,233	59.09
Christians	1,090,429	0.55
Buddhists	687,418	0.35

Source: Census of India 1991 and Bangladesh Population Census 1991.

ANNEXURE III

Table 3

Percentage of Religion-wise Population Growth of Bangladesh from 1941-1991

Census Year	Muslim	Hindu	Buddhist	Christian	Other
1941	70.3	28.0	—	0.1	1.6
1951	76.9	22.0	0.7	0.3	0.1
1961	80.4	18.5	0.7	0.3	0.1
1871	85.4	13.5	0.6	0.3	0.2
1981	86.7	12.1	0.6	0.3	0.3
1991	88.3	10.5	0.6	0.3	0.3

Source: Bangladesh Population Census 1991.

SECTION IV

INDO-MYANMAR RELATIONS - IMPLICATIONS FOR NORTHEASTERN REGION

13

Burma Policy and its Impact on India's Northeastern Region

—SUBIR BHAUMIK

Burma is one of India's six neighbours with whom she shares a long land and maritime boundary, a historical bond of culture and tradition, and some shared values that grew out of the anti-imperialist struggle. But Burma is far from India's heartland and its capital, Delhi. Indian foreign policy decision-making, obsessed with Pakistan, has rarely given sufficient importance to Burma after the initial post-colonial engagements. Only in 1990s, when India grew alarmed at the growing Chinese influence in Burma, did the Pagoda nation begin to get much attention in India's defence and diplomatic circles.

India's Burma policy has always been greatly influenced by the "China factor" ever since the 1950s. The Burmese understand that. Addressing the Burma Council of World Affairs on 20 July 1950, Burmese scholar-diplomat U Tun Nyoe said: "India's special interest in Burma cannot be denied owing to her geographical proximity. Her own security requires that no foreign power has a permanent interest in Burma.[1] In fact, as early as August 1945, Pandit Jawaharlal Nehru had talked of a 'South Asia Federation', which would include Afghanistan, Iran and Burma along with India.[2] Though he never elaborated on the rationale behind the idea, which never took off, some later-day analysts see this as an attempt to develop an India-centric power bloc in rim land Asia.[3]

Apart from the "China factor", India's interest in Burma has much to do with the security of her own sensitive Northeastern region, her desire to access markets in South East Asia, including Burma, her concern to stop the inflow of drugs and weapons from Burma's turbulent frontier region, and to a lesser extent, ensure the safety and security of the people of Indian origin, who continue to live in Burma. This paper will examine how each of these concerns has influenced India's Burma policy since the 1950s and it will seek to assess the impact of that policy on India's Northeast.

The Shadow of the Dragon

Immediately after Independence, Burma was ravaged by Communist insurgency that threatened to overthrow the Government. India promptly extended military and monetary support, even before Burma had asked for it. When asked about it, Prime Minister U Nu said on 8 January, 1951: "Why India gave us help, it is her concern, not ours".[4] One obvious explanation for this was India's own concern about the spread of Communist insurgency into India's Northeast, where a Communist rebellion had just been put down in Tripura and an incipient one had been controlled in Manipur.[5] One leading Communist guerrilla commander in Tripura later said that the Indian Communist leadership had indeed considered a "tactical tie-up" with the Burmese Communists as early as the 1948 World Youth Conference in Calcutta, which was attended by several revolutionaries including the Comintern representative, Lawrence Sharkey.[6] He said the legendary Manipuri Communist leader Hijam Irabot Singh was the one given this task, but he was arrested on his way to Burma.

A Chinese backed Maoist insurrection that would engulf the whole of the Northeast by spreading out of Burma was one of the worst case scenarios projected by Indian intelligence in the early fifties.[7] So acute was the Indian concern for maintaining Burma's stability, independence and territorial integrity that one Asian writer felt this "has been pushed to the point of actual interference in Burma's internal affairs".[8]

In the early 1950s, thousands of Kuomintang troops fled into northern Burma with Communist troops in hot pursuit. At the peak of the Korean War, the CIA sent two senior officials into north Burma (through India with active cooperation of Indian intelligence) to organize the Kuomintang stragglers for an overland attack into China's Yunnan province. This was seen as an attempt to force China divert troops from Korea, but the overland attack was decisively beaten back by the Communist troops and the mission of the two CIA officials, Richard Stillwell and Desmond Fitzgerald, failed.[9] Immediately after this, several incursions by the Communist Chinese troops were reported from north Burma even as the Chinese embassy in Rangoon displayed maps of China that showed large parts of Burma's Kachin, Shan and Wa regions' as the Chinese territory. A concerned Burma turned to India, provoking a sharp response from Delhi. Speaking at the UN General Assembly on April 17, 1953) V.K. Krishna Menon said: "India felt any violation of the honour of Burma or any wrong done to that country was as significant as any wrong done to India. What hurt Burma would hurt India because of links of friendship, geography and history between the two countries".[10]

The Burmese reciprocated the gesture. Its second Prime Minister U Ba Swe said that "although the two countries are geographically separate entities, our hearts beat in unison". On July 7, 1951, a five-year Treaty of Peace and Friendship was signed between India and Burma, and that had put the Indo-Burmese bilateral relationship on a firm footing. The Chinese never took kindly to the growing Indo-Burma relationship. In 1955, the Chinese troops occupied Burmese territories at certain border pockets. A year later, its forces were involved in several border skirmishes and incursions on the borders of India and Burma. India was quick to provide Burma with diplomatic support inside and outside the UN. In an interview with Michael Brecher, Nehru said on June6, 1956: "The only way to get over that fear is for common steps to be taken so that this fear of the other party having an advantage does not come in the way".[11] Characteristic of Nehru, the common steps" were never worked out and Burma resented it.

India wanted to ensure that she should get Burma on her side to pressurize China to accept the Macmahon line as the legitimate boundary between China and India and China and Burma. But the Burmese were unnerved by the Chinese claims over vast stretches of Burmese territory - nearly 250,000 sq. miles - and slowly succumbed to the Chinese pressure to sign a boundary settlement on her terms. Between 1956 and 1962, governments changed thrice. The government of U Ba Swe, U Nu and the military caretaker of General Ne Win all maintained good relations with India, but they just could not afford to keep China hostile. China was not only in a position to aggravate the Communist insurgency by backing it, it could effectively nibble away at Burma's frontiers without being challenged by the Burmese because large parts of their common border were not controlled by the Burma army. On being requested by his Burmese counterpart, Nehru met with Zhou En-Lai, urging him to settle the border with Burma. He said later: "I send a message to Premier Zhou saying that I was sorry that this small matter of Burma-China frontier was continuing and was not being settled and I hope it would settle down".[12] The Burmese did not want the friendship with India to be too obvious because that might, in the context of deteriorating Sino-Indian relations, affect her relationship with China and make the latter hostile. So U Ba Swe told the press in Calcutta in October 1956: "There was no question of asking India to act as a mediator in the Sino-Burmese frontier dispute".[13]

On 28th January 1960, when Burma finally signed the Boundary settlement treaty with China, India protested about certain parts of it. The tri-junction between the three countries was a subject of dispute. India said it fell at the Talu Pass, but the Chinese insisted it fell at the Diphu Pass. Burma did not accept the Chinese position but it nevertheless went ahead with the boundary settlement because it could not risk dropping the entire agreement on this rather minor issue, now that the Chinese had accepted the Macmahon line as the boundary between China and Burma. Said Prime Minister U Nu: "Burma is a tender gourd among the two cactus (India and China) and there is not much we can do about it". [14]

During the 1962 border war between India and China, Burma maintained strict neutrality because she felt that "she should playa positive role in bringing about peace between the two Asian giants".[15] This was apparent by the role Burma's new military ruler General Ne Win played in the December 1962 Colombo conference that paved the way for peace on the Sino-Indian border. The Indians knew that the Chinese were trying to woo Burma for its strategic location. So she was trying to break out of her isolation in Southeast Asia and was cultivating Burma. When General Ne Win visited Delhi in February 1964, the Indians did their best to woo him. The joint communique issued at the end of Ne Win's visit said: "A common outlook on international issues resulting from the pursuit of non-alignment has helped in the development of close and good neighbourly relations between the two countries".[16]

The Dragon and Insurgencies on Indo-Burma Frontier

But more than the boundary, the support given by China to insurgents from the Northeast India was becoming a matter of great concern for Delhi. In June 1966, the first batch of Naga rebels left for China and reached Yunnan through Burma's Sagaing Division and Kachin state. The group returned after six months and again several groups followed. The Nagas were followed by the Mizos and then by the Manipuri rebels. Since all these rebels were using the Hkamti-Kachin corridor of Burma to reach Yunnan, India was keen Burma's new military government should take action. Then in 1967, the Burmese Communist party, CPB (White Flag) unleashed a massive offensive against the Burma Army over a wide front along the China border.[17] Since Burma's military ruler Ne Win was convinced that the offensive had been planned and executed in close coordination with the Chinese authorities, which were arming, supplying and sheltering the Burmese Communist leadership, he turned to India. The first attempts at military coordination to fight the insurgents started in 1968. On March 29, 1969, Ne Win visited Delhi again and met Prime Minister Mrs Indira Gandhi. Addressing a banquet hosted in his honour by Mrs Gandhi, Ne Win said: "Though we may not agree on every single point, we have similar responses to many problems, especially to some of the international issues".[18] By the end of 1968, the Burmese army was attacking the second batch of Naga rebels returning from China and heavy casualties were reported. Other Northeast Indian rebel columns headed for China were also attacked. What upset the Burmese military authorities was the attempted takeover of some frontier towns by the Mizo rebels in the Chin Hills in 1968-1969.[19]

For the first time, the Burmese were unhesitantly cooperating with the Indians in military terms. By the mid-1970s, the effect was showing. Rebel columns from the Northeast were still going to China, but in much smaller numbers because they feared attacks by the Burmese army on the way and could not afford much casualties. In fact, the Manipuri rebels avoided the Burma route totally. They send their guerrillas in very small batches to Lhasa using the Assam-Nepal route. The first batch of Naga rebels who went to China through Burma for training in 1966 (led by Thinoselie and Muivah) numbered well over 300. A Mizo rebel batch, which failed to make it to China because of floods on the Chindwin river in 1968 numbered well over 400. But the first batch of Manipuri Peoples Liberation Army trainees (later called pioneers or Ojhas) who went to China in 1976 led by Nameirakpam Bisheswar Singh numbered below 20.

By the beginning of the 1980s, the Burmese army had grown stronger and Ne Win was cultivating China assiduously, primarily to ensure cessation of the Chinese support to the Communist rebels in north Burma. By mid-1980s, they had started attacking the Naga rebel bases in Sagaing Division. The biggest attack was reported in 1985 when journalist Bertil Lintner was staying in the headquarters of the National Socialist Council of Nagaland (NSCN)'s headquarters at Challam.[20] For 20 days, the Nagas were under heavy attack and only the onset of monsoon, which makes military logistics difficult to maintain, forced the Burmese to move back. Two Burmese light infantry regiments were involved in the attack.

But the process of military cooperation that was just beginning to happen between the two countries suffered a setback when India grew suspicious of Burma's growing relations with China. In the early Eighties, the Chinese had begun to scale down support to the Burmese Communists and other rebel groups they had helped in a big way since the Cultural Revolution. They also stopped assistance to guerrillas from the Northeast India. But while China's relations with India did not pick up appreciably, it began to improve with Burma in a noticeable way. The Burmese Communist radio station, Voice of the People of Burma (VOPB), which had been functioning in a Chinese border village, was stopped. Even weapons supplies to the Burmese Communists were scaled down![21] And Ne Win received red carpet welcome in his many visits to Beijing during the decade, while the Burmese Communists came under steady pressure to close down camps and other establishments along the Sino-Burma frontier.

According to a Chinese foreign policy analyst, there were many reasons for this policy shift in Beijing as far as Burma is concerned. She says that Beijing was beginning to emerge from the Maoist era and under Deng Hsiao Ping was trying to grow out the culture of "exporting revolution". And by the end of the Seventies, China was convinced that the Burmese communists would never be able to capture the State power. "So China was not keen to back a losing horse any more and lose a winning horse".[22]

When the student uprising erupted in Burma in 1986 and gathered momentum in 1987, hundreds of Burmese students and political dissidents began to take shelter in India's frontier states. Initially undecided, Delhi finally started sheltering them. The Burmese students first opened offices in Manipur and Mizoram and finally moved over to Delhi, opening an office even in the house of socialist MP (now Defence Minister) George Fernandes. Public opinion in India supported the pro-democracy upsurge - all major political parties came out in open support of the movement to oust the military regime.

The fact that Aung Sang's daughter Suu Kyi had taken over the leadership of the movement further enthused India. Suu Kyi had studied in Delhi when her mother was Burma's Ambassador to India. The Rajiv Gandhi government came out in open support of the "cause of democracy in Burma".

Gandhi's external affairs minister (and later Prime Minister) P V Narasimha Rao told journalists on return from the United Nations in 1987: "As the world's largest democracy and as a neighbour of Burma, India cannot look the other way when Burma struggles to establish democracy after having lived under a military dictatorship for 25 years. We will give the pro-democracy movement all forms of support".[23]

The support to Burma's pro-democracy movement was reflected in the shelter India provided to hundreds of Burmese students and politicians who fled into the country. Most of them opened offices in Delhi and, after the movement was crushed in a military coup in 1988, they started getting refugee status from the UNHCR.[24] But analysts have argued that India's support to the Burmese pro-democracy struggle was not merely motivated by a desire to help topple a corrupt and repressive military dictatorship -behind it lay the plan to curb China's growing influence in Burma and bring down a military dictatorship that had increasingly become close to Beijing ever since she scaled down support to the Burmese Communists.[25]

In the late eighties, India's relations with the Burmese military junta further deteriorated and its relations with China improved. When the Burmese Communist Party collapsed like a house of cards in 1989, its tribal fighters threw out the Burman commissars and formed separate drug-peddling armies, China has no further reason to give any support the communists. Many senior Burmese communist leaders continue to live in Yunnan but under strict instructions not to undertake political activity. The major sore in the Sino-Burmese relations vanished overnight. On the other hand, Indian support for the pro-democracy groups in Burma increased.

In 1990, two years after the pro-democracy movement was ruthlessly crushed, the Indian embassy in Bangkok was accused by Burma's military rulers of "funding" the Burmese government in exile called National Coalition Government for the Union of Burma (NCGUB).[26] India denied the charge but the Burmese military intelligence insisted they knew it all. When two Burmese youth activists hijacked a Rangoon-bound Thai Airways flight to Calcutta on 10 November, 1990, India decided to provide them shelter, if not formal asylum. Though the case against them were not dropped, one of the hijacker Soe Myint was even allowed to run a news agency with a website, Mizzima. This upset the Burmese all the more. Later, Burmese army chief and vice chairman of the ruling State Law & Order Restoration Council (SLORC) Than Swe, in a secret circular dated February 2, 1991, described India as a country, "which encourages and supports internal insurgents and interferes in Burma's internal affairs, acts which are not expected of a friendly neighbour".[27]

At this stage, India was not only cultivating the pro-democracy opposition led by Daw Aung Sang Suu Kyi, but was also forging covert ties with the Democratic Alliance of Burma (DAB), a grouping of twenty-three ethnic rebel armies. India's external intelligence outfit Research and Analysis Wing (RAW) forged particularly close ties with the Kachin Independence Organisation (KIO) and even supplied the rebels with a lot of weapons and ammunition from an Indian army base at Vijaynagar just before the Burmese army launched a massive offensive against the KIO-held areas. The KIO was allowed to maintain a liaison office in Delhi and a particularly trusted confidante of the KIO chief Maran Brangsein was sent to Delhi to liaise with the RAW.[28]

But the KIO's demand for weapons and ammunition was far too much and India, which was trying to win world opinion against Pakistan to fight the separatist campaigns in Kashmir and Punjab, was not willing to be seen as supporting insurgency in a neighbouring country after the LTTE connections had backfired in 1987. Her purpose to support the Kachins was limited: ensure that the Kachins, who had trained and armed a whole generation of rebels from the Northeast India in the 1980s, withdrew all forms of support to the rebels from the Northeast India and deny them the corridor to go to China.[29]

India also started cultivating the Chin and the Arakanese rebels in western Burma. The Chin National Front (CNF) and the National Unity Party of Arakans (NUPA) were not only allowed to set up bases in India's Mizoram State but were supplied with a limited quantity of weapons and some training. The Indian patronage to the Burmese rebel groups was pretty much limited, compared to the support that Delhi had provided to the Shanti Bahini rebels in Bangladesh's Chittagong Hill Tracts or the LTTE in Sri Lanka. Her limited tactical objective in extending such support was to deny the Northeast Indian rebel groups any base area or support in Burma's border provinces and there are evidence that the Burmese rebel groups were, at least in one instance, used to spy on and attack rebels from the Northeast India.[30]

In the meantime, China stepped up its support for the junta With China firmly supporting the military rulers in Rangoon with huge transfers of military hardware and aid to infrastructure projects. In the 1990s, the total value of military hardware given to Burma by China was valued at $ 2 billion dollars.[31] With both China and Burma facing a degree of global isolation due to the 1989 Tianammen massacres and those perpetrated by the Burmese army in 1988, it was but natural for both autocratic regimes to draw close to each other. But within India's foreign policy, defence and intelligence establishments, the policy of "limited support" to the Burmese rebels and the pro-democracy movement was opposed by a group of officials who felt it was necessary to emulate the ASEAN policy of "constructive engagement" with the junta. This group included senior military officials like army Chief General Shankar Roychoudhuri and the military intelligence chief Lt. General Ravi Sawhney, some senior Navy and RAW officials and a few in the foreign ministry. They argued that if India did not develop relations with the junta - and since a democratic transition was a far cry - Burma would become a Chinese satellite.

In 1994, India started making fresh approaches to the Burmese generals. Within the SLORC, a group who opposed total dependence on China pushed for closer ties with India. But the whole process received a temporary setback during the Operation Golden Duck. The Burmese army was requested to help out and it obliged by holding up some escape routes during the first phase of the operation. As the Indian army dragnet closed in and the rebels were desperate, Delhi gave the Nehru Peace Prize to Aung Sang Suu Kyi. The Burmese army pulled back its units involved in the operation, much to the consternation of the Indian army's Eastern Command.[32]

But by 1996, friendly contacts were resumed. Intelligence sharing and military coordination for anti-insurgency operations were started at command levels after few border level meetings. The whole process received a boost with the coming to power of the BJP-led coalition government. India began taking up several projects, the most important being the construction of the 160-kms all-weather road from Tamu on the Indo-Burma border to Mandalay. And in 1998, the Indian Army and Navy killed six top NUPA leaders after having called them to the Andamans for allegedly handing over an island base. Thirty-six other rebels, 24 Arakanese and 12 Karens, are still being held in Port Blair, without trial.[33]

The Indian Defence Ministry however said that the six were gunrunners and had been killed, after the Navy in the high seas chased their vessels. The action was christened "Operation Leech." Repeated appeals by the NUPA to secure the release of the 36 guerrillas have been rejected by Delhi, despite some lobbying on behalf of the Arakanese rebels by Defence Minister George Fernandes. In fact, the army has managed to largely neutralize Fernandes in the formulation of India's Burma policy. In 1999, the India's Eastern army commander Lieutenant General H R S Kalkat went to the extent of saying that the Burma policy better left to the Army. He said: "We are soldiers, they (Burmese junta) are soldiers and our blood is thicker than the blood of the bureaucrats and politicians".[34] A BBC analyst, while commenting on the situation, said: "Though the Indian army is largely apolitical unlike its counterparts in Pakistan and Burma, it is increasingly resentful of what it sees as the inept handling of national security issues by the political leadership".[35]

The Burmese junta needed nothing better than "Operation Leech" to be convinced of India's intentions of dropping support to insurgent or pro-democracy groups in Burma. Ever since then, the Burmese refugees, pro-democracy activists and ethnic rebels have been under enormous pressure to close down bases and camps and scale down activities. One instance that would highlight the difference in policy is the treatment meted out to the 1990 hijacker Soe Myint. After the hijack, he was granted bail and allowed to stay in India, even run a news agency, Mizzima. But in April 2002, his case was reopened immediately after External Affairs Minister Jaswant Singh's visit to Burma and he was arrested in Delhi and brought to Calcutta to stand trial.

In July 1999, Indian home secretary Kamal Pande and Burmese deputy minister for Home Thure Mying Maung held a meeting in Delhi to work out an agreement to provide for "increased cooperation to tackle cross-border terrorism and drugs trafficking."[36] Later, the agreement was signed in Kohima, Nagaland. "According to the new agreement, India and Burma will coordinate future military campaigns against ethnic separatists in border areas and take joint action against drug trafficking. Four new border trade points will also be opened.[37] In January and July 2000, Indian army chief General Ved Prakash Malik visited Rangoon to concretize military cooperation for anti-insurgency operations. While he met his counterpart General Maung Aye in his first visit, he was granted audience by the Burmese Head of the State, Than Swe during his second visit. Covering his second visit, a BBC analyst said, "While India was successful in getting Burma to make arrangements for conducting joint military operations against the rebel groups in future, Burma managed to strike deals for supply of military gear from India".[38] The Burmese were trying to diversify their sources for importing military equipment to avoid over-dependence on China and India was only to keen to play ball.

The arrangements for conducting joint operations against the rebels were finalized during General Maung Aye's week-long visit to India in November 2000. He had met Indian military officials during a visit to Shillong earlier that year. Maung Aye met Prime Minister A.B.Vajpayee, Home Minister L.K. Advani and External Affairs Minister Jaswant Singh. Defence Minister George Fernandes, a vociferous critic of China and Burma for their suppression of democracy was a notable omission in the list of senior Indian dignitaries who met Maung Aye.[39] So, in the first year of the new millennium, India and Burma finalized arrangements for military cooperation. In the last two years, the two armies have coordinated their campaigns against the rebels on the borders. Several bases of the NSCN (Khaplang group), the ULFA and the Manipuri rebel groups have been attacked and destroyed by the Burmese forces, while the Indians have similarly shut out the bases of the CNF and the NUPA, while KIO has gone quiet after signing a ceasefire deal with the Military junta in 1994.

However, there have been some hiccups in this emerging military relationship. In 1995, when the Burmese forces pulled out of "Operation Golden Duck" when India gave the Nehru Peace Prize to Aung Sang Suu Kyi, giving the trapped northeast Indian rebel column a chance to escape. In November 2001, the Burmese army raided seven camps of three Manipuri rebel groups in the area around Tamu and captured nearly 200 guerrillas, along with 1600 weapons and huge quantity of gold and currency.[40] This was easily the single biggest catch of insurgents and weapons anywhere along the Indo-Burmese border during the past 35 years. But then in December 2001, Western press reports sourced to Indian intelligence suggested, that Burma has given shelter to two Pakistani nuclear scientists close to Taliban and had then spirited them off to China when the story broke. The Burmese were furious; deputy chief of Burmese military intelligence Colonel Kyaw Thein denied the reports as "baseless" and said "this was designed to provoke the US against Burma".[41] India's former ambassador to Burma, Vivek Katju reported to Delhi that the Burmese had started releasing the arrested Manipuri guerrillas immediately after these press reports. By end of February 2002, all the arrested guerrillas had been released, though the Burmese retained the weapons and equipment seized from them.[42] Some military officials scheduled for a visit to the Indian army's Eastern Command also cancelled their visit. At the time of writing this paper, India was trying to restore its relationship with Burma - some of the misunderstanding had been cleared by Jaswant Singh during his visit to Rangoon during April 2002 and one BBC analyst suggested that the arrest of Soe Myint involved in the 1990 hijacking was an attempt by India to placate Burma.[43]

Gas, Roads, Trade & Other Issues

General Maung Aye visited Delhi with several ministers dealing with power, commerce and industries. While Delhi is desperately seeking ways to import gas from Burma after it became clear that Bangladesh was not forthcoming, Burma has made it clear it is more than willing to sell gas to India through a pipeline, either laid through Bangladesh or below the sea. The Myanmar Oil and Gas Enterprise (MOGE) and the Gas Authority of India Limited (GAIL) are believed to be close to an agreement on the pipeline and the only issue holding it up is the "Bangladesh factor". India is intensely lobbying with Bangladesh to allow it lay a pipeline through that country to enable it to import Burmese gas.[44] In fact, the GAIL has already picked up a stake in the Korean company Daewoo's gas hunt venture in Burma. So sure is India about receiving Burmese gas through a pipeline in Bangladesh, if not Bangladesh itself, that the GAIL has started laying its network of pipelines from West Bengal onwards to major consumption points in North and South India.[45] Indo-Burmese economic relationship, which has so far been restricted to an annual $200 million dollars bilateral trade (and an illegal contraband trade that's believed to twice to thrice as much), will grow by leaps and bounds once Delhi starts importing Burmese gas.

Burma is also looking to increase tourist traffic from India and so allowed the Indian Airlines to resume the Calcutta-Rangoon flight, suspended since 1962, in 2000. The two countries are believed to be close to deal to open consulates, the Burmese have said they will open it at Calcutta and the Indians say they will open it at Mandalay. The road to Mandalay from Tamu on the border with Manipur has been opened. Efforts are on to increase border trade between western Burmese States and the Northeast Indian States though snags on currency rates continue to affect it. The Chambers of commerce in both the countries are visiting each other and suggesting more items for trade. The economic relations between the two countries that began in the fifties with the controversy round rice imports from Burma and the separation debts are a thing of the past and both countries are looking for avenues to increase trade and tourism. Burma says it is also looking of major Indian investments in areas like power generation.

Implications for Northeast India

Analysts have suggested that once separatist insurgencies are controlled, Indian companies can start setting up large-scale manufacturing units in West Bengal and Northeast Indian States, taking advantage of the favourable investment concessions announced for export units by Delhi. They say Burma will not only be an important market for such products but once the trans-Asian highway connecting the Northeast India to Thailand through Burma comes through, Indian companies can access markets in other parts of South east Asia right up to Indo-China.[46] It is still very much into the future rather than the present but the possibility of big business groups investing in manufacturing units in the Northeast to access markets in Burma and rest of Southeast Asia and perhaps China's frontier regions are not remote. Foreign trade and nothing else can push through industrialization of the Northeast and the breakthrough in Burma will be crucial. But if the Indian industry miss out on this potential, the Northeast India will be flooded with cheap Chinese goods coming in through Burma, as is the case at the moment.[47]

The Indo-Burma military cooperation, once resumed and institutionalized, can prove effective in controlling trans-border insurgency movements. Once assured that the Burmese will push hard to deny rebels from northeast India a base area in western Burma, India can concentrate on a diplomatic offensive to pressurize Bangladesh and Bhutan to deny base areas to northeastern rebel groups. In fact, the Indo-Burmese joint military campaigns can become an effective model for combating insurgencies that can be emulated with other neighbours like Bangladesh. And once trade and military ties improve between the two countries, things are bound to get better for Burmese nationals of Indian origin since the country is slowly moving away from socialism and allowing a return of the free market economy. Since rampant nationalization forced many Indians to leave Burma since their trade was adversely effect, the return to free market economy will be more than welcomed by the large Indian trading class.

The steady improvement of Indo-Burma relations since the BJP took power in Delhi can have the following implications for the Northeast India:

(a) Growing Indo-Burmese military cooperation is bad news for the Northeast Indian rebel groups and can effectively deny them one of their longest and safest base areas.

(b) Better bilateral economic ties between the two countries can provide the necessary boost to industrialization of northeast India.

(c) Growth in bilateral trade can also favourably impact on the local economies of the Northeast India. But this will only be at the cost of Indian support for Burma's pro-democracy movement.

NOTES

1. Reported in the *New Times of Burma*, 26th July 1950.
2. S. Gupta, *India and Regional Integration in Asia*, Popular, Bombay, 1964.
3. Subir Bhaumik, India and her neighbours, seminar paper presented at the North Bengal University in July 1996.
4. *Burma*, Vol 1, No.3, 1951, P.34.
5. See *Amrita Bazar Patrika* (Calcutta) June 18, 1949.
6. Late Bipulananda Kar Choudhury alias Mohan Choudhury, chief commander of Shanti Sena, armed wing of the CPI in Tripura, in interview with author, 17th February 1985.
7. See Chapter 5 "The Communist and the Clenched Fist" in Subir Bhaumik, *Insurgent Crossfire: Northeast India*, Lancers, Delhi 1996, where excerpts suggesting possible Chinese involvement in the Tripura insurrection have been extensively quoted. Though these intelligence reports were alarmist and unfounded, they do reflect the establishment's mindset.
8. Ton That Thien, *India and South East Asia*, Geneva, 1963, p. 181.

9. Jonathan Powers, *Richard Helms: The Man who kept the Secrets*, New York, 1982. (A Pultizer Award winning biography of Richard Helms, the longest serving CIA chief).
10. Official Records of UN General Assembly, 7th Session, First Committee, April 1953.
11. Michael Brecher, *The New states of Asia*, London, 1964.
12. *Rajya Sabha debates*, Part II, Vol. XXVI, No.23, September 10, 1959, Cols 3907-08.
13. *The Burman*, 1st November 1956.
14. *Burma Weekly Bulletin*, Vol 3, No .39, 1959.
15. *Guardian* (Rangoon), Vol X, No 3, April 1963.
16. *Forward* (Rangoon) Vol III, No 14, March 1, 1965.
17. For details of this offensive, see Bertil Lintner, *Burma in Revolt: Opium and Insurgency since 1948*, Silkworm Books, Thailand, 1999.
18. *Selected Speeches of Indira Gandhi* (Jan 1966-August 1969), Delhi, 1971.
19. For details on the Mizo National Front offensive in Chin Hills, see Nirmal Nibedon, *Mizoram: The Dagger Brigade*. Lancers, Delhi, 1983 and Subir Bhaumik, Operation Jericho and After in Insurgent Crossfire: Northeast India, Lancers, Delhi, 1996.
20. Bertil Lintner, *Land of Jade: Journey through Insurgent Burma*, White Lotus, Bangkok, 1990.
21. Bertil Lintner, *Burma in Revolt: Opium and Insurgency since 1948*, Silkworm Books, Thailand, 1999.
22. Li Feiyu of Beijing College of Diplomacy, later Sincan Fellow at Oxford University, in interview with the author at Oxford, 1st February 1990. Feiyu admitted that her status paper on Burma policy was accepted by the Foreign Ministry as sound and Beijing shifted from emphasizing party-to-party relations with the Burmese Communists to state-to-state policy with Ne Win's government.
23. Narasimha Rao in interview on BBC World Service Radio with Mark Tully, 12th October 1987.
24. Cross Border Human Traffic: A Case Study of the Burmese refugees in Northeast India, paper presented by C. Joshua Thomas at *XVI European Conference on Modern South Asian Studies*, held at the University of Edinburgh, September 6-9,2000.

25. Subir Bhaumik, India and her neighbours, seminar paper presented at the North Bengal University in July 1996.

26. Bertil Lintner, The Indo-Burmese Frontier: a Legacy of Violence in *Jane intelligence review*, January 1994. Lintner says that a Burmese spokesman even claimed to know details of payment made by Indian intelligence to the NCGUB - the first installment, according to him, was 300,000 Thai bahts.

27. *Ibid.*

28. Maran Brangsein in interview with Subir Bhaumik at London, 17th April 1992. Released by the India Abroad News Service and published in India Abroad and in several Indian newspapers between 19th and 22nd April 1992.

29. Former Additional Secretary, RAW, B.B. Nandi, interview with author, 6th March 2002.

30. The Indian army used the NUPA to spy on and even attack a group of about 200 Naga, Manipuri and Assamese guerrillas when they were bringing in a huge consignment of weapons brought from Southeast Asia and off loaded at Wyakaung beach, south of the Bangladesh's resort town of Cox's Bazar. The army christened this "Operation Golden Duck" and between 21st April-7th May, 38 rebels were killed, 114 captured and huge quantity of weapons were seized. Those captured included ULFA's "foreign secretary" Sasha Choudhury. For details on this operation, see Sunday 21-28 May 1995 and BBC World Service reports by Subir Bhaumik, 24th April-12th May, I995. The NUPA's role in the Operation was made known to the author by "Major" Saw Tun of the Arakan Army in an exclusive interview on 3rd January,1998.

31. Andrew Selth, *Power without Glory: Burma's Tatmadaw*, Eastbridge Press, US, 2002.

32. India's eastern army commander Lieutenant General Ramesh Batra, interview to author, 6th May 1995. Batra told the BBC World Service: "The right hand should know what the left hand is doing. The Award should have been given at least after we finished the operation successfully."

33. Subir Bhaumik, Treachery: How an Indian agent betrayed Myanmarese rebels in *Times of India*, Calcutta edition, 15th April 2001.

34. Lieutenant General H R S Kalkat in a weekend guest speech delivered at the think-tank, Bengal Initiative, in the house of industrialist Rusi Mody, 13th October 1999.

35. Subir Bhaumik, *BBC News Online*, 7th January 2000.
36. *BBC News Online*, 30th July 1999.
37. *BBC News Online*, 13th November 1999.
38. Larry Jagan, *BBC News Online*, 4th July 2000.
39. Vir Singh, *BBC News Online*, 18th November 2000.
40. Subir Bhaumik, *BBC News Online*, 15th November 2001.
41. Kyaw Thein's press conference in Rangoon's Defence Officers Club was reported in the *www.burmanet.org* on 12th December 2001.
42. Subir Bhaumik, *BBC News Online*, 23rd February, 2002.
43. *Ibid.*, 15th April 2002.
44. *www.petrowatch.com*. Vol.6, 27th March,2002.
45. *www.petrowatch.com*. Vol.7, 6th April, 2002.
46. Nazeeb Arif, Secretary-General, Indian Chamber of Commerce, interview to author in Saaf Katha, a chat show in ETV Bangia, 21st February 2002.
47. Subir Bhaumik, Boom Time for Counterfeit border trade, *BBC News Online*, 13th March 2002 (Report from Tamu).

14

Indo-Myanmar Relations Since 1988: Its Implications on India's Northeast

—KONSAM IBO SINGH

The year 1988 was a landmark in Myanmar's history. From March to September a number of events took place. Provoked by pressing economic problems, withdrawal of high denomination currency notes from circulation, rice shortages black marketeering etc., there were widespread protests and demonstrations in the country. Removal of Home and Religious Affairs Minister Major General Min Gaung and the Yangon Police Chief Thien Aung from the office and the dismissal of the Prime Minister Maung Maung Kha and the resignation of General Ne Win, Myanmar's strongman from the chairmanship of the Burma Socialist Programme Party (BSPP) - the only political party allowed to function did not abate the crisis.

After Ne Win's resignation Sein Lwin, the butcher[1], head of the hated security police and a senior member of the BSPP was elected to the chairmanship of the party's Central Executive Committee also as Chairman of the State Council and as State President. His election provoked student riots in a large scale. Widespread protests and demonstrations continued in which nearly half a million took part but without violence. On 10 August a group of doctors and nurses were shot by the army outside the Rangoon General Hospital killing five of them on the spot.[2] The students called for general strike and forced Sein Lwin to resign on 12 August only after 17 days of his office. He was replaced by Dr. Maung Maung, a civilian and Ne Win's official biographer. However, the demonstrations continued unabated. In September students and Buddhist monks controlled municipal governments of many towns. Widespread opposition against the existing military regime could be seen.

Fully realizing the consequences of the strong opposition the BSPP, in a move to contain it, convened an emergency congress in September. It decided (i) to hold free elections within three months; (ii) to dissociate armed forces, police and bureaucrats from the BSPP.[3] Immediately after the announcement, General Saw Maung seized power on 18 September. He formed a nine-member State Law and Restoration Council (SLORC) and abolished the People's Assembly, the State Council and the Council of Ministers, banned demonstrations imposed dusk to dawn curfew and killed not less than 1000 students but promised for holding a multi - party democratic election.[4]

After the killing of the students a systematic repression continued. Unable to bear the sight the Indian diplomatic mission in Yangoon encouraged the students, who took shelter at the Indian embassy, to cross over to the Indian territory and assured them for asylum. The Myanmarese government knew the support extended by the Indian diplomatic mission. They even accused the mission for its alleged instigation and involvement. At the same time the kind of coverage that the All India Radio, Myanmarese Service gave, it was alleged, overtook the BBC coverage on Myanmar. In short it was quite open that India supported the movement for the restoration of democracy in Myanmar spearheaded by the students.

One of the outcomes of the movement was that more than 7000 students fled to the border areas for fear of military reprisal. Out of this figure around 3000 students crossed over to Thailand where the figure of Myanmarese refugees stood at 1,60,000.[5] Around 1,33,000 to 1,70,000 Rohingyas (Arakanese Muslims) crossed over to Bangladesh. Lastly, 1400

Nagas and 800 to 1000 Myanmarese many of them students, were able to cross over to the Indian side. Later number of refugees in India was estimated at 10,000, which included many Nagas and Chins.[6] These students were given asylum on humanitarian considerations. Many of them were scattered along the Indo-Myanmar border. Some of them even settled down in the Northeast India. It is also alleged that around 400 students who reluctantly returned to Myanmar lost their lives.[7]

India's encouragement and support to the movement created displeasure to the military junta. No doubt, India's relations with Myanmar were never close mainly due to the Nationalization Law of 1963, which forced the Indians and others to leave the country without compensation, and the Citizens Act of 1982, which discriminated against the Indians and others. However, it is to be noted that attempts were made by Indira Gandhi during the last years of rule (1980-84) and Rajiv Gandhi's tenure as Prime Minister[8] to have better ties. However, difference in the political systems followed could have contributed much for distant relationship. It was during this period that India expressed its sympathy with the students, especially those who protested for the restoration of democracy. India was quite critical of the military regime in Myanmar, which was evident from the remark made by the then President of India R.Venkataraman when the newly appointed Myanmarese ambassador to India Mr. Wynn Lwin met the former to hand over his credentials. The President expressed his serious concern at the "delay and uncertainty" in the restoration of democracy in Myanmar and also dissatisfaction over the refusal to release Nobel Laureate Aung San Suu Kyi who was then under house arrest.[9]

India's relations with Myanmar from 1989 to 1992 were "characterized by mutual disenchantment". SLORC was of the opinion that India was unnecessarily interfering in the internal affairs while India expressed its reservations about the suppression of democracy in Myanmar.[10]

The period from 1989 to 1992 also happened to be the one during which there was widespread condemnation of the

SLORC regime specially for its (i) repressive measures and unimpressive record of human rights abuses; (ii) undue delay in honouring results of the elections held in May 1990 in which the opposition National League for Democracy (NLD) won 392 seats while ruling National Unity Party (NUP) and its allies - Peasants, Workers and Youths organizations won only 10 seats out of a total of 485 seats. The widespread condemnation came from industrialized Western democracies and Japan. They even asked India to join them. However India declined to do so now.

The United States, since the suppression of Pro-democracy movement and the SLORC coup in 1988, suspended all aid, refused to appoint an ambassador to Yangon, used its influence on financial institutions to discourage from granting aid and called for international community to isolate Myanmar for its human rights abuses. In September 1991, 18 industrialize democracies, including 12 European Economic Community members issued coordinated statements calling on the regime to accept the results of May 1990 election and release the leaders from imprisonment.[11] The appeals were renewed calling for a worldwide arms embargo against Myanmar. In short, all these countries have suspended aid. Japan the largest donor of foreign aid to Myanmar believed that gentle pressure on SLORC would achieve results than outright confrontation.[12] It provided more than two-thirds of bilateral Official Development Aid (ODA) between 1973-1988. Myanmar was one of the top ten recipients of the Japanese aid.

Myanmar's external relations after 1988 drastically changed. It was more drastic with China. The Sino-Myanmar relations were not very cordial prior to 1988 though diplomatic relations were restored in 1978. The two also signed a Treaty of Friendship and Mutual Non-aggression in 1960 after a settlement of long-standing border dispute. An aid pact was concluded in July, 1979 which was followed by Ne Win's visit to China as BSPP Chairman in May 1985, following a March visit by Chinese President Li Xiannian. Despite these developments, China was never so close to Myanmar as it is today. Its support to the ethnic based insurgents and the Communist Party of Burma (White Flag), which fought against

Yangon was considered to be playing the role of an instigator. However after 1988 uprising China has become Myanmar's "Principal aid donor, arms supplier, source of consumer goods". Frequent exchange of official visits, significant increase in the bilateral volume of trade. Myanmar's heavy dependence on China for arms supply, China's increasing participation in the developmental process of Myanmar, the expansion of China's border trade with Myanmar, and the Chinese economic penetration reaching India's Northeast are some of the steps taken by both. In October 1989, Lt. General Khin Nyunt, SLORC's Secretary No.1 paid an official visit to China at a moment when SLORC was at its height of unpopularity and condemnation. His visit was followed by another visit of General Saw Maung. Chairman of the SLORC in August in 1991, which was reciprocated by Chinese Premier Li Peng's visit to Myanmar in December 1994. In fact, during the last 10 years or so there has been a series of mutual visits exchanged at the highest level of political, military and commercial ones, a symbol of closer ties.

What is significant in the improvement of relationship between China and Myanmar is that China has taken the second place in terms of import and export after Singapore the position previously held by others. From 1994 to 1996 and even after the Chinese export to Myanmar ranges from 24 percent to 30 percent (i.e $ 400 million and $ 600 million) whereas the import from Myanmar comes to around 14 percent of Myanmar's total.[13] Cross border trade, formalized in 1985, is estimated to be around $ 1 billion a year.[14]Northern Myanmar has become a centre of Chinese commercial activities, connecting southern China's Yunnan provincial capital Kunming reaching Mandalay in a big way.

China's main interest is, no doubt, economic. However, following the 1989 visit of Khin Nyunt and 1991 visit of General Than Swe to Beijing, Myanmar purchased arms worth $1.2 billion the largest arms deal in Myanmar's history.[15] Apart from trade and commerce China is largely responsible for imparting training to the Myamarese Army personnel and the modernization process of the armed forces.

Apart from the aforesaid expansion of Chinese economic activities, it has also developed Myanmar's naval base at Hianggyi Island; upgraded the naval facilities at Sittwe (Akyab), Mergui etc., radar station at Coco Island, quite close to Indian islands of Andaman and Nicobar. These facilities are viewed by India to be "serious encroachments into India's sphere of influence", as they were created for monitoring Indian missiles tests conducted between Orissa and the Andamans.[16]

Improvements of the Sino-Myanamar economic and strategic relations have sent alarms to both ASEAN and India. Keeping in view of the growing the Chinese involvement in Southeast Asia, the ASEAN group initiated what it called "constructive engagement", a policy of non-interference in the internal affairs of Myanmar, while actively participating in the economic activities of the country. This opportunistic economic approach is largely determined by the vacuum created by the suspension of aids by the US and European Union. In simple terms, China along with ASEAN especially, Singapore, Thailand, Malaysia and Indonesia are the most benefited ones. This is a new development in the post-Cold War Southeast Asia, which is also conditioned by the political developments inside Myanmar. Then what could be its implications on India and its Northeast region?

India's Response

Chinese economic and strategic penetration into Myanmar is a serious concern to India. India's security concern is visible in the context of its Northeast political scenario. Before we discuss the Indo-Myanmar relations and its implications on India's Northeast, it would be worthwhile to highlight the history of the Indo-Myanmar relations.

India's relations with Myanmar remain almost cool prior to 1988. Even though India is alarmed at Myanmar's closer ties with China it is the consensus view that Myanmar desires to maintain good relations with both the neighbours, China and India. Further, it believes that "its security is best maintained by being friendly with all nations and allied with none"[17]. However, aftermath 1991 India's policy towards Myanmar was guided by the following imperatives:

i) Myanmar should not form an exclusive area of influence of other great powers. Attempts should be made to normalize relations whatever the government is in control of Myanmar;

ii) Myanmar is geo-strategically important to India as it falls between China and Bangladesh. Its closeness to the Indian territories of the Andamans and Nicobar islands is relevant to India's security. Indo-Myanmar cooperation is necessary to counter drug smuggling, drug crimes, insurgency and security threats to India's Northeast.

Keeping these two important imperatives in mind India reviewed its earlier policy of distancing Myanmar. Exchange of visits of U Ba Swe, Vice Foreign Minister of Myanmar to India in the middle of 1992 and J.N. Dixit, Foreign Secretary of India from 11-13 August 1992 underlined three important aspects: i) India should not be concerned about the internal developments in Myanmar; ii) Myanmar acknowledges security and political concerns affecting both the countries and agrees to cooperate to counter the smuggling of drugs and contraband; iii) Both outlined the importance of increasing economic and technological cooperation with India.[18] Beginning with the above visits and identification of areas of interest J.N. Dixit visited Myanmar from 29 March to 1st April 1993. At the end of his visit, both the countries signed an agreement to control smuggling and illegal trafficking in drugs. Draft agreements for economic and commercial cooperation were exchanged. India offered to build a road from Kalemyo to Tamu and from there to Mandalay (as the Chinese did in Yunnan and Kachin area) and also to increase communications and trade between the two countries. Taking the advantage of the exchange of visits, views also were exchanged with Lt. Gen Khin Nyunt Secretary No.1 U Ohn Gyaw, Foreign Minister and Brigadier General Win Tin, Minister for Home Affairs regarding the import of arms, the Chinese interest in the establishment of a naval base in the southern part of Myanmar quite close to the Indian territories of the Andaman and Nicobar islands. The Myanmarese authorities explained that the Chinese arms were necessary for the maintenance of internal security and defence purposes. Regarding the establishment of a Chinese naval base they cleared India's doubts saying that they will never allow any permanent foreign military presence in Myanmar.[19]

Coming back to our main theme Indo-Myanmar relations since 1988 has far reaching implications, especially on India's Northeast. These implications can be discussed on the basis of the following premises: i) border trade; ii) control of drug trafficking; iii) containment of insurgency.

Discussing the first one i.e. border trade it is worthwhile to point out that an agreement for border trade was signed between the two countries represented by Tijinder Khanna, Secretary, Ministry of Commerce for India and Lt. Colonel Kyaw Myint, Director General, Directorate of Trade, Ministry of Trade, Myanmar on 21 January 1994 in New Delhi. The border trade was to be conducted at two different sectors - i) Moreh in India (Manipur) and Tamu in Myanmar: ii) Champai in India (Mizoram) and Rib in Mynamar. Though illegal border trade was thriving since a long time it was formalized on 12 April, 1995 by the Commerce Minister, Mr. P. Chidambaram. Value of trade between 12 April 1995 to 15 September 1998 was estimated at Rs.123,94,69,256 of which Indian export to Myanmar was Rs. 67,66,14089, whereas corresponding import was valued at Rs. 56,28.55,167 20 well below the Sino-Myanmar border trade value. The second Sector, Mizoram-Myanmar border trade at Champai and Rih is yet to be formalized.

Another important item which figures prominently in the bilateral relationship, is control of drug trafficking. Here it may not be out of place to mention that Myamnar cultivates opium poppy in the areas that constitute more than 50 percent of the world's total area used for the purpose (see Table 1 below). Further, in terms production, it ranks second after Afghanistan ranging the contribution from 28 percent to 40 percent except for the year 1999 (see Table 2 below).

As the tables below show opium cultivation and production is substantial in Myanmar. In terms of area used for cultivation it is the highest in the world and in terms of production it is the second highest. Further the highest number of HIV/AIDS cases are recorded in the neighbouring provinces of Myanmar i.e. the Yunnan province of China where 80 percent of China's HIV/AIDS total infected cases live, Manipur of India where 56 percent of India's HIV/AIDS total live, while Thailand has 80,000 and Myanmar has 400,000 cases.[20] These figures are quite shocking and the drug abuses assumed epidemic proportions. In view of this, restrictions on drug trafficking have become all the more urgent. Incidentally, this drug comes mainly through Moreh (to India), an important centre of border trade.

Table 1

Opium Poppy Cultivation In Hectares (1994-1999)

COUNTRY	YEARS				
	1994-1995	1996	1997	1998	1999
Afghanistan	71,47053,759	56,824	58,416	63,674	90,583
Myanmar	146,600154,070	163,000	155,150	130,300	89,500
(Percentage of the area world total)	(54%) (62%)	(63%)	(62%)	(55%)	(41%)
World Total	**272,479249,919**	**257,615**	**251,848**	**237,935**	**217,000**

Table 2

Opium Production In Metric Tons (1994-1999)

COUNTRY	YEARS					
	1994	1995	1996	1997	1998	1999
Afghanistan	3,416	2,335	2,248	2,804	2,693	4.565
Myanmar	1,583	1,664	1,760	1,676	1,303	895
(Percentage of the world total production	(28%)	(37%)	(40%)	(35%)	(30%)	(15%)
World total	**5,620**	**4,452**	**4,355**	**4,823**	**4,348**	**5,778**

Source: Drug Control and Crime Prevention, United Nations, World Drug Report 2000 (Oxford University Press, New York, 2000, P.160).

However, the most important of all this, is the agreement on containing insurgency on both sides. Insurgency in both the countries is ethnic based and some of them operate on both sides of the countries. Some of them had China connections e.g. the National Socialist Council of Nagalim (NSCN), the People's Liberation Army (PLA) operating in Manipur. Many of the cadres of the Northeast outfits received training inside Myanmar like those of United Liberation Front of Assam (ULFA), PLA, NSCN etc. They had plans to form a common front, which means a big security threat to India. In Myanmar too, ethnic-based insurgency drained out a huge amount of money from the State exchequer. However, majority of them have agreed to have ceasefire with the intervention of China, while on the Indian side, the NSCN is having a ceasefire extended from time to time. Reports indicate that arms purchase is done in Southeast Asia brought through Myanmar and reaches India. In the later part of 1995, the Bangladesh army and navy near seized a huge consignment of arms at Cox Bazar. The Thai Navy intercepted the second consignment in May 1997 from the PLA insurgents and the Myanmarese nationals, while smuggling arms in a motorboat. Another huge consignment consisting of rocket propelled grenades, AK-47 rifles, M-79, heavy machine guns and an assortment of pistols in all 145 weapons, 40,000 rounds of ammunition and four motor boats mounted with anti-aircraft guns were seized in the high seas near the Andamans and Nicobar islands in a combined operation conducted by the Indian army, Navy, Air Force and Coast Guards in which six people were killed and 72 were nabbed. Security forces suspected these militants could belong to PLA, ULFA and NSCN. The point is huge consignment of arms are coming through Myanmar. In another incident the Myanmarese army captured 192 militants during raids on seven camps of various Manipur outfits around Tamu in Sagaing division in November 2001. It is believed that UNLF Chairman R.K Meghen and PLA commander Jibon were among the captured. At the same time, the Myanmarese army captured 40 kg of gold, currency worth of millions, currency printing machines and 1600 weapons allegedly supplied by China. India asked Myanmar to extradite them. However, Myanmar replied that they were

Myanmarese. Later on, they were released on the Chinese pressure.

The above four incidents clearly establish the presence of the Northeast militants in Myanmar, the use of the country as transit point both for weapons and drugs. The same is true in Bangladesh too, and now Bhutan, where ULFA and the National Democratic Front of Bodoland (NDFB) have permanent camps.

Whether they have shifted their camps or not after the expiry of dateline i,e. 31 December 2001 is not the point. But many of the militant outfits of the Northeast have formed a ring covering Myanmar, Bangladesh and Bhutan for various reasons. It would not be a surprise if militants in the Northeast had set up a common command. In view of this, the maintenance of good relationship and cooperation with all these neighbours has become all the more important and crucial. The economic communities in Bangladesh, India, Myanmar, Sri Lanka and Thailand are also going to play an important role. The trans-Asian highway, reopening of the old Stillwell road will become topics of talk. The exchange of visits and contacts of military commanders as India and Myanmar do at present, will become a regular feature. Joint military operations are expected along the Indo-Myanmar border. The exchange of visits between India and Myanmar like that of India's External Affairs minister Jashwant Singh's visit to Myanmar to open a 'gift road' connecting Kalewa and Kalemyo, and the seven-day visit of General Maung Aye, Vice Chairman of the State Peace and Development Council, Myanmar leading a high power delegation in November 2000 are symbols of growing cooperation between the two countries. The improvement in the relations is yielding mutual benefits — legitimacy for the military government in Myanmar, and protection of India's security interests in its Northeast frontiers. However, that would mean the the restoration of democracy, which India strongly supported over the past years, is going to be a distant dream to be realized now.

NOTES

1. He has been nicknamed so for his role in dynamiting Rangoon University Students' Union building in 1962 and 1971. See

Maureen Aung-Thwin, "Burmese Days", *Foreign Affairs* (New York. 68(2, Spring 1989). pp.143-161.

2. *Ibid.*
3. *The Europa Yearbook 1990* (London), p. 1813.
4. *ibid.* See also *Working People's Daily* (Yangon), 23 September 1988.
5. *Assam Tribune (Guwahati)* 21 March 1992. See also *Eastern Courier (New* Delhi), 16 February 1992.
6. *The Far East and Australia 2000* (Europa Publications: London, 1999), p. 758.
7. *The Burma Review* (Rego Park. New York), vol. 31, January 1992, p. 13.
8. J. N. Dixit, *My South Block Years: Memoirs of a Foreign Secretary* (New Delhi, 1997 reprint of 1996). p.154.
9. *Eastern Courier.* 19 February 1992.
10. J. N. Dixit, *op.cit.*
11. Arthur S. Banks, Thomas C. Muller, eds. *Political Handbook of the World 1998: Government and Inter-governmental Organizations as of January 1.1998* (New York. 1998) p. 639.
12. John Bray, *Burma: The Politics of Constructive Engagement* (The Royal Institute of International Affairs, 1995) p.51.
13. *The Europa World Yearbook 1999*, Vol. 2 (London) p. 2520.
14. John Bray, *op. cit.* p.46.
15. *Ibid.*
16. There are a number of recent works dealing with Chinese influence and activities in Myanmar having security implications on India's Northeast and Eastern borders. See for instance, Andrew Selth, "The Burma and the Strategic Competition between China and India". In: John J. Brandon (ed.), *Burma/Myanmar in the Twenty-First Century: Dynamics of Continuity and Change* (Washington/Bangkok. 1997), pp.146-168. Maj.Gen (Retd), Dipankar Banerjee, *Myanmar and North East India* (Delhi Policy Group, New Delhi); J.Mohan Malik, "Sino-Indian Rivalry in Myanmar: Implications for Regional Security" *Contemporary Southeast Asia* (Singapore) vol. 16.no. 2. September 1994, pp. 137-156. also Malik. "Myanmar's Role in Regional Security: Pawn or Pivot", *ibid.* vol.19.no.1. June 1997, pp. 52-73. The same is also discussed in Jaya Jaitley and Jaya Roy, eds. *Report on*

the International Convention for the Restoration of Democracy in Burma (New Delhi, n. d), pp.132-159.

17. R. G. Sawhney, "Burma". In: U.S. Bajpai (ed.), *India and its Neighbourhood* (Lancer International, New Delhi 1986), p. 351.
18. J. N. Dixit, *op.cit.*, p.167.
19. *Ibid.*
20. Department of Commerce & Industries. Government of Manipur, *Notes on Indo-Myanmar Border Trade for the Visit of Parliamentary Standing Committee on Home Affairs during Their visit at Moreh, Manipur. 12-14 October* 1998 (Imphal)? n.d.), p.1.

15

Geo-economic and Geo-Strategic Importance of Myanmar in India's Look-East Policy

—UDAI BHANU SINGH

Introduction

India's "Look East" policy initiated in the early 1990s coincided with the timing of liberalization. It slowed down as the Southeast Asian region went through a phase of economic crisis. The policy has once again resumed with vigour. Geographically, India is the pivot of Western, Southern and Southeast Asia. In the post-Cold War period a new strategic and economic scenario began to emerge in which the Asia Pacific gained prominence. In the emerging strategic scenario, Myanmar is expected to play an important role because the dynamics of economics, geography and politics have placed it in a crucial position. Since India's Looks East policy is born of the conviction that the Pacific is bound to be the nerve centre of the future, Myanmar will continue to take priority in Indian thinking.

The Look East policy is premised on the assumption that India understands that the ASEAN region is important, placed as it is, between the Indian and the Pacific Oceans, it controls major trade routes and sea-lanes. Indian and ASEAN interests have become intertwined as became evident with ASEAN inviting India to an ASEAN-India Summit.[1] Economic cooperation has a great potential as India's Look East policy coincided with the timing of the economic liberalization. India had sought membership of Asia Pacific Economic Cooperation (APEC) forum. It is already an outside member of two workshops: science and technology; and energy. But because of the moratorium on membership its aspirations could not be fulfilled. India's concern for the region is evident from the fact that it is an active member of forums such as BIMST-EC, Ganga Mekong Project, and IOR-ARC. India has many economic and security reasons for adopting a Look East policy:

- India's large dimension and sharing maritime boundaries with ASEAN
- Need to protect resources like fisheries, oil and gas
- As a pioneer investor under UN Convention on the Law of the Sea (UNCLOS) it has a natural interest in the Indian Ocean.
- Need to tap alternative oil suppliers in Southeast Asia.
- India's opposition to link between trade and non-trade issues like labour standards and human rights. It seeks to coordinate policy with ASEAN in forums such as the World Trade Organization (WTO) and the Post Ministerial Conference (PMC) of ASEAN.
- India seeks to improve its bilateral trade with countries of East and Southeast Asia
- India is in a position to provide Information technology and educational facilities to some of these countries.

Background of India's Policy towards Myanmar

India's relations with Myanmar have seen many ups and downs. From being a buffer against China during British rule, the Burmese leadership developed a close understanding with its counterpart in India in the post-independence phase. Nehru supported U Nu (with military assistance) in tackling the insurgencies, which then riddled Burma. However, when General Ne Win captured power in 1962, he was not willing to reciprocate by helping India tackle its Naga problem in the frontier region. This was due to the fear of the People's Republic of China.

India's moral support to the pro-democracy forces in the 1988 uprising did not endear it to the Myanmarese regime, especially its request to the SLORC seeking the release of Aung San Suu Kyi. But realizing the limitations involved in pursuing its earlier policy when the rest of the world had adopted the policy of "engaging" the SLORC regime, it initiated a change of tack. In 1991 it was decided to discontinue criticism of the Myanmarese regime in All India Radio's (AIR) Burmese broadcasts. This policy was continued in the following year and in 1993, the Indian Foreign Secretary's visit to Yangon marked the coming closer of the two countries. An attempt was simultaneously made to curb the anti-SLORC activities of Myanmarese students in India.[2] But a section of the Indian intelligentsia, which supports the pro-democracy movement, is of the opinion that even the objective of neutralizing the Chinese influence does not justify collaboration with Yangon.

The change in policy can be appreciated in the context of the need to improve trade and commerce with neighbouring Southeast Asia in order to stimulate economic growth in India's Northeastern States; need to combat drug trafficking from the notorious Golden Triangle region ; need to obtain support of the Yangon regime in order to check insurgency in India's Northeast; ASEAN's own policy of "constructive engagement" of Myanmar (to the extent of according it membership of ASEAN); and the need to improve Sino-Indian relations and hence the requirement to meet China in Myanmar.

Geo-Strategic Importance

For India Myanmar's geo-strategic location at the tri-junction of East Asia, Southeast Asia and South Asia (between 10 and 28 degrees North latitude) is of critical significance. A boundary agreement between India and Myanmar was signed in 1967. Second, maritime boundary between the two countries was defined by a maritime delimitation agreement in 1986. Four Indian States border Myanmar - Arunachal Pradesh, Nagaland, Manipur and Mizoram. Similarly three

Myanmarese States border India - Kachin, Sagaing and Chin. Third, Myanmar shares land border with the other major Asian power - viz. China. Fourth, Myanmar's border with Bangladesh to its northwest is also crucial from India's perspective because it provides an alternative route (and a crucial one at that) to Myanmar and Southeast Asia. Here it is important to remember that the Northeast, through which the route to Myanmar traverses, is only tenuously linked (by a narrow stretch of land) to the rest of India. A route through Bangladesh would reduce the distances for most Indian states passing through our Northeastern states. Fifth, Myanmar shares borders with two Southeast Asian States: Thailand and Laos to its east. Sixth, both India and China understand Myanmar's maritime significance. In the south, it is washed by the Bay of Bengal, and in the southwest, by the Andaman Sea. China, which otherwise has no opening into the Indian Ocean can gain access through Myanmar. It is in close proximity to India's maritime trade routes. Myanmar's Coco Islands are cheek by jowl with India's Andaman and Nicobar islands.

The country's geography has played a significant role in shaping its ethnic profile and history. The horseshoe of mountains (comprising the Arakans in the west and the Shan plateau in the east) encloses the central Irrawaddy plain in the middle, which was the cradle of many cultures. The Irrawaddy river, which traverses from north to south (about 2,170 km) to complete its journey in the Andaman Sea, is central to the nation's life and economy. Its vast delta (240 km wide and 290 km long) provides the right conditions for rice cultivation. In Myanmar, it was the north-south flowing rivers (the Irrawaddy-Chindwin and the Salween), which provided the natural route of migration of peoples from Central Asia into the plains of Myanmar[3] just as the Himalayan passes in India's northwest provided invaders the route to settle in the Ganga-Yamuna *doab*. Once inside they were protected from invading Armies on all sides by the mountain ranges.

Border Management

India's interest in Myanmar can be explained in terms of that country's enormous strategic importance for us. India shares a 1643 km long border with Myanmar and a long maritime boundary. India wants Myanmar to ensure that the area west of Chindwin river (a tributary of Irrawady) remains free of the Chinese or Pakistani influence. Four States in India's Northeast border Myanmar: Arunachal Pradesh, Nagaland, Manipur and Mizoram. Secondly, it is important to seek stability on the Northeastern border by ensuring economic prosperity of the region especially in view of the fact that it is a land-bridge to the South East Asian region. Thirdly, there is a need to regulate border trade in order to curb drug trafficking and smuggling.

Growing Chinese influence in Myanmar

Relations with China have always been of supreme importance to Burma. In Myanmarese usage, Chinese are *toyok* or *pauk paw* (distant cousins) while all the rest are *kala* or foreigners. Myanmar's international isolation gave China an important opportunity to befriend the military regime. Sino-Myanmarese relations were "built on the basis of the clinical rationale of geography, strategy and politico-economic complementarities." Myanmar (then Burma) withdrew from the Non-Aligned Movement (NAM) at the sixth conference held at Havana (Cuba) on September 7, 1979. Myanmar's action was regarded as a veiled attack against the Soviet Union, aimed at pleasing China.

China provides support to Myanmar in international forum like the UN. (For instance, the PRC sought to stall resolutions in the UN Commission on Human Rights in Geneva in 1989 and 1990 and the UN General Assembly in 1990, critical of the SLORC's human rights record).[4] China and Myanmar have exchanged high level visits in the recent past.

The Chinese President Jiang Zemin paid a four-day visit to Myanmar in December 2001 when a border security pact was signed and agreed to expand cooperation in infrastructure construction and human and natural resources development. The Chinese military aid[5] plus the increased defence expenditure and modernization of the armed forces has meant that the SPDC has assiduously consolidated its base and the military intelligence has been strengthened.[6]

Sino-Myanmar Trade and Transit

Indian Defence Ministry Annual Reports have time and again pointed out India's concern. It has been noted that Beijing is engaged in building strategic road links from its border towns to railheads and seaports of Myanmar. It is helping to develop these ports.

Myanmar's northern cities like Mandalay are witnessing a slow demographic change, with Chinese immigrants from the bordering Yunnan province purchasing estates after "buying" Myanmar citizenship. Moreover, China is engaged in modernising Myanmar's infrastructure in order to expand its trade network further. There are also plans to build a 1,350-km railway through Laos, Myanmar and Kunming in China going up to Bangkok.[7] The rail network from Myitkyina near the Chinese border to Yangon via Mandalay has brought remote parts together and opened up Myanmar to Chinese economic expansion. China has also sold railroad equipment to Myanmar.

The old Stillwell road, which links Yunnan with north Myanmar, is already operational. China has built roads from three districts (i.e. Yinchaing, Lungchuan and Tengchung) of Yunnan province to Myanmarese towns.[8] A road was opened from Yinchaing to Taihone in January 1993; the second from Lianghe to Bahmo in April 1993; and the third from Myitkyina to Mangmin in May 1993.[9] The aim is to enable Yunnan to export to third countries via Myanmar. Access to the Indian Ocean would provide China an alternative route to vital markets. For the first time in 30 years a Chinese language newspaper, *Myanmar Morning Post* was allowed by the junta to be published.[10]

Chinese Interest in the Indian Ocean

Another major factor that draws India's attention to Myanmar is the problem of growing Chinese influence in Myanmar and influence in the Indian Ocean. A General of the Chinese Academy of Military Sciences has spoken of the Chinese Navy extending its naval operations into the Indian Ocean in order to prevent the Indian Ocean becoming "India's Ocean" and as such sought strategic outposts on Myanmarese islands. Factors such as these could have led India to station a tri-service Far Eastern Command in the Andamans and Nicobar islands.

Chinese Tapping Markets in SA/SEA

China-Myanmar trade had reached $750 million in 1995 but due to the economic crisis fell to $640 million in 1997 and $580 million in 1998. In comparison India-Myanmar trade stood at $ 216.52 million only in 1999-2000. However, its exports to India totalled $141.14 million making India its largest export market.[11] It is interesting to note that the Myanmarese Foreign Minister U Win Aung suggested at a meeting in Laos (which India's Foreign Minister also attended) including China in the Mekong Ganga Cooperation forum, as it was a Mekong country.

Pakistani Interests in Myanmar

Pakistan Chief Executive Pervez Musharraf's visit to Myanmar was preceded by port calls in the Bay of Bengal by two Pakistani warships.[12] A Pakistani presence in such close proximity to India's Northeast concerns New Delhi because of the possibility of Pakistani collaboration with insurgents. Pakistan supplied arms worth $2.5 million in March-April 1999.[13] It sent two delegations to visit Coco Islands in 1997-98.

The Problem of Drug Trafficking, Small Arms and AIDS:

Myanmar is the second largest producer of illicit opiates accounting for nearly 80 per cent of the world's drug supply. It forms part of the 'Golden Triangle' (which also includes Laos and Thailand) where the drugs problem has persisted for the last 20 years. Large tracts of land (99,300 hectares in 1999) are devoted to opium cultivation. 'Designer drugs' like amphetamine-type-stimulants (ATS) ('speed', 'ice' and 'ecstasy') are also produced.[14]

Yangon claims that it is doing all it can to control the drugs menace. It ratified the 1988 Vienna Convention against trafficking in illegal drugs. It has sought international help to deal with the problem. The world at large is equally concerned at the menace because the opium from Southeast

Asia finds its way into affluent countries like the United States: so in seeking to help they have their own vested interest in view. A major part of the funding to overcome the drug menace comes from Japan, the United States and the UNDCP (United Nations Drug Control Programme). The UNDCP launched the Wa Alternative Development Programme (a crop substitution project in northern Shan State) three years ago with a projected target of US$15.8 million. Under this project it hopes to spend another US$1.5million next year. However, it is feared that the US commitment to curb terrorism will constrain contributions to anti-drug projects.[15]

In 1976 the Americans had agreed to help but the stoppage of aid put a halt to that process in 1988. Though the US is in the forefront of the movement against drugs, it bears recounting that it was the American Central Intelligence Agency (CIA) which had in the initial period, supported the Kuomintang (KMT) to grow poppies in that border region for purely ideological and economic ends.[16]

It is interesting that the Chinese have evinced interest to cooperate with Myanmar on drug issues.[17] Both Beijing and Yangon sought to make political capital out of the reported surrender of Khun Sa in January 1996 to the State Law and Order Restoration Council. While China used this occasion to justify massive arms transfer ($400 million) to Yangon,[18] Myanmar attempted to clear itself from allegations of a nexus with the drugs trade. But Khun Sa's surrender did not quite deter drug movements.[19]

The officials of China, Myanmar, Thailand and Laos met in May 1993 to decide on linking the Golden Triangle area with a Golden Square Highway Network.

It is to tackle the drugs menace that the Myanmar-India joint coordination meeting on transnational crime involving drugs was held in Kalemyo.[20] Because of the proximity India is also concerned about the danger the drugs, AIDS, and illegal small arms pose to its Northeast. The war in Afghanistan and the tightening of security on the Indo-Pakistan border has reduced the supply of drugs from the west, but white heroin may be smuggled in from Myanmar in greater quantity.

Smuggling is two-way from the higher reaches of Manipur (as the Moreh border is better patrolled now). This means that ingredients (like ephidrine, psedoephidrine and acetic anhydride) required to purify opium into heroin, are first smuggled out from the Northeast into Myanmar, and then heroin is smuggled into India via the same route.[21]

It would be difficult for any Government to disregard international opinion on the drugs issue and Yangon is no exception. National commissions to check drug abuse, which were established in Myanmar and Laos respectively, have met periodically since 1990. On October 26, 1993 these countries signed the Memorandum of Understanding in New York to check drug abuse. More recently the ASEAN Summit in Brunei addressed this problem.[22]

Opposition leaders like Suu Kyi herself have drawn attention to the problem of drug abuse and the associated problem of spread of AIDS through the use of infected needles.[23] Myanmar has formed a National AIDS Committee and has laid down a four-year Master Strategic Plan-2002-2005 for HIV/AIDS prevention, control and care, in which both non-governmental and governmental agencies will participate.[24] Yangon also organised drug control training course with Japanese assistance for its police force.[25] It has also started drug detection course with Australian help.[26] As part of their anti-drug operations, the SPDC raided an opium refinery in Kokang, Shan States on information from the Chinese authorities.[27]

Tackling Insurgency:

Insurgent groups in India's Northeast and in Myanmar have been a source of concern for both the countries. The insurgents fleeing across the border and the existence of the light arms and drugs nexus have aggravated this problem. Close coordination between the security agencies on both sides is required for curbing insurgency in the border. The problem is aggravated by the fact that people of the same ethnic communities are found across the border. This makes detection and tracking them down that much more difficult. Second, following the opening of the Indo-Myanmar border to trade, the problem of controlling insurgency along the international border has increased. The two armies have cooperated closely, for instance, they held discussions in Kalemyo, Myanmar in November (2001) after the Myanmarese army arrested some 40 Manipur insurgents when it raided three underground camps at Tamu, Namphalong and Khunjao, near the Manipur border. These insurgents belonged to the United National Liberation Front, People's Liberation Army and People' Revolutionary Party of Kangleipak and were arrested between 2 and 10 November.[28] Some of the Northeast insurgent groups receive their supply of armaments through Myanmarese territory and it comes via Thailand and partly by the sea route. With the setting up of the base in Andamans and the patrolling of the Malacca Strait it is hoped that some check on insurgent activity could be possible.

Developing Military to Military Contacts

Lt. Gen Kalkat led a delegation on a study tour of Myanmar in September 2001 and he was received by Gen Maung Aye, Vice chairman of the SPDC. [29] India's Chief of Naval Staff Admiral Sushil Kumar visited Myanmar in January 2001. India's Home Secretary Kamal Pande participated in the annual security interaction in Myanmar in August 2000. India's Army Chief Gen. V.P. Malik visited Myanmar in July 2000 at the invitation of Gen Aye and was joined by the latter for a visit to Shillong in return. Myanmar's Gen. Aye and its Home Minister Tin Oo visited New Delhi in November 2000. Its Deputy Foreign Minister U Khin Maung Ming visited India twice – in May and October 2000.

Yangon has sought to diversify its arms procurement but it still does not favour procurement from India.[30]

Socio-Cultural Importance: Managing the Ethnic Diversity

Managing the kind of ethnic diversity that Myanmar has, is a challenging task indeed. The SPDC/SLORC was able to put pressure on a number of ethnic groups. The junta has negotiated several cease-fire agreements with the ethnic minorities. It negotiated cease-fire agreements with the Shan armies following the breakup of the Communist Party of Burma (CPB). To a certain extent this has allowed peace on the border. The problem faced by Myanmar today is, in some sense, a legacy left behind by the British colonial rulers who adopted the "divide and rule" policy. Myanmar is a land of remarkable ethnic diversity with a historical record of "divide and rule" under British colonial rule. What emerged as a consequence then was a distinct "Burma Proper" inhabited by the majority Burman community[31] and "Outer Burma" inhabited mainly by the minorities. While "Burma Proper" was directly administered under British India, the minorities were allowed greater autonomy.[32] According to Myanmar's Foreign Minister U Win Aung the problem of disunity was a legacy of the British Raj. He said: "Right now, we are 135 national races living together in the union.... We cannot afford to disintegrate... we are living between two most populous nations - India and China. How can we afford to have small pieces? It will not do any good for the security of both (these) countries too. Also, if we disintegrate into small pieces, our region will not have stability."[33]

The Burmans, the largest ethnic group, and mainly Buddhist, are concentrated on either side of the Irrawaddy in central Myanmar.[34] In number they are estimated to be from half to two-thirds of total Myanmarese population.[35] The Karens are the largest minority group but no reliable statistics are available for the post-independence period. It was the 1931 census, which attempted to give the ethnic breakdown of the country. Presently the Karen population is roughly estimated to be 3 to 4 million. Shans and Mons are approximately 4 million each. After them are the Buddhist Arakanese (Rakhine), the Muslim Arakanese (Rohingyas), the Chins, Kachins and Palaung-Wa.[36]

The Karen opposition group, which constantly faced the government's wrath, was the Karen National Union (KNU). Following the failure of talks with the KNU the government launched an attack in February 1997 on Karen enclaves along the Thai border. There are more than 70,000 refugees in these camps. The Karenni National Progressive Party (KNPP) is too weak to be a real threat to the SPDC.[37] The SLORC/SPDC led several attacks on the Karen positions. The most significant was the fall of Manerplaw, the headquarters of the Karen National Union (KNU) on the Thai-Myanmar border on January 26, 1995.[38] This was followed by the successful attack on the smaller Karen enclave at Kawmoora, some 60 km south of Manerplaw.[39]

Indian Minority Community:

The Indian government is today exercised over the issue of safeguarding the interests of people of Indian origin in Myanmar. As it happens, the Indian community has prospered under the military regime. At present, their number exceeds 500,000 (428,000 by the last census). Buddhism is our greatest asset in Myanmar and India is still referred to as *Madhyadesa*. Till the period extending up to World War II, Indians held positions in the security organizations and administration of Burma and controlled a large part of the Burmese economy. In fact, the Chettiars held 62 per cent of land as a consequence of their money lending business, and Rangoon then had a population, which comprised 52 per cent Indians.[40] It was Gen. Ne Win's policy of nationalization that led to a mass exodus of (150,000) Indians from Burma and a decline in Indo-Burmese relations.

Geo-Economic Importance: Developing our Northeast

Overview

A stable economy is a necessary precondition for a stable government. Though SPDC heads a country with considerable natural resources, it still remains a poor country in South East Asia with a low per capita income. There is rising inflation, marginally reduced foreign investment, erratic electric supply, fall in tourist inflow and collapse of property prices. A realistic estimate for GDP growth in 1999/2000 would be 6 per cent and not the exaggerated 10.9 per cent claimed by Myanmar Government.[41] The exchange rate of the currency has gone out of control. Myanmar Government claims to have checked inflation rate but it is still high. Myanmar follows the fixed exchange rate system where the rate of exchange of the currency has been artificially managed by the State. The value of the *kyat* (Myanmarese currency) corresponding to the US dollar in the market plunged dramatically in October 2000 falling to about Kt. 450 to the dollar. But Yangon is wary of devaluation, which it fears could fuel inflation further. It has also found it difficult to keep the fiscal deficit in check. The SPDC also dismissed rumours of demonetization of the currency.[42] In the midst of all this, the parallel economy is flourishing. Smuggling on its borders with China, Thailand and India continues apace.

Infrastructure Development

In keeping with the understanding of holistic approach to security, further development of the communication link between India and Myanmar is necessary. In order to bring prosperity through trade physically connecting the underdeveloped Northeast to the business centres of Southeast Asia now seems the most obvious thing to do. "The Northeast could well turn out to be the gateway to Southeast Asia," said Manipur chief minister Okram Ibobi Singh.[43]

First road and communication constitute important elements of infrastructure in any country's economy. [44] Second, India has helped Myanmar build roads so that surface transport gives a boost to trade and tourism. Third, it is our only road link to Southeast Asia. India has a long land border with Myanmar, which has become an ASEAN member. Fourth, growing economic linkages (especially, trade and commerce) with Southeast Asia are important for the development of our Northeast. On the one hand these states are in the grip of law and order problems and on the other they have somehow been left out of the national mainstream in terms of development. Good road network on our borders with Myanmar will reduce the response time in dealing with insurgents. Fifth, roads are an important factor in view of Myanmar's strategic location between India and China.

India's External Affairs Minister, Mr. Jaswant Singh inaugurated the 160km long Tamu-Kalewa-Kalemyo road on February 13, 2001. The national highway 39 which terminated at Moreh in Manipur was extended. It now links Moreh town to Kalemyo in central Myanmar. Kalewa will get further linked to Mandalay once the Monywa-Yargyi-Myoma-Kalewa Road project is completed. (Monywa is already connected to Mandalay). It would be an important segment in the proposed Asian Highway linking Singapore with Istanbul. Myanmar

Foreign Minister U Win Aung suggested the possibility of India and Myanmar developing a deep sea port at Kyaukpyu, providing a linkage to Mizoram in India.[45] The air link between India and Myanmar was restored after a gap of two decades in December 1995.

The road link to Myanmar is important for at least three reasons: as a link to rest of Southeast Asia; economic reasons and in order to tackle insurgency across the border. Myanmar Foreign Minister U Win Aung said: "Good communication and ease of transport will not only enhance security but will also spur the movement of goods between the border region and the interior of the country."[46] Later, India signed a Memorandum of Understanding (MoU) with Myanmar by which it undertook the responsibility for the maintenance of the road for the first six years.[47] This has to be seen in conjunction with other developments occuring at a hectic pace simultaneously. The Eurasian land bridge plan - the Silk Road - is being actively developed.[48] Hence the need for India to link up with Southeast Asia by the road route.

Myanmar Foreign Minister U Win Aung suggested the possibility of India and Myanmar developing a deep seaport at Kyaukpyu, providing a linkage to Mizoram.[49] India and Myanmar are already cooperating in the field of hydel projects and in information technology.[50]

It is in this context that the call for building an airfield at Pygmalion Point (Indira Gandhi Point) and an airbase at Cambell Bay for the surveillance and policing of the Straits of Malacca[51] becomes relevant. A proposal in 1975 to develop the airfield was not taken up then because of the high cost involved and for fear of offending the Indonesian and Malaysian governments.[52] But in the changed international and regional environment, such a move may not elicit an unfavourable response from the ASEAN.

Earlier on, an important development was the signing of a border agreement on March 10, 1967. For economic recovery of Myanmar "a resumption of aid from multilateral agencies is the key", according to Scott Rosenberg of the Broker Group, a business and trade consultancy of Indochina. Japan had been the major source of aid to Myanmar till the crackdown on the democratic movement.

Trade

India's total trade of $216.52 in 1999-2000 does not compare favourably with China's trade of $580 million in 1998 with Myanmar. Myanmar set up in 1996 a Committee for the Promotion of Myanmar-China Economic Cooperation. While Singapore and Thailand are the top trading partners of Myanmar, China is the third. India and Myanmar signed a border trade agreement in April 1994. Moreh (Manipur) - Tamu (Sagaing division, Myanmar) border trade began a year later in April 1995.

Tourism

As part of India's Look East policy there are attempts to enhance tourism, trade and economic cooperation with Southeast Asia. On April 4 this year the Guwahati-Bangkok flight was inaugurated and it is hoped this will lead to a growth in tourism in the North East. India and Myanmar were brought closer to each other when air link between India and Myanmar was restored after a gap of two decades. Indian Airlines introduced bi-weekly flights from Calcutta to Yangon from December 7, 1995 but facilities will need to be improved for the Northeast to attract more tourists[53] . The Northeast accounts for only 0.5 per cent of the tourist traffic into the country, though it has excellent natural heritage.[54] The proposed setting up of a Hotel Management Institute in Shillong[55] will fill the gaps in terms of facilities for tourists. China too has been active. On April 1, 2002, the Chinese Yunnan Airways inaugurated an air link between Kunming (China) and Mandalay (second largest city of Myanmar).[56]

Investment

Investment is important to any country. Hence it is not very surprising that pressed by the advancing market forces and the need to supplement Chinese aid the Yangon regime began wooing foreign capital and nations were vying with each other to bag contracts from Myanmar. It has liberalized its foreign investment laws giving a three-year tax holiday and allowing repatriation of profits. In drafting its Foreign Investment Law in 1998, it sought to streamline procedure and provide guarantees and incentives to investors.

By April 1997 the total foreign investments had risen to $6 billion from $5.3 billion in December 1996. The largest investments have been in the oil and natural gas sectors In 1997 the United Kingdom replaced Singapore as the top investor in Myanmar with an investment of $1.3 billion as against Singapore's $1.2 billion.[57] In fact, foreign investors became more daring, especially after Singapore Prime Minister Goh Chok Tong's visit in March 1994.[58] After Myanmar became a full-fledged member of the ASEAN, the possibilities of trade and investment with the ASEAN further increased. It also became member of BIMST-EC,[59] the organization to promote economic cooperation in the sub-region,(not a trade bloc) when the grouping met in Bangkok on December 21, 1998.[60]

Myanmar's British legacy of English language, an effective legal system and an already existing patent and copyright law are expected to attract foreign investors. These developments have entailed a need to be more responsive to the Western call for improving the human rights status.[61]

Energy

Thailand had been an important market for Myanmar's natural gas but with the contract due to expire soon and not likely to be continued, India could be a likely market. The gas pipeline could be laid through Bangladesh (provided Dhaka does not raise political objections) under BIMST-EC auspices.[62] From India's perspective, it is worth considering Myanmar as a source of energy in the light of the fact that our overall import dependence for energy, which is currently 14 per cent and likely to increase to around 40 percent by 2010, would increase still further by 2020. India is the fourth largest oil consumer in the Asia Pacific.[63]

Myanmar has recently confirmed plan to commission a 10-MW nuclear reactor from Russia. At the same time reports stated that Myanmar had given refuge to two Pakistani nuclear scientists – something strongly denied by Yangon. [64]

Armed Forces

The growth of military power can be estimated by the various indicators like the quantum of military expenditure, strength of armed forces and paramilitary forces. Myanmar has been rapidly modernizing its armed forces and equipping them with sophisticated aircraft, air defence weapons and upgrading its naval capabilities. The *Tatmadaw Yay* (Navy) controls a few bases[65] and Naval Infantry has been deployed for counter-insurgency operations in Arakan and Tenasserim coastal regions and to the Irawaddy delta.

It procures arms from many countries like China, Israel, Pakistan, Portugal, North Korea and Singapore.[66] An arms deal worth over $1 billion was struck with China during Gen Than Shwe's visit to Beijing in 1989. Myanmar signed a second defence contract in November 1994 with China for the supply of helicopters, armoured vehicles, field guns, assault rifles and patrol boats.[67]

Singapore is the other important arms supplier to Myanmar. It provided 84mm rockets for Myanmar's M2 Carl Gustav recoilless guns, which were made in Singapore under license from a Swedish company.[68] Singapore also sold second-hand RPG2 grenade launchers and 57 mm anti-tank guns.[69] Pakistan sold $2.5 million worth of arms to Myanmar in 1999, while India remained content with supplying some "military support" equipment.[70] Myanmar signed a contract worth $130 million for 10 MiG-29s from Russia and has since taken delivery of the fighter aircrafts.

Myanmar's defence expenditure has shown a steep and steady incline: it is one country in Southeast Asia, which has witnessed massive infusion of resources into the defence sector for two decades. The defence expenditure has seen a significant increase from K1.35 billion in 1980 to K 1.80 billion in 1986 to K 8.3 billion in 1994 to K 32 billion ($2.1 billion) in 2000. The armed forces have been increasing substantially since nearly two decades: in 1985 the figure stood at 186,000; in 1994 - 286,000 and in 2001 at 444,000.[71] New artillery and infantry battalions in the northern State of Kachin have been planned.[72] The expansion of Myanmar's military has caused concern to neighbours like Thailand. It is true that the strength of the armed forces is an indicator of Myanmar's growing military power. However, unless the sharp increase in the manpower and military equipment is accompanied by generating a suitable catchment area, and fine-tuning of the recruitment and training and maintenance processes, there could be problems in the long run. The military has a unique place in Southeast Asian countries. The military tends to be eulogized in Myanmar and the military permeates all sectors of society. It is said to have become a "state within a state".[73] Military-civilian fissures have the potential to create disruption in any traditional society, but in a country with great disparities this becomes even more likely.

Military doctrine had been dominated by the imperatives of counter-insurgency in the past; it is now adjusting the doctrine to the requirements of more conventional roles. Myanmar has borders with five countries- Laos, Thailand, Bangladesh, India and China. The presence of identical ethnic groups across borders further complicates the problem as ethnic insurgents seek refuge in neighbouring countries (as in Thailand and India).

There has been a re-organization of the SPDC leadership. While Secretary-3 Lt-Gen Win Myint and Deputy Prime Minister Lt-Gen Tin Hla were both dismissed, Secretary-2 Lt-Gen Tin Oo died in a helicopter crash.[74] Ten regional commanders were recalled to Yangon. The Triangle Region Commander Maj-Gen Thein Sein took over as the Adjutant General and Northeast Commander Maj-Gen Thiha Thura Tin Aung Myint Oo as the Quartermaster General. Earlier, Lt Gen Win Myint and Lt-Gen Tin Hla were dismissed from their post of Adjutant General and Quartermaster General respectively.[75] It has been surmised that the reorganization was done to check the growing power of the regional commanders.

It is significant that Myanmar has been rated among the top ten exponents of information warfare. A Directorate of Defence Services Computers (DDSC)[76] was created around 1990. Singapore's help was taken to install a network linking Yangon with the 12 Regional Military Commands. A basic course for C4I warfare and a computer science course are on offer for the defence forces.[77]

Conclusion

Myanmar will continue to be important to India since India's Look East policy is destined to shape our attitude towards the Asia Pacific for the foreseeable future. Myanmar's military junta appears to have weathered the domestic political storm and the economic and political turbulence in the region. If economics is the final arbiter of rule-legitimacy, then SPDC is on test. Yangon's success and survival would depend on its domestic acceptability and the extent to which it succeeds in establishing stability rather than the response it evokes from outsiders.

NOTES

1. India is already an ARF member, ASEAN's full dialogue partner and a CSCAP member.
2. Suhas Chakma, "Burma's rulers and the emerging alliances," *Pioneer,* January 21, 1994.
3. Martin Smith, *Burma: Insurgency and the Politics of Ethnicity* (London and New Jersey: Zed Books, 1991), p.31.
4. For details on the extent of this support see, Udai Bhanu Singh, "Recent Trends in Relations between Myanmar and China", *Strategic Analysis* (New Delhi), 18 (1), April 1995, pp.61-72.
5. Andrew Selth, 'Burma's Arms Procurement Programme', *Working Paper No. 289*, Strategic and Defence Studies Centre, Australian National University, 1995
6. Details in, Andrew Selth, "Myanmar revamps its military intelligence apparatus", *Asia-Pacific Defence Reporter*, Jun-July 1998, pp.11-12.
7. J. Mohan Malik, "Sino-Indian rivalry in Myanmar: Implications for Regional Security", *Contemporary Southeast Asia* (Singapore: Institute of Southeast Asian Studies) 16 (2), September 1994, pp.1099-1113.
8. Mya Maung, "On the road to Mandalay: A case study of the Sinonization of Upper Burma", *Asian Survey*, 34 (5), May 1994.
9. *Ibid.*

10. There were six Chinese language newspapers in the 1960s until their permits were terminated on January 1, 1966. Refer, British Broadcasting Corporation, *Summary of World Broadcasts: Far East* (hereafter cited as BBC-SWB)-3376, B/ 1, Nov 5, 1998.
11. Amit Baruah, "India steps up efforts towards engaging Myanmar," *The Hindu* February 12, 2001.
12. Atul Aneja, "Pakistan naval ships in Myanmar on eve of Musharraf visit," *The Hindu* May 1, 2001.
13. Atul Aneja, "India, Myanmar discuss security," *The Hindu,* November 19, 2000
14. Ananda Rajah, *Burma: Protracted Conflict, Governance and Non-Traditional Security Issues*, IDSS Working Paper No.14, Institute of Defence and Strategic Studies, Singapore, May 2001.
15. "Burma: UN agency earmarks 1.5m dollars on Wa drug project-paper," The Myanmar Times web site, Rangoon, in English, November 5, 2001, in *BBC Monitoring Global Newsline-* Asia Pacific Political, November 14, 2001.
16. Sunanda K. Datta-Ray, "A nuclear China weighs heavy on ASEAN's mind", *Pioneer* (New Delhi), January 16, 1995.
17. See, "Visiting Chinese Official Urges Cooperation on Drug Issues", *SWB-FE-2485, B/3,* December 13, 1995. Cited in *IDSA South East Asia Newsreview* (New Delhi), January 1996.
18. In December 1994 Chinese Prime Minister Li Peng had voiced the need to check the drug problem in Myanmar.
19. According to the Bureau for International Narcotics and Enforcement Affairs of the US State Department, the opium yield for 1996 was 9 per cent more than in 1995.
20. "Burma: Anti-drug coordination meeting held with India," Radio Myanmar, Rangoon, in Burmese, September 14, 2001 in *BBC Monitoring Global Newsline*, Asia Pacific Political, September 16, 2001.
21. Chitra Subramnyam, "Heroin may flow in from Myanmar," *Indian Express*, January 2, 2002.
22. "Burma: Lao national assembly president visits to further cement ties," *The New Light of Myanmar* web site, Rangoon, in English, November 18, 2001 in *BBC Monitoring Global Newsline-* Asia Pacific Political, December 20, 2001.

23. "Suu Kyi expresses concern About 'Growing' Drug Problem", *BBC-SWB-FE-2479*, B/1, December 30, 1995. Cited in *IDSA South East Asia Newsreview*, January 1996.
24. "Leader Khin Nyunt says Burma committed to fight HIV/ AIDS as national cause," Radio Myanmar, Rangoon, in Burmese December 1, 2001 in *BBC Monitoring Global Newsline*- Asia Pacific Political, December 3, 2001.
25. "Burma: Drug Control Training Course opens with Japanese aid," *The New Light of Myanmar* web site, Rangoon, in English, December 4, 2001 in *BBC Monitoring Global Newsline- Asia Pacific Political*, December 5, 2001.
26. "Burma: Australia-sponsored drug detection course opens in Mandalay," TV Myanmar, Rangoon, in Burmese, November 19, 2001, in *BBC Monitoring Global Newsline- Asia Pacific Political*, November 21, 2001.
27. "Burmese authorities raid opium refinery in Kokang, Shan States," *Democratic Voice of Burma*, Oslo, in Burmese, November 13, 2001, in *BBC Monitoring Global Newsline* - Asia Pacific Political, November 16, 2001.
28. *BBC Monitoring Global Newsline*- Asia Pacific Political, November 24, 2001.
29. "Burma: Maung Aye receives head of India's Eastern Command," TV Myanmar, Rangoon, in Burmese, September 26, 2001 in *BBC Monitoring Global Newsline* - Asia Pacific Political, September 28, 2001.
30. It is felt in Yangon that Chinese weaponry suffers from the lack of accuracy and durability. Since Moscow is the principal arms supplier to India it is preferred over India as it is the 'mother' supplier.
31. "Burman" refers to an ethnic community while "Burmese" pertains to the nationality.
32. Gottberg Andeson,ed., *Insight Guides: Burma* First edition (Hong Kong: Apa Productions, 1981).
33. PS Suryanarayana, "Myanmar needs firm democracy", *The Hindu* (Delhi), December 20, 1998.
34. John Bray,"Ethnic minorities and the future of Burma", *The World Today*, August/September 1992, p. 145.
35. *Ibid.*
36. Smith, n.3.

37. Bruce Hawke, "Burma's ceasefire agreements in danger of unravelling", *Jane's Intelligence Review,* November 1998. Pp.23-27.
38. "The fall of Manerplaw: The Karens are in disarray as SLORC scores big", *Asiaweek,* February 1995
39. "SLORC's successes," *Times of India* (New Delhi), February 24, 1995.
40. Malik, PMS, "South East Asia and Myanmar: Political and Military Implications for India". Proceedings of a seminar on the Emerging Security Environment in South East Asia with Special Reference to Myanmar, CASS, Pune, India, 2-3 December 1995.
41. For details, *Regional Outlook: Southeast Asia 2001-2002,* Institute of Southeast Asian Studies, Singapore, 2001.
42. 'Burmese junta blames "unscrupulous persons" for demonetization rumours,' Radio Myanmar, Rangoon, in Burmese, November 17, 2001, in *BBC Monitoring Global Newsline* - Asia Pacific Political, November 19, 2001.
43. Syed Zakir Hussain, N-E CMs welcome road link to Thailand, *The Asian Age* (New Delhi), April 9, 2002.
44. Yangon seems conscious of this and communication network is being enlarged. It launched the country's first FM station in November. ("Burma: Rangoon development committee launches FM radio station," The Myanmar Times website, Rangoon, in English, 21 November 2001, in *BBC Monitoring Global Newsline*- Asia Pacific Political, 23 November). Further, it ushered in e-Education starting January 2001.
45. Amit Baruah, "We will help combat insurgency: Myanmar", *The Hindu*, February 17, 2001.
46. Interview: Myanmar Enters the New Century, World Affairs, April-June 2001, Vol.5, no.2.
47. Amit Baruah, "India to maintain Myanmar road,"*The Hindu*, May 26, 2001.
48. Ramtanu Maitra and Susan Maitra, "India awakens to land-bridge potential," *Executive Intelligence Review*, January1, 1997.
49. Amit Baruah, "We will help combat insurgency: Myanmar", *The Hindu*, February 17, 2001.
50. Amit Baruah, "We will help combat insurgency: Myanmar", *The Hindu*, February 17, 2001.

51. Lt Gen. J.F.R. Jacob, "Delhi should build relations with Rangoon", *The Asian Age*, Novemebr 10, 1994, p.13.
52. *Ibid.*
53. *BBC/SWB/FE/2479*, A/2, December 6, 1995.
54. Sobhapati Samom, "Manipur misses the boat", and Krishna Das, "Passage to Bangkok," *Northeast Sun*, April 15-30, 2002, Vol. 7, No.8. At the national level the tourist arrival figure rests at 2.6 million only. Only 0.9 per cent of the tourists come from Southeast Asia (while 58 per cent come from Europe and 18 per cent from United States).
55. *Ibid.*
56. Xinhua, "Chinese Yunnan Airways Opens Air Link with Myanmar," *FBIS-CHI-2002-0401*
57. *Asian Development Outlook 1998*. For detailed study see, Joseph L.H. Tan, *Singapore's Foreign Direct Investment in Indochina & Myanmar: Opportunities & Challenges* (New Delhi: Research and Information System for the Non-Aligned and Other Developing Countries).
58. Michael Vatikiotis, "Burma: Catching the Wave", *Far Eastern Economic Review*, February 16, 1995.
59. "Burma takes its place at BIST-EC table", *Bangkok Post* (Bangkok), December 19, 1997
60. Its precursor was BIST-EC (before Myanmar elongated the acronym) with its proclaimed objective of "creat[ing] an enabling environment for rapid economic development, through identification and implementation of specific cooperation projects in the sectors of trade, investment and industry, technology, human resource development, tourism, agriculture, energy and infrastructure and transportation". See V Jayanth, "A forum for co-operation: Another sub-regional grouping in Asia," *Frontline,* July 11, 1997. Also see, V Jayanth "Myanmar to find place in regional grouping," *The Hindu,* November 27, 1997
61. "Significant Initiative by Burma Junta", (editorial), *Le Monde* (Paris), September 22, 1994 in *Guardian Weekly*, October 2, 1994, vol.151, no.4.
62. "India, Myanmar take stock of ties," *The Hindu*, October 10, 2000.
63. The top three are Japan, China and South Korea. India's demand for petroleum products is set to increase from US$96 million tonnes currently to 195 million tonnes per annum by

2011-12. India would have to reduce its dependence on West Asian oil and gas, and diversify its sources of energy. Similarly our import dependence on oil is around 40 per cent, which is likely to increase to 70 per cent by 2010. Our import dependence on natural gas is likely to rise to 43 per cent by 2010. For more details, G Parthasarathy, 'Look East for Energy Security", *Pioneer* (New Delhi) 5 July 2001.

64. Yangon has sought to put at rest international apprehensions on its nuclear programme. It explained that Myanmar joined IAEA in 1957, signed the nuclear Non-Proliferation Treaty in 1992, signed (1995) and ratified (1996) the SEA Nuclear Weapon Free Zone Treaty, and participated in UN's non-proliferation effort through its chairmanship of the First Committee of the UN General Assembly in 2000. The NPT recognizes the sovereign right of the signatories to strive for the peaceful use of nuclear technology. See "Burma gives reasons for planned nuclear research reactor project," *TV Myanmar*, in Burmese, January 21, 2002, in *BBC Monitoring Global Newsline*- Asia Pacific Political, December 23, 2002. Also see "Russia confirms plan to commission nuclear reactor in Burma," *ITAR-TASS* news agency, Moscow, in Russian, January 22, 2002 in *BBC Monitoring Global Newsline* - Asia Pacific Political, December 23, 2002. Editorial in *Washington Post*, January 6, 2002.

65. These are: Bassein, Mergui, Moulmein, Yangon, Seikyi, Sittwe (Akyab), Sinmalaik, Hanggyi Island, Kyaukpyu, and Sandoway.

66. Micool Brooke, "Myanmar's Security Challenges for the 21st century," *Asian Defence Journal* (Kuala Lumpur), July 2001.

67. *Jane's Defence Weekly*, November 30, 1994.

68. This was reported by Bertil Lintner and cited in Andrew Selth, 'Burma's Arms Procurement Programme', *Working Paper No. 289*, Strategic and Defence Studies Centre, Australian National University, 1995.

69. *Ibid.*

70. Brooke, n. 36

71. Various issues of *Military Balance*.

72. "Burmese junta to build new artillery, infantry battalions in north," *Democratic Voice of Burma*, Oslo, in Burmese, January 11, 2002,in in *BBC Monitoring Global Newsline - Asia Pacific Political*, January 13, 2002.

73. Report on the International Conference on Myanmar organised by Georgetown University, USA in February 2001.
74. "Burmese opposition radio reports military shake-up," Democratic Voice of Burma, Oslo, in Burmese, November 14, 2001, in *BBC Monitoring Global Newsline- Asia Pacific Political*, November 21, 2001.
75. *Ibid.*
76. Nicknamed 'Cyber Warfare Department'. It is also tasked with enhancing Myanmar's Signals intelligence (SIGINT) capabilities.
77. William Ashton, "Myanmar boosts cyber war abilities," *The Defence Reporter: Australia and Asia-Pacific*, October 2001.

SELECT CHRONOLOGY: INDIA-MYANMAR RELATIONS 1991-2002

1991:

- May: All India Radio's Burmese service discontinues its broadcasts critical of SLORC.
- November: New Delhi calls for unconditional release of Aung San Suu Kyi.

1992:

- China and Myanmar sign agreement on cooperation in tourism.
- August: Director General of the Myanmar Foreign Office visits India.
- August 11-14: Myanmar's U Aye, Director-General of the Political Affairs Department of the Ministry of Foreign Affairs meets Indian Government officials (MEA, MOD, Home and Commerce).
- December: India votes in favour of a UN resolution on Myanmar calling for an early restoration of democracy and human rights and immediate and unconditional release of Aung San Suu Kyi.

1993:

- March 29-31: Indian Foreign Secretary JN Dixit visits Myanmar.
- June: The Council for Security Cooperation in the Asia Pacific (CSCAP) founded.
- September: India's Surveyor General visits Myanmar to work out a schedule for joint inspection and maintenance of boundary pillars.

- October 27: India, Myanmar and Thailand sign a Tripartite Maritime Agreement determining T-point in the Andaman Seas.

1994:

- January 19-24: Myanmar's Deputy Foreign Minister U Nyunt Swe visits India. An MoU on Cooperation between Civilian Border Authorities and a Border Trade Agreement are signed.
- April 21: Border Trade Agreement signed between India and Myanmar.
- May: India's Army Chief visits Yangon.
- December: Institute for Defence Studies and Analyses (IDSA) admitted as Associate Member of CSCAP.

1995

- April 14: Border trade between Moreh (Manipur) and Tamu (Sagaing Division) opened.
- November 14: Aung San Suu Kyi is conferred Jawaharlal Nehru Award for International Understanding for 1993 in New Delhi.

1996

- July: India participates for first time in the Post Ministerial Conference and the Third ARF held in Jakarta. India's Minister of External Affairs IK Gujral represents India as Full Dialogue Partner of the ASEAN.

1997

- June: Bangladesh-India-Sri Lanka-Thailand Economic Cooperation (BISTEC) is launched.
- November: SLORC dissolved and is reconstituted as State Peace and Development Council (SPDC).
- December: Myanmar is admitted to BIST-EC, making it BIMST-EC

1998

- April 28: The Second ASEAN-India Joint Cooperation Committee (JCC) meeting held in Singapore through April 29. It was decided to establish a Working Group on Trade and Investment.
- July 26: India participates in the32nd ASEAN-PMC and the Sixth ARF Session held in Singapore. Led by External Affairs Minister Jaswant Singh.

1999

- India and Myanmar sign an agreement on science and technology
- July: Myanmar's Deputy Home Minister visits India.
- December: Myanmar's Railway Minister visits India.

2000

- January: India's Chief of Army Staff General VP Malik visits Myanmar
- May: Myanmar's Deputy Foreign Minister U Khin Maung Ming visits India.
- June 1-3: India's External Affairs Minister Jaswant Singh visits Singapore. Speaks on "India and ASEAN: Security Paradigm AD-2000".
- July 4: Indian Chief of Army Staff General VP Malik makes his second visit in 2000 to Myanmar at the invitation of Gen. Maung Aye.
- July 6: BIMSTEC's third meeting held in India.
- August 28-31: India's Home Secretary Mr Kamal Pande leads delegation to Yangon for the annual security interaction (to discuss drug trafficking and trade related issues).
- September: India's Secretary (Bio-technology) Mrs Manju Sharma visits Myanmar.
- October 18: Myanmar's Deputy Foreign Minister U Khin Maung Win pays his second visit during the year to India.
- November 8-11: India's External Affairs Minister Jaswant Singh visits Laos. The Mekong Ganga

Cooperation (MGC) is launched at Vientiane by India, Cambodia, Laos, Vietnam, Thailand and Myanmar.

- November 14-21: SPDC Vice Chairman Maung Aye visits India.
- November: Myanmar's Home Minister Col. Tin Oo visits India.
- November 21, New Delhi: India-Myanmar Joint Statement.

2001

- China and Myanmar sign an MoU on the implementation plan for outbound travel to Myanmar by Chinese citizens.
- January: India's Chief of Naval Staff, Admiral Sushil Kumar visits Myanmar.
- February: India's External Affairs Minister Jaswant Singh visits Myanmar. Inaugurates the 160 km long Tamu-Kalewa-Kalemyo road.
- February: SPDC Secretary-2 Lt. Gen. Tin Oo killed in a helicopter crash.
- July 27: India participates in the seventh ARF session held in Bangkok.
- November 10: SPDC Secretary-3 Lt General Win Myint; and Deputy-PM and Minister for Military Affairs Lt Gen Tin Hla "retired" from office. Five others reported retired include two Deputy PMs-Vice -Admiral Maung Maung Khin (72) and Lt. Gen Tin Tun (70); and Culture Minister Mr Win Sen, Cooperative Minister Mr Aung San and Immigration Minister Mr. Saw Tun.
- December 12: Chinese President Jiang Zemin arrived in Yangon for a four-day visit marking the first such visit since 1985.

2002

- February 27: All India Radio (AIR) launches its digital satellite home service for Southeast Asia and the Indian subcontinent.

- March: Relatives of Ne Win arrested for plotting coup against Yangon government.
- March: Myanmar's Police Chief Col. Soe Win; head of the air force- Commander in Chief Air Major General Myint Swe; and Brigadier General Chit Than were sacked in connection with the attempted coup.
- April: It was revealed that India's Cabinet Committee on Security (CCS) cleared in February a proposal for joint patrolling by India and the United States of the Malacca Straits.
- April 4: Air India's first Guwahati-Bangkok flight launched.
- April 4: India's External Affairs Minister Jaswant Singh arrives in Bangkok.

APPENDIX 1

Myanmar: SPDC Troika:

Name	Position
1. Senior General Than Shwe	Chairman, SPDC; PM; Minister of Defence; C-in-C of TatmadawHead of State
2. General Maung Aye	Vice-chairman, SPDCDeputy C-in-C of TatmadawC-in-C of the Army
3. Lt.-General Khin Nyunt	Secretary-1 of the SPDC; Chief of Military Intelligence.

APPENDIX 2

Myanmar: New Assignments to senior military posts (Ministry of Defence) in Yangon for the 10 former Regional Commanders: (shifted in November 2001)

	Name	Command
1.	Maj-Gen Khin Maung Than	Chiefs of Bureau of Special
2.	Maj-Gen Ye Myint	Operations.
3.	Maj-Gen Maung Bo	
4.	Maj-Gen Aung Htwe	
5.	Maj-Gen Thura Shwe Mann	Joint chief of staff of the Army, Navy, and Air Force
6.	Brig Gen Myat Hein	Chief of Staff of Air Defence
7.	Maj-Gen Tin Aye	Chief of Military Ordnance
8.	Maj-Gen Kyaw Win	Chief of Military Training. Chairman of the Committee for Holding 57th Armed Forces Day
9.	Maj-Gen Thein Sein	Adjutant-General
10.	Maj-Gen Thiha Thura Tin Aung Myint Oo	Quartermaster General

Source: Table derived from "Burmese junta to build new artillery, infantry battalions in north," *Democratic Voice of Burma*, Oslo, in Burmese, January 11, 2002, in *BBC Monitoring Global Newsline-Asia Pacific Political*, January 13, 2001

APPENDIX 3

Myanmar: Military and Police Force

Name	Position
Military:	
Rear Admiral Kyi Min	C-in-C of Navy
Brig-Gen Myat Hein	C-in-C of Air Force
Police Force:	
Col Soe Win (dismissed in March 2002)	Director General
Col Hla Tun	Deputy Director General

APPENDIX 4

Myanmar: 12 Regional Commands and some newly appointed commanders

Command	Place	Commanders
Northern Command	Myitkyina	Brig-Gen Maung Maung Swe
North East Command	Lashio	Brig-Gen Myint Hlaing
Eastern Command	Taunggyi	Brig-Gen Khin Maung Myint
Triangle Region Command	Keng Tung	Brig-Gen Sein Lin (temporary)
Central Command	Mandalay	Brig-Gen Ye Myint
South East Command	Moulmein	Brig-Gen Thura Myint Aung
Coastal Region Command	Mergui	Maj-Gen Aye Kywe (dismissed March 2002)
Southern Command	Taungoo	
South West Comnmand	Bassein	
Western Command	Akyab	Brig-Gen Maung Oo
Yangon Command	Yangon	Brig-Gen Myint Swe
North West Command	Monywa	Brig-Gen Soe Naing

Sources: "Burma appoints three new army commanders," *Democratic Voice of Burma*, Oslo, in Burmese, December 26, 2001, in *BBC Monitoring Global Newsline- Asia Pacific Political*, December 29, 2001 and
"Burmese Opposition radio says junta confirms new army postings," Democratic Voice of Burma, Oslo, in Burmese,December 21, 2001, in *BBC Monitoring Global Newsline- Asia Pacific Political*, December 23, 2001.

APPENDIX 5

India and Myanmar, 1999: Human Development Indicators and Per Capita Income

	Life expectancy at birth (years) 1999	Adult literacy rate1999 (% age 15&above)	GDP per capita (PPPUS$) 1999
India	62.9	56.5	2,248
Myanmar	56.0	84.4	1,027*

Source: *Human Development Report, 2001* (UNDP), oup, 2001.
Note: *Data refer to a year or period other than that specified, differ from the standard definition or refer to only part of a country.

APPENDIX 6

Myanmar: Oil and Natural Gas Reserves 1998

Country	Oil (m barrels)	Gas (bn cm)
Myanmar	40	300
(Southeast Asia) Total	11,543	5,660

Source: Petroleum Economist, National energy sources.

APPENDIX 7

Myanmar: Oil and Natural Gas Production 1998

Country	Oil (b/d)	Natural Gas (bn cm)
Myanmar	10,000	1.8
(Southeast Asia)Total	2,580,800	136.7

Source: Petroleum Economist, National energy sources.

APPENDIX 8

Myanmar: Per Capita Oil Consumption 1990-1998

Country	1990	1998	Total growth(%)
Myanmar	0.1	0.2	29
(Southeast Asia) Total	1.7	2.2	33

Source: Harold Thaler, *Energy in Southeast Asia,* (London: The Petroleum Economist Ltd, 1999).
(Thaler's calculations based on EIA and UN Data).

APPENDIX 9

Myanmar: Military Expenditure in billion Kyats, 1991-2000

1991	1992	1993	1994	1995	1996	1997	1998	1999	2000
5.9	8.4	12.7	16.7	22.3	27.7	29.8	37.3	...	...

Source: SIPRI Yearbook 2001.

APPENDIX 10

Myanmar: Military Expenditure as percentage of GDP, 1991-1999

1991	1992	1993	1994	1995	1996	1997	1998	1999
3.9	4.5	5.1	4.6	4.7	4.6	3.6	3.3	...

Source: SIPRI Yearbook 2001.

APPENDIX 11

Inflow of Tourists in Manipur

Year	Domestic	Foreign	Total
1991-92	91,664	374	92,038
1992-93	62,374	221	62,595
1993-94	72,890	350	73,330
1994-95	·82,798	370	83,168
1995-96	84,025	288	84,313
1996-97	87,074	219	87,293
1997-98	91,620	173	91,793
1998-99	95,897	294	96,191
1999-00	99,399	335	99,734
2000-01	1,03,854	409	1,04,263

Source: Sobhapati Samom, "Manipur Misses the boat", North East Sun, Vol. 7, no.8, April 15-30, 2002.

APPENDIX 12

India's Trade with Southeast Asia

	1993-94	1994-95	1995-96	1996-97	1997-98	1998-99	1999-00	2000-01
India-ASEAN Trade (US $ Million)								
India's Exports	1675.55	1901.99	2710.01	2857.68	2421.84	1592.48	2191.59	2835.97
India's Imports	1101.67	1940.10	2688.06	2921.16	3382.30	4142.64	4918.86	3864.37
India-Myanmar Trade (US$ Million)								
India's Exports	-	-	-	-	-	-	-	-
India's Imports	120.90	126.80	162.60	177.34	224.28	173.72	171.80	204.20
India-ASEAN Trade (% change)								
India's Exports	34.79	13.51	42.48	5.45	-15.25	-34.24	37.62	29.40
India's Imports	-10.19	76.11	38.55	8.67	15.79	22.48	18.74	-21.44
India-Myanmar Trade (% Change)								
India's Exports	-	-	-	-	-	-	-	-
India's Imports	4.46	4.88	28.23	9.07	26.47	-22.54	-1.10	18.86
Source: Economic Intelligence Service, Foreign Trade & Balance of Payments, Centre for Monitoring Indian Economy (CMIE), Mumbai, various issues.								
India-Myanmar Trade (% Change)								
India's Exports	-	-	-	-	-	-	-	-
India's Imports	4.46	4.88	28.23	9.07	26.47	-22.54	-1.10	18.86

Source: Economic Intelligence Service, Foreign Trade & Balance of Payments, Centre for Monitoring Indian Economy (CMIE), Mumbai, various issues

SECTION V

LOOK-EAST POLICY, SECURITY ASPECTS - IMPLICATIONS FOR NORTHEASTERN REGION

16

Importance of Northeastern Region in India's Look East Policy

—P.D. SHENOY

Introduction

The location and features of the Northeastern region have been beautifully summed up by well known writer and journalist B.G. Verghese. According to him, "The region is virtually landlocked, with a narrow 37 km-wide corridor connecting it to the Indian heartland against external boundary of over 4500 km marching with Nepal, Tibet/China, Bhutan, Myanmar and Bangladesh. Partition fractured connectivity and caused serious market disruption, greatly aggravating the prevailing geo-political and emotional isolation of the "Northeast" which had suffered constitutional and political "exclusion" under the Raj. The Northeast truly defined, lies north and east of the Siliguri choke point. South East Asia commences at Siliguri"[1].

The Northeast region, comprises of seven States - Arunachal Pradesh, Assam, Manipur, Meghalaya, Mizoram, Nagaland and Tripura, well known as 'seven sisters', has an area of 2,55,500 sq. kms. It represents approximately eight percent of the country's geographical area and four percent of its population. Its ethnic, linguistic, cultural, religious and physio-geographical diversity is well known. It is connected with the rest of the country through a narrow Siliguri corridor in the North Bengal whereas 98 percent of its borders are with other countries. There is tremendous variety in its physical features ranging from the mountain terrain in the Arunachal Pradesh to the plains of mighty Brahmaputra.

The statistical analysis is given below in Table 1:

Table 1

States (1991 Census)	No. of Districts	State Capital	Area (Sq.km)	Population (Provil. 2001)
Arunachal Pradesh	13	Itanagar	83743	1091117
Assam	23	Guwahati	78438	26638407
Manipur	9	Imphal	22327	2388634
Meghalaya	7	Shillong	22429	2306069
Mizoram	8	Aizawl	21081	891058
Tripura	8	Kohima	16579	1988636
Sikkim	4	Agartala	10486	3191168

Development Scenario in the Northeast

Pace of development in the plains and the hill areas differs considerably. The economic development of the region is not uniform. Certain areas in Arunachal Pradesh or say Mon and Tuensang districts of Nagaland are least developed, whereas the valley regions of the Brahmaputra, Imphal and plains of Agartala are well developed. As the resources and skills move towards developed regions it leads to a regional imbalance.

The regional disparities of the Northeast had their roots in the British imperialism. Development efforts in the region during pre-independence era were concentrated more on the cultivation of tea. To facilitate the expansion of tea growing areas, land revenue rates were eventually increased compelling indigenous farmers to abandon their land to make room for the mushrooming of the British tea industry. Labourers were drawn from outside in large numbers. Along with the expansion of tea cultivation, steamer services were introduced and railway lines were constructed. Road construction was also improved in the region. However, no efforts were made to modernize and commercialize cottage industries and also the arts and crafts of the region for creation of employment opportunities and increasing the income of common people[2]

With the dawn of Independence and adoption of planned process for economic development, vistas were opened for balanced regional development of the Northeastern States, but the Partition gave a severe blow to the connectivity of the region with the mainland. Due to geographical and emotional distance, people of the region felt alienated. However, successive development plans and massive investment in infrastructure development has made the people of the area equal partners in taking the engine of growth towards improved standards of living.

Initiatives taken by the Government to Accelerate Development in NER

To promote economic development through a coordinated regional plan the North Eastern Council was set up in 1972 following the enactment of North Eastern Council Act, 1971. The Council is an advisory body. It can discuss any matter in which some or all of the States represented in the Council, have a common interest and advise the Central Government and the Government of each State concerned as to the action to be taken on any such matter. For securing the balanced development of the Northeastern area, the Council forwards proposals, formulating for the States represented in the Council a unified and coordinated regional plan in regard to matters of common importance. The Council also reviews, from time to time, the implementation of the projects and schemes included in the regional plan. The Council has also been entrusted with the task of reviewing from time to time, the measures taken by the States represented in the Council for the maintenance of security and public order therein.

The Council presently consists of the Governors as well as the Chief Ministers of the seven Northeastern States, namely, Arunachal Pradesh, Assam, Manipur, Meghalaya, Mizoram, Nagaland and Tripura. The President of India nominates one of the members of the Council as its chairman.

Outstanding Achievements of NEC

a. The Council provides an important platform where representatives of the constituent States can voice their needs and aspirations and chart out a common programme for regional development;

b. Completed Power Projects with totaled installed capacity of more than 500 MW, which represents a big increase in power generation as compared to the installed capacity of 200 MW in 1971.

c. Completed 1887 ckt Km of power transmission lines.

d. Completed investigation of 19 Hydro Electric projects having power potential of 3836.15 MW.

e. Completed 4800 Kms of roads.

f. Completed two major bridges across the Brahmaputra at Tezpur and Jogigopa.

g. Completed Regional Institute of Medical Sciences (RIMS), Phase-I.

h. Established Regional Dental College, Guwahati.

i. Established Regional Nursing College, Guwahati.

j. Established North Eastern Regional Institute of Water and Land Management (NERIWALM), Tezpur.

k. Established Regional Para-medical and Nursing Training Institute, Aizawl.

l. Established North Eastern Police Academy, Umsaw.

Funding of NEC

The Council acts as a funding as well as a planning agency. The investment of NEC funds, State-wise, since the inception of the Council, has been as follows (Table 2):

It is proposed to amend the North Eastern Council Act to include Sikkim within the ambit of the North Eastern Council. This will facilitate faster economic development of the Northeast Region. However, the new Department of Development of Northeastern region has a mandate to develop the State of Sikkim on par with the seven sisters.

Table 2

Investment of NEC funds in States

(Rs. in Crores)

States	Total funds released since inception up to the end of 2000-2001
Arunachal Pradesh	1610.63
Assam	857.52
Manipur	379.66
Meghalaya	338.99
Mizoram	353.95
Nagaland	875.16
Tripura	286.42
Total	4702.39
NEC Secretariat and other agencies	202
Grand Total	4904.75

Prime Minister of India, Shri Atal Bihari Vajpayee had convened a conference of the Governors and Chief Ministers of North Eastern States and Sikkim in January 2000 at Shillong to review the economic development and security related issues of the region. Therein, the Prime Minister announced an agenda for socio-economic development of Northeastern States at an estimated cost of Rs.10,721 crores, which has now been revised to Rs.13, 390.29 crores. The agenda includes 28 programmes/schemes covering inter-alia the power sector, border trade, horticulture, rural infrastructure, roads and air links, medical education and health services, industrial training institutes, information technology, border fencing and upgrading of the policy infrastructure. Progress of implementation of PM's Package for economic development can be seen at the web site: pmindia.nic.in

The Northeastern States and Sikkim (NE Region) are categorized as special category States wherein 90 percent of the Central Assistance for the Plan Schemes is given as grant from the Central Government. The experience has been that even though adequate funds have been earmarked for various socio-economic development projects, utilization of funds has been tardy due to various factors including procedural delays and absence of an efficient centralized machinery for monitoring the implementation of the development projects. In this context, a new Department was created, viz., Department of Development of North Eastern Region (DoNER) on 1st September 2001.

Presently, the total volume of central transfers and central plan assistance to the Northeastern States is of the order of Rs.12,000 crore annually. This excludes expenditure on account of central sector and centrally sponsored schemes. The DoNER will be tasked to monitor and ensure proper utilization of these flows. In addition, subjects of North Eastern Council and Central Pool of Resources for the Northeast have been allocated to the new Department. In the year 2001-02, the Plan Budget Estimates for NEC is Rs.450 crores. From the Central Pool Resources, Rs.491 crores were disbursed during 2001-02. In future years, these two heads will imply direct development expenditure by the Department of Development of North Eastern Region of the order of Rs.1, 000 crores.

Non-Lapsable Central Pool of Resources

The Union Government on December 15, 1997 decided (in principle) to constitute a (non-lapsable) Central Pool of Resources from out of unspent amounts from 10 percent of the Budget of the Union Ministries and Departments (except those specifically exempted) earmarked for the Northeast (and Sikkim) to support development projects and schemes benefiting the Northeastern region.

The Prime Minister, Shri Atal Bihari Vajpayee, announced the constitution of a Central Pool in a Meeting of Chief Ministers of the Northeastern States and Sikkim held on 8th May 1998. The announcement also indicated that the benefits from the Central Pool of Resources might also be availed by the Government of Sikkim. The commitment of the Government of India in this behalf was also reflected in the Budget Speech of the Finance Minister for the financial year 1998-99. The Central pool became operational during the financial year 1998-99.

Objective

The broad objectives of the Non-lapsable Central Pool of Resources scheme are to ensure the speedy development of the Northeastern region (and Sikkim). The Non-lapsable Central Pool of Resources focuses on taking up appropriate projects, which would reduce the existing Basic Minimum Services (BMS)/infrastructure gaps in the States of Northeastern Region (and in Sikkim). Specific projects/schemes related to physical and social infrastructure are extended financial support under the Central Pool. Installment payments are made from the Pool on project specific basis.

Release of Funds

So far, during the last four financial years since the operationalization of the Central Pool, an amount of Rs.1346.72 crores has been released from the Central Pool for the various projects in the Northeast and Sikkim. The details are given below in Table 3.

Table 3

Central Pool for the various projects in the Northeast and Sikkim

(Rs. in Crores)

State	Funds	Released			
	1998-99	1999-2000	2000-01	2001-02	Total
Arunachal Pradesh	15.00	19.65	43.96	74.24	152.85
Assam	28.81	105.86	69.31	89.18	293.16
Manipur	20.34	121.67	23.85	18.56	184.42
Meghalaya	8.79	3.00	32.63	22.39	66.81
Mizoram	9.00	62.15	27.06	69.86	168.07
Nagaland	20.01	44.08	15.91	52.16	118.16
Sikkim	10.00	32.01	23.78	49.71	115.50
Tripura	10.00	22.50	67.08	115.71	215.29
Common to NE		9.00	9.46	-	18.46
Total	121.95	419.92	313.04	491.81	1346.72

As may be seen, the releases from the Central Pool for the various projects in the Northeast and Sikkim aggregated to Rs.491.81 crores during 2001-02, which was the largest in any single year in the last four financial years. DoNER since its inception in September 2001 gave emphasis on proper utilization of funds released from the Pool during the last financial years on the one hand and increased frequency of meetings of NLCPR Committee to at least once in each month on the other hand, to expedite sanction of fresh proposals received for assistance under the Central Pool.

The largest amount (Rs.293.16 crores) has been released from the NLCPR for the various projects in Assam during the last four financial years followed by Tripura (Rs.215.29 crores).

Monitoring

A system has been established to monitor the progress of implementation of projects under the Non-lapsable Central Pool of Resources. The Department of Development of Northeastern region (DoNER) is the nodal organization for the matters concerning the Non-lapsable Central Pool of Resources and the monitoring of the projects being supported from the Pool.

The State Governments are required to submit their periodic feed back regarding progress of implementation of the projects under the Central Pool to the DoNER in the form of utilization of Certificates and Quarterly Progress Reports on the proforma prescribed for these purposes which contains critical items of information on the financial and physical progress of implementation of the project. The release of next installment of funds is made strictly on satisfactory performance of the project.

Chief Secretaries of the State Governments are expected to hold monthly meetings to review the progress of implementation of the ongoing projects under the Central Pool. Monitoring and Evaluation of implementation of the project are also undertaken through field inspections by the DoNER officers.

Achievements

An illustrative list of projects/schemes which have either been completed or commitment from the Central Pool has been fulfilled is indicated below in Table 4:

Table 4
Projects/Schemes Completed or Commitment from the Central Pool

Sl. No.	Projects/Schemes	Rs. in Crores
1	Srimanta Sankardev Kalakshetra Project,Assam	4.85
2	90, Minor Irrigation Schemes, Assam	11.21
3	Sankardeva Netralaya, Assam	1.00
4	Guwahati Medical College, Assam	8.00
5	Infrastructure for National Games, Manipur	10.00
6	ACA for BMS, Manipur	16.00
7	ACA for BMS, Mizoram	14.91
8	Administrative Training Institute, Nagaland	1.00
9	Railway Over Bridge at Dimapur, Nagaland	3.50
10	Rural Water Supply Schemes, Sikkim	13.50
11	Anti-erosion and Land Slides Works (6Nos), Arunachal Pradesh	11.30
12	Limakhong Heavy Fuel Based Power Project, Manipur (Commissioning of the Project is expected shortly)	126.00

Militancy in the Northeast and Efforts to Curb the Same

The States of Sikkim, Arunachal Pradesh, Mizoram and Meghalaya are generally peaceful. The area covered by Mizoram, which witnessed the height of militancy by the Mizo National Front activists, has become most peaceful after the Mizo Accord and it has also got a peace bonus. There is sporadic militancy in some parts of Assam, Manipur, Tripura and Nagaland and also in some areas of Tirap and Changlang districts of Arunachal Pradesh.

Following are the major militant groups in the Northeast:

Assam

1. United Liberation Front of Assam (ULFA)
2. National Democratic Front of Bodoland (NDFB)

Manipur

1. People's Liberation Army (PLA)
2. United National Liberation Front (UNLF)
3. People's Revolutionary Party of Kangleipak (PREPAK)
4. Kangleipak Communist Party (KCP)
5. Kanglei Yawol Kanna Lup (KYKL)
6. Manipur People's Liberation Front (MPLF)

Nagaland

1. National Socialist Council of Nagalim (Isak/Muivah) (NSCN-IM)
2. National Socialist Council of Nagaland (Khaplang) (NSCN-K)

Tripura

1. All Tripura Tiger Force
2. National Liberation Front of Tripura

Meghalaya

1. Achik National Volunteers Council (ANVC)
2. Hynniewtrep National Liberation Council (HNLC)

All the above groups have been declared as "Unlawful Associations" under the Unlawful Activities (Prevention) Act, 1967 (37 of 1967). In addition there are numerous other insurgents groups like, the Bodo Liberation Tiger (BLT), People's Liberation Front of Meghalaya (PLFM), Dima Halim Daoga (DHD), Bru National Liberation Front (BNLF), United People's Democratic Solidarity (UPDS) etc.

A number of Muslim organization like the Muslim Liberation Front of Assam (MLF A), Muslim United Liberation Front of Assam (MULFA), Muslim Liberation Tigers of Assam (MLTA), Muslim Volunteer Force (MVF), Islamic Liberation Army of Assam (ILAA), etc. have come up in Assam. The proclaimed aim of these organizations is to safeguard the overall interests of Muslims in Assam. However, reports indicate that some Muslim fundamentalist elements are supporting militant activities also.

The most serious insurgency affected States/area, viz., the whole of Manipur, Nagaland and Assam as well as the Tirap and Changlang districts of Arunachal Pradesh and a 20 km belt from Assam in the neighbouring States have been declared as 'disturbed area' under the Armed Forces (Special Powers) Act, 1958 as amended in 1972. The Government of Tripura has also declared the entire area under 22 Police Stations and part of areas under five Police Stations as 'disturbed areas'.

The strength of State Police Force in the Northeastern States is as follows (Table 5):

Table 5

Strength of State Police Force in the Northeastern States

State	Police Stations	Civil Police	Armed Police	Total	India Reserve Battalions
AP	66	2987	2913	5900	2
Assam	240	22977	30946	53923	4
Manipur	57	4743	9241	13984	2
Meghalaya	26	5955	2626	8581	1
Mizoram	31	2948	3852	6800	1
Nagaland	45	7367	9020	16387	1
Tripura	44	7786	4596	12382	2
Total	**509**	**54763**	**63194**	**117957**	**13**

Units of the Central Para Military Forces (CPMF) and Army have been deployed in aid of civilian authorities in the insurgency-affected States. While deployment charges for CPMF units in Assam are presently levied at 10 percent of the normal charges, the other six Northeastern States are totally exempt from such charges in view of their poor resource position.

Despite deploying Central Para Military Forces far beyond authorized limits, it has not been possible to meet the demands of the States. The concept of Indian Reserve Battalions was mooted by the Ministry of Home Affairs, in the background of increasing problems of law and order and emerging internal security scenario in the country, which put considerable pressure on the Central para military forces.

The Government of India categorically rejects violence as a means of achieving any objectives. It believes in solutions to problems through talks and negotiations to bring about peace, stability and development. Its doors are open to all insurgent groups.

Ceasefire with NSCN (IM) and NSCN (K)

The Government of India had entered into formal ceasefire with the Isac-Muivah group of the National Socialist Council of Nagalim since August 1,1997 and the ceasefire with this group has been extended up to 31st July 2002.

There have been persistent demands from the public in Nagaland, NGOs, Church leaders and the State Government that formal ceasefire should be entered into with other militant Naga groups. As a result, the Government of India has entered into formal ceasefire with NSCN (K) for a period of one year on April 28, 2001. The Government of India hopes that this would enlarge the area of peace in Nagaland. This would also meet the longstanding demand of the people of Nagaland for entering into ceasefire with this group.

In response to the policy of the Central Government for peace negotiations, the Bodo Liberation Tigers (BLT) unilaterally suspended its operations from July 14, 1999. In this context, Union Home Minister made a statement in both the Houses of Parliament on March 15, 2000 about the suspension of operations against BL T. Simultaneously, Chief Minister, Assam made the announcement at Guwahati. The peace talks with the Bodo Liberation Tiger (BLT) are progressing satisfactorily. The level of violence attributable to the BLT has come down drastically following initiation of peace talks with the BLT. The other insurgent groups in the Northeast have, however, not yet responded to the peace overtures of the Central Government within the parameters indicated.

Reimbursement of Security Related Expenditure

The Northeastern States have been facing serious insurgency/militancy for the past several years. This has resulted in these States having to incur huge expenditures for maintaining peace and tranquility. Furthermore, the disturbed conditions in these States have adversely affected the economic development of the region, which in turn had a debilitating impact upon the revenues of these States. Lack of adequate income coupled with additional burden due to militancy/insurgency compelled these States to come up with requests to the Central Government for the reimbursement of additional security related expenditure (SRE) borne by them due to the prevailing security situation in the Northeast.

The Central Government has accordingly formulated a scheme for reimbursement of security related expenditure under which expenditure on certain identified item is reimbursable. These include expenditure incurred by the State Governments, including transportation, on new vehicles/bullet proofing of new/existing vehicles, purchase of automatic/semi-automatic weapons along with ammunition, bullet proof jackets and other protective gear and procurement of latest communication equipment both mobile and static, bomb detectors, explosive detectors, computers, etc.

In addition, additional expenditure incurred in connection with capital works on jails and detention centres attached to police stations, special training provided to State Police and Prison Administration Personnel for counter insurgency purposes, expenditure on raising India Reserve Battalions. The expenditure incurred by the State Governments in making necessary provisions for CPMFs/Army deployment, expenditure on ex-gratia grant and gratuitous relief of the victims of extremist violence, and expenditure incurred for transporting arrested militants to jails outside the State or those arrested from outside the State and brought to the State by special flights etc is also reimbursable.

During his visit to Shillong on January 22, 2000, the Prime Minister has announced that the Government of India will further expand the list of items of expenditure incurred by the police, eligible for reimbursement, which would include 50 percent of PLO (petrol, oil and lubricants) costs, village guards, village defence committees and home guards (subject to guidelines). The SRE reimbursement facility will be extended to Meghalaya and Arunachal Pradesh. The total additional reimbursement would be Rs. 40 crores per annum.

The amount released/approved for release to the Northeastern States as on 31-3-2001 is given in Table 6.

Table 6

Amount Released/Approved under SRE to the Northeastern States

(Rs. in Crores)

State	Released in				Total
	1997-98	1998-99	1999-2000	2000-01	
Assam	131.91	78.86	52.19	63.97	326.93
Nagaland	0	35.61	17.88	7.50	56.34
Manipur	0	19.43	3.44	14.17	37.34
Tripura	0	28.55	17.53	15.00	61.08
Arunachal Pradesh	-	-	-	1.00	1.00
Meghalaya				3.21	3.21
Total	**131.91**	**162.45**	**91.04**	**104.85**	**485.90**

Modernization of Police Forces

The condition of Police Forces in the Northeastern States is quite poor. Many of the militant groups have far more modern arms and equipment than the State Police. The financial position of the State Governments in the Northeast is also such that it has not been possible to equip their forces with modern arms and equipment.

The Ministry of Home Affairs have taken up a 100 percent Centrally funded Special Scheme for Modernization of Police Forces in the Northeast with emphasis on supply of (i) arms and ammunition, (ii) vehicles, (iii) communication equipment and (iv) other essential equipment in kind by the Central Government.

The entire scheme has been approved for a sum of Rs.285 crores for five years from 1997-98 to 2001-02. During 1997-98 vehicles and arms and ammunition amounting to Rs.35.63 crores were provided as assistance to the Northeastern States under the New Scheme. During the year 1998-99, 1999-2000 and 2000-01 an expenditure of Rs.12.48 crore, Rs.50.90 crore and Rs.67.42 crore, respectively was committed.

Surrender and Rehabilitation Policy

Central Government have formulated a 100 percent Centrally funded Surrender and Rehabilitation Scheme, effective from 1.4.1998, to wean away the misguided youth and hardcore militants that have strayed into the folds of militancy and now find themselves trapped into that net. The scheme also seeks to ensure that the militants who have surrendered do not find it attractive to join militancy again.

Under the scheme, applicable for militants who surrender with weapons, the surrendered militants are to be initially, for a period of up to one year, lodged in a Rehabilitation Camp, run by an NGO with support from security forces, where they will be imparted training in a trade/vocation of their liking befitting their aptitude.

They shall be paid a monthly stipend, not exceeding Rs.2000 per month, for a period of 12 months, and all attempts shall be made to settle the surrenderees during this period. Minor criminal cases against successfully rehabilitated surrenderees will be withdrawn. Monetary incentives have also been built into the scheme for the surrendered weapons/ammunitions.

However, the experience of the Northeastern States under this scheme has not been very encouraging. There is a need to review the scheme. A proposal has been initiated to amend the said scheme.

Border Fencing

There is a constant, consistent and persistent infiltration of the Bangladeshis into India. This has assumed alarming proportions. With a view to prevent infiltration of the Bangladeshi nationals into India and in pursuance of the Assam Accord, a project for construction of roads and fence along the Indo-Bangladesh border in the States of Assam, Meghalaya, Mizoram, other Northeastern States and West Bengal, has been taken up since 1987. The progress has been tardy. The Government of India has sanctioned a sum of Rs.1334 crores to complete the task by March 2007. Table 7 gives the details of the works:

Table 7

Border Fencing and Construction of Roads along the Indo-Bangladesh Border

State	Roads (kms)	Fence (kms)	Tentative Cost (Rs. In Crores)
Assam	77.50	71.50	167.00
Meghalaya	204.00	201.00	198.00
West Bengal		1021.00	440.00
Mizoram	246.50	400.00	254.00
Tripura	269.00	736.00	275.00
Total	**797.00**	**2429.50**	**1334.00**

India's Relations with Neighbours

Ministry of Home Affairs has a comprehensive mechanism for bilateral discussions with the Government of Bangladesh at the level of Home Secretary and Joint Working Group at the level of Joint Secretary. The Chiefs of the Border Security Force of India and Bangladesh Rifles meet regularly. During these discussions security related issues, cross border movement, trans-border crimes, smuggling of arms and explosives, trafficking of women and children, border incidents, review in existing visa regime are also discussed. There is constant interaction at the Foreign Secretary level also. Apart from this as a follow up action on the Indira-Mujib Agreement, 1974, Governments of the two countries have set up two joint working groups to deal with boundary issues.

In addition Ministry of Commerce and Industry, Roads and Highways, Railways, Water Resources have their own mechanism for interaction with the Government of Bangladesh. These interactions have resulted in agreements on the Farrakka Barrage, Kolkata-Dhaka-Agartala Bus service etc. for better economic cooperation and understanding of security concerns. However, camps of certain Indian militant groups continue to flourish in Bangladesh. India and Bhutan have a long standing close cultural and economic bondage. At the request of the Government of India, King of Bhutan has initiated steps for vacating some of the camps of NDFB and ULFA from the soil Bhutan.

A memorandum of understanding on cooperation between civil border authorities of Myanmar and India was signed in January 1994 in pursuance of that regular interaction is taking place at the Home Secretary level and joint Secretary level in the Ministry of Home Affairs with their counterparts of the Government of Myanmar. The Ministry of Commerce handles matters relating to trade, while the Ministry of External Affairs looks after other developmental works. Recently, India and Myanmar friendship road stretching 160 kms between Tamu, Kalemyo, Kalewa was inaugurated by our External Affairs Minister. The Ministry of Defence looks after work relating to coordination. Several high-ranking dignitaries of Myanmar including General Maung Aye have visited India. It is reported in the press that Government of Myanmar has smashed certain Indian militant camps in the border areas of Myanmar and recovered huge cache of arms.

Mechanism exists for consultation and cooperation between other neighbouring countries like China and Thailand to promote better relations, improved security concerns, trade and commerce. Ninety eight percent of the Northeast's external borders have boundaries with the foreign countries like Bhutan, China, Myanmar and Bangladesh. Therefore, external economic relations are of extreme importance in terms of trade and transit. There has been consistent improvement in our relations with Myanmar, China and Bangladesh. The Seven Sisters have shown keen interest to resume their cultural ties and trade with neighbouring countries. Bangladesh has an unfavourable balance of trade with India. The ties between East Bengal and the Northeast got scrapped due to the Partition. But they have restored fully to improve the trade and transit between these two regions. According to Shri S.P. Shukla, Bangladesh has locational advantage in supplying the Northeast with various goods and services in the Northeast. Bangladesh could also provide a market to the Northeast for several agricultural products, cement and limestone. Simple border trade in head-loads or small quantities would benefit local communities on either side and would be important in itself quite apart from substantive inter-country trade.

Transit also holds out considerable mutual benefits. Revival of traditional water-routes along the Brahmaputra, Meghna/Barak and Karnaphuli rivers would enable Indian vessels to navigate through Bangladesh between West Bengal and Dhubri and Karimganj in Assam or via Chittagong to Dhemagiri in Mizoram and vice-versa. Bangladesh would find a cheap means of moving its goods into various parts of the Northeast and thence, using existing or prospective road and rail facilities, to market its goods in Bhutan and Myanmar.

In the pre-independence era there were several rail links between West Bengal and East Bengal and the Northeast. This could be reconnected and some could be expanded. This would be beneficial to both the Indian Railways and the Bangladesh Railways. A portion of water way is being used for inter-country transport. This could be expanded. Bangladesh would definitely benefit by transit through rail and road through India, Myanmar, Bhutan and China. At present the informal trade has assumed gigantic proportions. There is a need to conduct a detailed study in all its dimensions so as to formalize a big chunk of the same. Kolkata-Dhaka bus service and proposed Dhaka and Agartala bus service would enhance the trade and transit. Air service in the region could also be expanded.

SAARC has provided a forum for sub-region cooperation between Nepal, Bangladesh, Bhutan and India. The gains have to be consolidated. Trans-Asian Highway and Railway, with spurs to Southwest China, have to be revived. An energy exchange/grid in the region would be mutually beneficial.

The recommendations of the Shukla Commission on this subject are given below:

"An inter-ministerial task force be set up to revive the entire Northeast border and inter-country trade issue, with particular reference to Bangladesh, Myanmar, Southeast Asia and Southwest China, and to report on trade opportunities, related manufacturing possibilities in the Northeast, required infrastructure and communication links, banking and warehousing facilities, necessary customs and security arrangements and manpower needs.

A similar review should be made of Indo-Bangladesh trading possibilities and transit routes in relation to the Northeast and the neighbouring countries, and of the transport connections or new facilities that might be useful and mutually advantageous to both sides.

The Ministry of External Affairs might examine what consular or other offices need to be established in the Northeast to facilitate trade and movement. Serious consideration should be given to establishing one or more export processing/special economic zones to promote external trade from the Northeast.

Bangladesh and Myanmarese trade and industrial delegations may be invited to visit the region and vice-versa.

The Commerce Ministry should consider opening an office and setting up one or more permanent exhibitions and showrooms in the region. Traveling in railways and steamer exhibitions might be exchanged between India and Bangladesh with strong Northeastern participation.

The Government should commission a study (or a joint study with Bangladesh) of the costs and benefits to both countries from trade and transit, including the use of Chittagong port as an entrepot for the Northeast. This should include the extent of up-gradation of infrastructure, if any, required in Bangladesh in various sectors for handling Indian traffic. Indian assistance should be forthcoming for consequent investments.

The programmes and related infrastructure requirements under this heading will need to be separately funded. Likewise, it would be desirable to earmark a fund for trade promotion and some suppliers credit to support the North East's external trade".[3]

According to Shri P. Rath,[4] the Northeast connection to mainland South East Asia would be important for the following reasons: a) It would connect the Northeast to a dynamic part of Asia. Trade and commerce would link it to that part of the world. This would make the North East at the centre of two regions of South Asia and South East Asia and dramatically reduce its isolation; b) There are a number of militant movements that straddle the Indo-Myanmarese border. Increasing political and commercial contacts between the Northeast and Myanmar would help us in coordinating with the Myanmarese on tackling of these movements, and finally, the Northeast could attract investment from South East Asia.

South Asian Sub-Regional Economic Cooperation

The Indian Chamber of Commerce, Kolkata took the initiative to organize first private sector forum on South Asian Sub-Regional Economic Cooperation in November 2000 at Kolkata. Several eminent personalities from India, Bangladesh, Bhutan and Nepal participated in it. Cooperation in the field of trade and investment, transport and communications and tourism were discussed in great detail and several recommendations were made. The concept of South Asian Growth Quadrangle emerged during the conference. Implementation of some of the recommendations would go a long way in ensuring faster socio-economic development of the sub-region.

On April 4, 2002 Guwahati was put on the international map as the first Air India flight from Guwahati to Bangkok took off, resulting in euphoria in the hearts of the people of Northeast. The connectivity provided by Air India between Guwahati and Bangkok should be utilized well and imaginatively for strengthening of relations between India and Thailand. It would be desirable to identify the areas of focus on the interest and potential of the Northeastern States. It is hoped that this would promote tourism and development of horticulture and floriculture business.

The Minister for External Affairs has participated in the India-Myanmar-Thailand meeting on transport linkages on 5th and 6th April 2001 at Yangoon, Myanmar. During the meeting, the Ministers agreed that the objectives of the trilateral cooperation shall be to develop and promote cooperation in multi-modal transport and other linkages, with a view to enhance trade and investment, tourism and people-to-people contact so as to further contribute to the economic development of the three countries and two regions.

Cooperation between the three countries shall be supportive and complimentary to BIMST-EC, Mekong-Ganga Cooperation as well as ASEAN-India Dialogue Cooperation shall include the participation of both private and public sectors as well as funding by countries regional organizations and international financial institutions.

The meeting agreed on the following areas for cooperation: a) Construction of a highway from Moreh in India to Mae Sot in Thailand through Bagan in Myanmar to be completed within a time frame of two years; b) Promotion of a highway from Kanchanaburi in Thailand to Dawei deep seaport in Myanmar and shipping links to seaports in India; c) Promotion of trade, investment and tourism through facilitation of movement of goods and people across borders; d) Cooperative efforts on human resource development and transfer of technology; and e) Collective efforts in acquiring funds and advisory services from countries, regional organizations and international financial institutions, for the transport linkages.

This agreement would not only be important economically but also would send out a political message about developing closer cooperation between India and its eastern neighbours.

Note: The views expressed in this article are his personal.

NOTES

1. B.G. Verghese, CPR, New Delhi. Article for *HT* based on an address at the meeting of NE Chief Ministers held at Shillong on 9.2.2002.
2. Seminar: Vision for NE Region in the New Millennium organized by NEC, Shillong.
3. S.P. *Shukla Commission Report on Transforming the North East High Level Commission Report to the Prime Minister*, March 7, 1997.
4. Additional Secretary, Ministry of External Affairs.

17

India's Eastern Neighbours and Insurgency, Small and Heavy Arms Proliferation and Narcotics in Northeast India

—SAJAL NAG

Northeast India has been facing the problem of proliferation of small arms and narcotics from the late 1940s. The fire of insurgency has engulfed this strategic region for the last half-a-century making it one of South Asia's most disturbed regions. The region has large variety of conflict dynamics, ranging from insurgency for secession to insurgency for autonomy from sponsored terrorism to ethnic clashes, problems of continuous inflow of migrants and the fight over resources. Due to the prevalence of variety of turmoil's in the region resulted in the massive influx of small arms and narcotics.

Definitions

The United Nations, panel of Government experts on Small Arms define the small arms as those weapons designed for personal use, weapons that are light and small and those that can be carried by a normal infantry soldier. Small arms can thus range from clubs, knives, and machetes to revolvers and self-loading pistols, rifles and carbines, sub-machine-gun, assault rifles and light machine guns.[1] However, the definition provided by Aaron Karp is the most exhaustive. According to him, there are four definitions of small arms.[2] They are:

1. Defining small arms by exclusion: Small arms and light weapons. Other weapons not covered in existing data collections on major weapons.
2. Small arms defined as weapons carried by infantry. These weapons than can be carried by a normal infantry soldier.
3. Small arms defined as those transported by animals and like vehicles.
4. Empirical definition of small arms. This approach defines the weapons of ethnic war empirically listing all the weapons actually used internecine conflict. A review of the history of many ethnic nears reveals that small and light arms may carry the burden of fighting but major weapons are not entirely absent.

Causes for Proliferation[3]

All the weapons used by the Northeast insurgents are small arms. There has been a massive proliferation and popularity of the and small arms as they are available easily. There are an estimated 55 million AK-47's which are let loose globally and there are around 500 million weapons of all types. Weapons continue to flow in the black market for conflict areas like Cambodia, Mozambique and Afghanistan. These arms are also available at a cheap price. In Cambodia an AK-47 could be as cheap as US $8. While in Mozambique an AK-47 can be exchanged for a little rice or a chicken. Moreover, these light weapons need little training and technical knowledge to use. The average age of 'fighter' in South Asia may be as low as 13. NSCN and the Tamil Tigers are known to have child soldiers. Besides, these weapons being light and small could be easily concealed by animal transport, head loads or under trucks and rail carriages. The possession of such weapons by a young boy give him a deep sense of power, with a weapon in hand, he can do anything that he likes. A young boy from Manipur who is in touch with insurgents told Bina Lakshi Nepram who interviewed him that he feared nothing. He is not afraid of anybody when he has a gun in his hand.

Arms in Possession of the Militants and their Procurement

The first insurgent group from the Northeast India was a 353-guerrilla detachment led by Thinoschie Medon Keyho and Thuingiland Muivah.[4] They were trained in China and most of the insurgent groups of the Northeast follow the Maoist principle. In 1969 when the three Naga groups came back from China after training, they brought with them a large stock of arms, which was superbly suited for jungle warfare of 'hit and run' based on Maoist bus war principle. Few arms which were listed[5]: 89 Semi-automatic rifles; 11 light Machine guns; 42 Sub-machine guns; 1 Rocket launcher; 6 mm Mortars and 14 Pistols.

During the late 1970s, the Chinese stopped this arming and training and it was then that the Myanmarese insurgent groups took over. From the very dawn of independence, Myanmar has been plagued with insurgencies. The country has 27 insurgent outfits, the main important ones being:

The KIA (Kachin Independence Army) in Myanmar initially helped the PLA (People's Liberation Army) with arms and training. Even the Mizo insurgents had the bases in Myanmar. It was the KIA, which trained the ULFA in the late 1970s and early 1980s. The first batch of ULFA and the boys from PLA of Manipur were sent back with a gift of around 10 weapons of various make which included some Chinese AK-47 and some M-20s.[6] However, unlike the Chinese, these Myanmarese groups extracted a costly amount or training and charged money for the weapons sold to the insurgent groups. It was said that for a three month training for a cadre, an amount of three lakh rupees was charged.

The various militant groups starting with the Naga National Council (NNC) of Nagaland had traditionally forged and maintained ties with similar moments in Myanmar primarily with the Kachins, who were instrumental in providing them sanctuary, training, weapons and access to the arms market of South East Asia.[7] Led by the NSCN, the movement was transformed into the most powerful insurgency in the Northeast; they displayed impressive fighting skills as guerillas with the variety of powerful small arms procured mostly from South East Asia and clandestinely smuggled into the Northeast.

United Liberation Front of Assam (ULFA) established its ties with the NSCN and with the Kachins with whose active support and help it raised small guerrilla army and procured their 'tools' of revolution. The NSCN and the KIA played a vital role in transforming ULFA into a formidable guerrilla outfit armed with sophisticated weapons.[8] It has also established contacts with various militant groups like, LTTE[9] and the Afghan Mujahideens fighting in Kashmir. At present, it also receives active political and material support from nations hostile to India while others provide sanctuary, base camps and transit routes.

In 1992, a section of leaders broke away from the ULFA and surrendered. These former militants though gave up the romance of revolution, they illegally retained their 'tools of revolution', which they use liberally to commit acts of violence. These militants popularly known as SULFA have added an entirely new dimension to the problem of small arms proliferation in Assam.

The sophisticated weapons of ULFA are kept in various camps in Bhutan,[10] Bangladesh and Myanmar. It has introduced militancy in Assam and also opened the gates for proliferation or small arms and light weapons from the conflict-ridden places of South East Asia.

Although numerically much smaller than the ULFA, both the Bodo Liberation Tiger Force (BLTF) and the National Democratic Federation of Bodoland (NDFB) cadres are extremely well armed and experts in the making and use of Improvised Explosive Devices (IED).

The ULFA and the NSCN had been instrumental in the spread of small arms in the Northeast as a whole and Assam in particular, from where it spread to the small militant outfits and even among civilians. The NDFB and the BLTF, though have only a fraction of the cadre strength of either the ULFA or NSCN (I-M), they are as well armed. There are other groups like, KNV, KPF, DHD etc., which are reported to be well-armed, being patronized by the NSCN (I-M).

Many of these groups also had been receiving the bulk of their supplies from Bangladesh and Pakistan's ISI. There are reports about the Pakistani ISI based in Bangladesh trying to recruit experienced pilots from Afghanistan for air dropping of arms by small aircrafts. It is estimated that ULF A has a stockpile of not less than 5,000 sophisticated small arms. The Nagaland-Manipur area alone has an estimated 15, 000 to 20,000 armed guerillas. The armouries of the rebels highlighted below (Sunday 15-21 June, 1997) show an organized network of smuggled weapons in this region.[11]

National Socialist Council of Nagaland (NSCN) (Isac-Muivah)

AK-47/56 rifles	300	303 rifles	400
M-22 SGM	50	Rocket launchers	10
M-16 rifles	200	2 inch Mortar	5
M-21 rifles	50	M-20 pistols	10
M-23 rifles	20	38 Revolvers	10
G-/3 rifles	50	Hand Grenades	700
SLR rifles	200	Land Mines	Several bundles
LMGS	30	W/T Sets	10
Carbine	60	Binoculars	50
Sten gun	10		

National Socialist Council of Nagaland (NSCN) (Khaplang)

90 M.M. Mortar	5	M-21/22/6 rifles	1000
60 M.M. Mortar	5	Sten Guns	100
2 inch Mortar	10	Rocket Launchers	10
LMG	50	W.T Set (14 regions)	2 each
G-2 3 4 rifles	200	9 MM Pistols	10

United National Liberation Front (UNLF)

LMG	4/5	Revolvers	2/3
SLR	5/7	Sten guns	5/7
.303 rifles	25/30	Hand grenades	50 (approx)
M-14 rifles	2/3	G-F rifles	3
M-16 rifles	6/7	2 inch mortar	3
M-20 rifles	6/7	9 MM Pistols	10
M-21 rifles	6/7	M-21 Pistols	5
M-2 rifles	2/3	Detonators	50/60
G-3 rifles	5/6	.45 Pistols	6/7

People's Liberation Army (PLA)

LMG	4/5	Revolvers	8/10
SLR	8/9	Sten guns	8/10
.303 rifles	30/35	Carbines	5/6
M-14 rifles	4/5	Hand grenades	/4050
M-16 rifles	4/5	G-F rifles	4/5
M-21 rifles	2/3	W/T/set	6/7
M-22 rifles	5/6	9 MM Pistols	10/13
G-3 rifles	5/6	M-20 Pistols	4/5
G-2 rifles	2/3	.45 Pistols	6/7

Kuki National Front (KNF)

LMG	7	DBBL guns	10
SLR	7	SBBL guns	40
Carbines	6	.303 rifles	89
Sten guns	4	.315 small arms	1
9 MM Pistols	2	Other small arms	2
.38 Revolvers	5	Hand grenades	25
.32 Revolvers	5		

Kuki National Army (KNA)

LMG	1	9 MM Pistols	1
M-21 rifles	8	Sten guns	5/7
.303 rifles	10	G-3 rifles	8
M-20 rifles	1		

People's Revolutionary Party of Kangleipak (PREPAK)

SBBL guns	3.4	.3 SC/Mame	
DBBL guns	2/3	Revolvers	2/3
.38 Revolver	¾	Hand Grenades	2/3

Though we have come to know about some of the arms being possessed by the militants, most of the stockpile of these clandestine weapons is still retained by these militant groups, which we are not aware of. Quantity of weapons confiscated by the security forces do not reflect the actual number of weapons available with the militants but the seizures list indicate the nature of weaponry in their possession.

Between 1993 and 1998, in the entire Northeast, a total of 928 weapons were seized including 729 weapons from ULFA in Assam alone. The first consignment supplied by the Karen National Union (KNU) to ULFA included:[12] 775 AK-56 rifles, 65 GMPGS, 10 Rocket Propelled Guns, 100 plus anti-tank, Anti-personnel shells, 50 Pistols and Assorted ammunitions.

In a press release issued by Superintendent of Police, Imphal stated: On April 12, 1994, the following were seized from a Manipur gun runner: two Chinese hand grenades, two Detonators and 40 live rounds of 9 mm ammunition.

The arrested man who hailed from Yummam Laikai, Imphal disclosed that he was indulging in smuggling of arms since 1981. He collects the weapons from Tammu Bazar in Myanmar. He gets arms from a Myanmarese national based in Mandalay too. He supposedly bought the grenades at a rate of Rs. 600 per piece including detonators and ammunitions at price of Rs. 25 per unit. He was due to supply to a lady based in Churachandpur from where it will be sent to Dimapur in Nagaland.

During the tri-services "Operation Week"[13] conducted in February 1998 over the high seas of the Andamans, the security forces killed six gun-runners, arrested 13 others and seized a huge consignment of arms. The illegal arms consignment included AK series rifles, rocket propelled grenades, Night vision fitted rifles and hand grenades. The end users of this particular consignment were mainly National Socialist Council of Nagaland (NSCN), the All Tripura Tiger Force (ATTF) and the Chin National Army in Myanmar.

The Assam Police has provided some lists of arms and ammunition being recovered by the Security Forces from ULFA and other outfits of Assam.

Routes of Their Distribution

It is estimated that about 13 sources of the influx of small Arms into the Indo-Myanmar Region and beyond has been identified[14]. They were: 1. Myanmarese insurgent groups/ arms bazzar; 2. The South-East Asian black market; 3. China; 4. South Asian countries (in black market) and Cambodia, Pakistan, Bangladesh, Nepal, Sri Lanka (State-sponsored); 5. South Asian militant outfits of L TTE, Jammu and Kashmir Outfits, Punjab Extremists, Maoist Communist Party Operating in Bihar, Andhra Pradesh, Nepali Communist Maoist forces; 6. Other parts of India, UP, etc., (pilferage from legal gun factories); 7. Criminal gangs operating in India and other South Asian countries; 8. The Indian Security Forces, Home Security Guards are the most vulnerable; 9. Other international markets, e.g., Romania, Germany; 10. Some tribes in the region produce their own weapons. British Intelligence Branch Report specifies that in China, "Almost every free man has a gun which he appears to keep in good order. Every village makes its own gunpowder", 'Small Arms' like knives, spears, daos, which are used sometimes are produced within the region itself. The Khasi's "poison arrows", a lethal weapon, was reportedly used in the 1992 communal riots in Shillong to kill non-tribals; 11. Arms are obtained from fellow militant outfits; 12. Of late, some Northeast

Table 1

Arms recovered by Police from Different Militant Outfits of Assam (1995 to 30.4.2000)

Year	Rocket Launcher	LMG	SLR	AK-56	AK-47	Other Rifles	Carbine/ Stengun	Pistol/ Revolver	DBBL/ SBBL	Others	Total
1995	-	-	3	-	1	5	5	48	13	2	77
1996	-	2	3	3	1	13	15	52	12	3	104
1997	1	6	3	16	3	21	18	139	28	23	258
1998	1	2	1	24	10	26	26	139	18	27	274
1999	2	-	5	15	6	34	19	150	18	19	268
2000	-	1	1	10	1	7	8	50	10	5	93
Total	4	11	16	68	22	106	91	578	99	79	1074

Table 2

Year-wise Recovery of Arms/Ammunitions from ULFA militants

Category	1991	1992	1993	1994	1995	1996	1997	1998	1999	2000	Total
Pistol/Revolver	382	92	118	80	26	39	72	70	56	26	961
CMPistol/Revolver/ Gun	15	-	25	18	24	12	63	47	33	8	223
Rifles including AK series	203	28	20	6	3	11	25	23	12	14	345
Sten/Carbine	58	12	17	14	2	11	8	11	7	5	145
Magazine	-	-	-	-	2	25	71	29	35	7	
Rocket Launcher	-	-	-	-	-	-	1	-	-	-	1
Line Rocket/ 2" Mortar Shell	-	-	-	-	-	-	1	1	-	-	2
UMG/LMG	8	-	1	-	-	1	2	-	-	2	14
Shot gun	2172	215	65	27	-	-	-	-	-	-	
Machine gun	-	-	-	-	-	-	1	-	-	-	1
Ammunition	-	-	-	-	447	1079	1045	2130	776	723	

Table 3

Year-wise Recovery of Explosives from ULFA Militants

Category	1991	1992	1993	1994	1995	1996	1997	1998	1999	2000 upto April
Grenade	-	-	-	-	2	20	26	15	56	6
Detonator	-	-	-	-	4	4		84	21	
Gelatin Sticks	-	-	-	-	1	2		-	-	
Flexible/Use Wire	-	-	-	-	-	-	22.5 m + 1 bundle	300 metres	-	
Bomb	-	-	-	-	-	-	7		7	
Explosives	-	-	-	-	3 boxes	1		4 Kg 950 Gms + 9 packets	31 Kg 127 gms + 11 packets	
Land Mines	-	-	-	-	8	-	-	-	-	-

politicians reportedly have become suppliers of weapons; and 13. The RAW (Research Ward Analysis Wing) has been known to arm some outfits operating in the region.

Table 4

Year-wise Recovery of Explosives from other Militants

Category	1991	1992	1993	1994	1995	1996	1997	1998	1999	2000 upto April
Pistol/ Revolver	-	-	-	-	5	6	10	19	39	9

CM Pistol/Revolver/Gun

Moreover, most of the weapons, which flow into the Northeast, originate in Cambodia. Weapons acquired from East European allies after the disintegration of the 'East Bloc' by South-East Asian arms cartels are routed through the small islands from where consignments are re-routed for distribution.[15] It is believed that the route to South Asia begins in the Rangong Islands off the Thai coast from where the arms are shipped through the Andamans and land in Cox's Bazaar.[16]

From Cox's Bazaar, arms are carried in smaller caches through different routes to various destinations in Myanmar and the northeast. Some of the arms move up the Chittagong Hill Tracts and enter the Northeast through Mizoram[17], Tripura or further up through Karimganj into Assam. It passes through the North Cachar Hills District and Karbi Anglong District into Nagaland.

Arms are carried even further up to Sylhet in Bangladesh and to Meghalaya through Dawki and Baghmara in the Khasi and Garo Hills districts respectively. From there the arms pass into Assam through Mankachar in the Dhubri district, and then through Siliguri and the Dooars into West Bengal and then to Bhutan.[18]

The other route from Cox's Bazaar is through the Arakans, the eastern Naga and the Patkai Hills in Myanmar. This region in Myanmar is rebel-held, which facilitates transfer

Table5

Year-wise Recovery of Explosives from NDFB/BLT/NSCN (I-M)/UPDS/DHD and other Militant Groups

Category	1991	1992	1993	1994	1995	1996	1997	1998	1999	2000 upto April
Grenade	-	-	-	-	2	14	4	25	56	4
Detonator	-	-	-	-	200	-	2	8910	26	-
Gelatin Sticks	-	-	-	-	-	-	-	2846	-	-
Bomb	-	-	-	-	-	3	-	-	-	4
Explosives	-	-	-	-	-	-	13 Kg + 79 packets	-	12 Kg-500 Gms	80 Kg
Land Mines	-	-	-	-	-	-	-	-	-	-
IED	-	-	-	-	-	-	1	2	4	-

of these arms through Khonsa in Tirap district of Arunachal Pradesh.

In an incident on December 17, 1995, a Russian-built AN-26 aircraft dropped a huge cache of arms which included, 241 AK-47 and AK-56 rifles, 77 anti-tank grenades, 10 rocket launchers, 11.9 pistols and over 24,000 rounds of ammunition through Purulia in West Bengal. Intelligence agencies believe that the consignment originated in Romania and was actually headed for Bangladesh through which it would have reached militants in the Northeast.

Arms after entering into the Northeast, reach the hands of its various militant groups. Dimapur in the Assam-Nagaland border and Shillong, the capital of Meghalaya have become the major clandestine markets of contraband weapons in the Northeast[19]. Apart from ordnance factory made weapons, the region has also witnessed a proliferation of country-made arms.

The huge funds required are accumulated primarily through extortion and occasionally through kidnappings for ransom. [The 600 odd tea gardens of Assam and now even those in the Dooars of West Bengal have become the 'golden source' for the ULFA, the NDFB and even the NSCN (I-M) to raise funds. The public sectors like ONGC, OIL, NEEPCO, BRPL, etc too have given substantial amount to these groups. Funds have also been raised from the government projects like the DRDA and government departments like those of excise and the revenue departments. It is estimated that the ULFA, between 1990-97 had collected not less than Rs. 500 crores mostly through extortion][20]. A substantial portion of such funds has also been invested in legitimate business through the 'front-men' of those outfits and the profits ploughed back into sustaining their movement.[21]

The use of small arms constitutes a serious threat to national and regional security. Ninety percent of all casualties in armed conflict have been victims of light small arms and light weapons. And up to 80 percent of all casualties and victims are civilians and a great number of them are women and children. The proliferation of small arms not only affects the communities but also the countries. And with the easy availability of small arms, it has become easier to seek a violent resolution to these conflicts.

Table 6 below reflects the casualties due to the proliferation of small arms.[22]

Table 6

Violent Incidents Committed by ULFA, NDFB, BLT, KNV, KPF, DHD, and NSCN (I-M), 1991 to April 2000

Name of Militant Group	No. of Incidents	Security Forces killed	Civilians killed	Militants killed	Total
ULFA	1969	248	538	562	1388
NDFB	997	134	923	29	1276
BLT	388	21	296	75	392
KNV/KPF (Karbis)	17	2	20	5	44
DHD (Dimasas)	34	19	19	11	49
NSCN (IM)	196	80	93	29	202

Amnesty International said in a report released at the start of the first UN Conference on Small Arms and Light Weapons that pistols, assault rifles, and other small arms used in the commission of violent human rights abuses in 100 countries around the world.[23]

The report by the London-based human rights organization also criticized gun-producing nations like the United States, Russia and China for trying to prevent the conference from agreeing on a programme of action that would address human rights issues related to the international trade in small arms.[24]

Amnesty's report also found that the violent abuses committed with small arms included cases of women being raped by soldiers at gunpoint, the arbitrary arrest and detention or peaceful protestors and small arms being used by Police, soldiers and prison oflicials during torture. Despite the reported abuses, Amnesty said major small arms-producing countries have tried to exclude references to human rights standards from the programme of action to be approved at the UN Conference.[25]

The UN is trying to adopt a global action plan against small arms trafficking by delegates from the UN's 189 member nations.

Narcotics and Northeast India

By the late 70's and early 80's, drug abuse became a common problem in Northeast India, especially in Manipur, Nagaland and Mizoram. It was around the same time that insurgency started in full swing too. Within decades, these States saw over 1,10,000 drug addicts and over 6,871 HIV positive cases, with Manipur contributing to nearly eight per cent of India's total HIV positive cases and ranked 3rd in India.

Reasons Leading to Drug Abuse in the Region [26]

The World Drug Report 1997 says that the rapid disintegration of traditional social structure has been a contributing factor to new pattern of drug abuse in the countries in transition; and feeling of marginalization, of non-identification with the cultural environment are attributed to reason for drug abuse. In many Northeastern States, heroin became a cultural pattern of youth to counteract the frustration, which is mainly due to unemployment and low quality of life. This becomes the breeding ground for insurgency and socio-political instability. Dr Paul Goldstein, a decade ago had formulated a tripartite conceptual framework of the relationship between drug and violence.

The second and most important reason is the acute proximity of the region with the Golden Pentagon Area (formerly Golden Triangle). The Northeast shares a 1642 Km long boundary with Myanmar, which is the world's biggest producer of opium. And 80 percent of all opium trade is controlled by the rebel forces, which train various Northeast insurgent groups.

The Northeast region is used by these forces as a transit route for many of the drug bound for the international market (US, Europe and other parts of South Asia). More than 12 drug trafficking routes have been identified. The most important of the routes are: 1. Tamu-Moreh-Imphal; 2. Bihiang-Singhat-Churachandpur-Imphal; 3. Tamanthi

(Myanmar)-Noklak (Nagaland-Myanmar border)-Kohima-Dimapur and many others.

Drug Scenario in the Northeast

The first district affected by heroin in the region is perhaps Churachandpur located in the southern part of Manipur, bordering northwestern Myanmar.[27] It was in this place that drug addiction among the youth as well as the children started. Most of the drug addicts belong to the age groups of 15 to 30.

According to the US Drug Enforcement Administration, Myanmar produces 80 percent of the heroin in South East Asia and is responsible for 60 percent of the world's supply. The demand for the Myanmarese heroin is because of its high purity. The region of Northeast falls in the trafficking route of the Myanmarese heroin and many of the heroin laboratories are located near the border. There are more than 39 trafficking routes from Myanmar and Northeast. An official report prepared in August 1989 pointed out that Manipur, Mizoram, Nagaland together accounted for the smuggling of at least 20 Kgs of heroin everyday. Intelligence reports reveal that the heroin smuggled into the region was not for consumption alone but a bulk of it is sent to different parts of the country for various destinations including foreign countries like US, Europe and major parts of India.

In the areas of Imphal and Aizwal, a kilogram of heroin costs around Rs. 3 lakhs but by the time it reaches its destination in Europe and the USA, it reaches around Rs. 50 lakhs[28]. At least ten percent of all heroin passing through the route, gets distributed in the Northeast, accounting for the rise in the drug addiction among the youth of the seven States in the past half-a-decade.

Manipur also grows fine quality of marijuana (Ganja) in the Ukhrul and Senapti districts. It is being smuggled in other parts of India and abroad, sometimes even with the help of security personnel. The reported arrest of the Inspector-General, Central Police Force (CRPF) Manipur and Nagaland for involvement in Ganja smuggling in 1996 shows the gravity or the situation[29]. The trade is a lucrative one. During the harvesting season (October-December), a kg of ganja costs

Rs. 40 to Rs 50, but it rises to Rs. 100 per kg when it reaches Orissa, Bengal, Bihar and Maharashtra, the price hikes up to even between Rs. 900 and Rs. 1000. During the off-season, the prices get doubled. Hence the farmers here can earn a decent amount by cultivating ganja.

The Northeast Region being in close proximity with the main bread basket of the opium trade, Myanmar has also started cultivating poppy in the area. During a recent survey of four districts of Arunachal Pradesh - Tirap, Changlang, Lohit and Yingkiong, bureau officials assessed that in about 103 villages poppy is being cultivated. The high incidence of opium addiction in Arunachal Pradesh and the lure of easy money have fuelled the growth of poppy plantations in the villages bordering Myanmar and China. The number of opium addicts in Tirap, Changlang, Lohit and Yingkiong is estimated to be over 3000[30].

The narcotics bureau is aiming at "total eradication" of poppy cultivation in the State through strict enforcement of rules and introduction of income substitution programmes. However, no such operation has been conducted in Tirap and Changlang since militancy reared its head in the two districts.

Recently the Narcotics Control Bureau has found out that the inflow of a lethal drug "Methani Phetamine" across the border from Myanmar into Mizoram is creating havoc. According to recent researches conducted by the National Institute of Drug Abuse in the US, the intake of methanephetamine tablets cause long-term brain damage and affects various functions of brain cells by altering brain chemistry. The drug also known as "Speed", "Chalk" or "Crystal" can be smoked, snorted, injected or even taken orally. The intelligence reports that the United State Army manufactures these tablets in clandestine laboratory inside deep jungles in Myanmar using inexpensive ingredients.

In Mizoram alone, 684 kg of ephedrines, an essential ingredient for manufacturing methamphetamine, have been seized since January 1999[31].

Besides, spasmoproxyvon abuse in Mizoram has also caused several deaths and amputation of legs and arms.[32] The abuses caused by repeatedly injecting through the veins under the most unhygienic conditions led to 'Septicaemia' and death, if the addicts are not hospitalized at the right time.

The NGOs in Mizoram, chiefly TNT and Salvation Army's Chan are, in fact, doing yeoman's service, to fight drug abuse and spread of HIV/AIDS. The NGOs in their mission are also being aided by individuals and public donations, government assistance from within the State.[33]

Acquired Immuno Deficiency Syndrome (AIDS), which has often been associated with the evil of the high society, has now percolated into the rural area. In this case Manipur is leading. Its sero-prevalence rate per one million population is six times higher than that of Maharashtra. The seriousness can be gauged from the fact that the HIV sero-prevalence rate in Manipur alone increased from 0 percent to 50 percent in just one year during 1990-91. This shot up to 80.70 percent in 1997[34] and the most important point is most of the AIDS victims happened to be drug users. 76 percent of the HIV positive cases in Manipur were IDUs (Intravenous Drug Users),[35] which are different from other States, where 76 percent of the HIV infections occur through sexual transmission. This is the kind of havoc drugs have created.

The HIV/AIDS epidemic is not only confined to Manipur, it is spreading in Nagaland, Meghalaya and Assam also. J. Warbah, Counselor of Northeast India Drugs and AIDS Control (NEIDAC) said: "the Shillong AIDS scenario is like a dormant volcano, which is bound to erupt within a short span, if left unchecked"[36]. Also the infection is no longer confined to IDUs. It has now spread to the female sexual partners and their children. The HIV sero-prevalence rate among the pregnant women in urban areas have increased from 1.97 percent during 1997 to 3.5 percent during 1998 whereas in the rural areas, it is found to be around 1.5 percent in 1998.[37] TB (Tuberculosis) associated AIDS is also becoming a public health problem in the region. Of late, there has been an increasing HIV prevalence among the TB patients (6.16 to 7.8%) and more than 60 percent of HIV positive cases developed TB as an infection of AIDS.[38]

To check presence of AIDS, the Eliza test is being conducted at Civil Hospital and Pasteur Institute free of cost for confirming the report, Western Blot Test is done in Kolkotta and the Rapid Test, which is accurate, fast but expensive is being conducted in private laboratories and hospitals and nursing homes.[39] NEIDAC has also been conducting AIDS awareness programmes in various localities.

Of course, due to growing various activities against AIDS, Manipur has also registered a decline in HIV positive cases. According to Marwah, the Governor of Manipur, the State has witnessed a decline in the "HIV sero-prevalence rate from 80 percent in 1997 to below 60 percent in 2001 among drug users. Most HIV positive cases in the state were detected among drug users.[40]

Alcoholism had been a problem confronting the tribal states, but with the advent of drugs they are more and more attracted to them. A recent report (Asian Age, 29 April 1997) disclosed that the scourge of drug addition among the youth of Nagaland was on the rise and the state at present has about 35,000 drug abusers.[41]

Bina Lakshmi Nepram has provided the statistics of number of drug addicts in the Northeast India.

Number of Drug Addicts in North East India

State	Number
Manipur	40000 to 45000
Nagaland	10000
Mizoram	Below 10000
Meghalaya	Data not known but number is increasing
Assam	Data not known but number is increasing

Thus, if the insurgency had kept the Northeast on the boil for over four decades, the problem of drug running and rise in drug addiction aggravated the situation.

The cases that have been registered for various drug seizers have shown a steep increase in 1994 compared to 1990. Drug wise analysis indicates that trafficking in almost all types or drugs have shown an increasing trend. The figures below give the information regarding the quantity of the various drugs that were seized during the searches conducted by the Law Enforcement Agencies (Source: Crime In India, 1994).[42]

Quantity of Drug Seized

Quantity in Kgs seized

Drugs	1990	1991	1992	1993	1994
Opium	2114	2145	1118	3011	2256
Morphine	6	6	35	36	51
Heroin	2193	622	1153	1088	1011
Ganja	39090	52633	64341	98867	187896
Hashish	6388	4413	6621	8238	6992
Methaqualone	2141	4415	7475	15004	45319

From the above information it is understood that drug trade has a thriving market and the money generated from the trafficking is capitalized through various money laundering processes.

Routes Through Which They are Distributed[43]

The Northeast route has become a new favourites of the drug cartels active in the vicinity of the Golden Triangle, a remote thickly forest area along Myanmar's border with Thailand and Loas. Earlier, the drugs used to reach Europe and the USA through Thailand and Singapore but due to the enforcement of stringent laws, the drug lords found the Northeast to be the easiest of the routes because of laxity in law enforcement and rampant corruption amongst the law enforcement officials. Some of the important trafficking routes in Northeast India are:

1. Behiang-Singhat-Churachandpur-Imphal;
2. Behiang-Singhat-Tipaimukh-Silchar;
3. Mandalay-Tahang;
4. Tamu-Moreh-Imphal;
5. Homalin-Ukhrul-Jessami-Kohima;
6. Mandalay-Tahang-Tiddim-Aizwal-Silchar;
7. Homalin-Kenjong-Shangshak Khullen-Ukhrul;

8. Myitkina-Maingkwan-Pangsain Pass- Manupong-Jairangpur-Digboi;
9. Putao-Digboi-Pasighat (Arunachal Pradesh)-other destinations;
10. Tamarthi (Myanmar)-Naklak (Nagaland-Myanmar border)-Kohima-Dimapur;
11. New Somtal (Chandel District)-Sugnu-Churachanpur-Imphal-Kohima-Dimapur;
12. Kheinan-Behiang-Churachanpur-Imphal-Kohima-Dimapur

Apart from these routes, there are numerous jungle tracks, which are used by smugglers for illicit trafficking of heroin. Once, heroin or other narcotic drugs reach Imphal, Aizwal, Kohima, Silchar or Dimapur, it is ready for its onward journey to Calcutta, Bombay, Delhi, etc and abroad. The lack of security posts at border points coupled with inadequate security staff has led to the "freely entering" of heroin into the region.

Champai, a border town in Mizoram, and other border points have become floodgates of heroin from the Northeast part of Myanmar. The routes identified are as follows: Tahan-Tiddin-Melbuk (all in Myanmar)-Champai-Aizwal-Silchar-Calcutta; also Aizwal-Bairabi Tripura-Bangladesh; Tahan-Tiddin-Hnahlan-Aizwal; Tahan-Vaiphai-Khawlailung-Serchhip-Aizwal; Tahan-Falam Dawn-Nagharchip-Khawlailing-Secrhhip-Aizwal; Falam-Daun-Thingsai-Hnahtial-Lunglei; Falam-Lungbun-Saitha-Bangladesh; and Churachandpur-Ngopa-Aizwal

The rapid increase of drug smuggling in Mizoram appears to be due to its strategic location having a 704 km international border with Bangladesh and Myanmar. Of late, some inhabitants of hilly terrain of Indo-Myanmar border in Aizwal and Chhimtuipui districts had cultivated opium poppy under cover of thick jungle.

Small Arms, Narcotics and Insurgent Groups Linkages

Illicit trafficking in small arms together with narcotic trafficking is one of the primary activities of the criminals.

This is both due to huge profits it provides and other causes such as the control of the territory wherein it operates, to oppose the government, to exert some kind of supremacy over the competitive or rival groups, to instill fear and to demonstrate for the same purpose its power through various types of military operative capacities, Arms are usually used in exchange of drugs, a traffic which can lead to far longer profits.

According to Stefano Drajani, the inter-relationship between illicit trafficking in small arms and drug trafficking are of two kinds.[44]

Firstly, it has been found that the same criminal organization carrying but both these illicit activities uses the same operational encouragements as well as the same operators, middlemen, carriers and routes.

Secondly, it is the relation between arms trafficker and the organizations specializing in drug trafficking. The arms-drugs units, according to Stefano Drajani fulfill two different requirements. One is that the drug traffickers have huge quantities of weapons to arm the forces which ensure the control and defence of vast plantation areas or redefining laboratories, even against armed interventions by the regular forces. The other requirement is that of arms traffickers who use arms in exchange for purchasing large quantities of drugs at a cheap rate.[45]

The inter-relationship between illicit arms and narcotic trafficking with terrorist groups are of two kinds. Firstly, the terrorist group is only a user or a client of the clandestine work, and secondly, the terrorist groups ask a trafficker both for its own needs and also act as a salesman or middleman for other groups to make money or even because of political and ideological affinities.

The alliance between drug traffickers and guerilla arose during the 1970s in response to the reciprocal needs of such groups due to the great pressure exerted by the regional security forces and also the terrorist in order to maintain their operational levels by restoring to self-funding of their activities set up such links. Both these factors gave rise to: a) The strengthening regional drug-trafficking groups, due to the expansion of their areas of influence and b) The strengthening and updating of the alliances of these groups with terrorist organizations which received economic support in return for their guaranteeing the security of illegal crops.

NOTES

1. Nepram Bina Lakshmi: *Insurgency, Narcotics and Small Arms in India's North East,* (i), The Sangai Express, Imphal, 29 September 2000.
2. Aaron Karp: "The Arms Trade Revolution – The Major Impact of Small Arms" and Brad Roberts (ed.) *Weapons Proliferation in the 1990s,* Massachusetts, MIT Press, 1995, pp. 63-65.
3. Nepram, Bina Lakshmi: *Society Under Seize – The Proliferation of Small Arms and Narcotics in India's North East Region,* Shillong, 2001.
4. *Ibid.*
5. *Ibid.*
6. *Ibid.*
7. Dasgupta, Anindita: "Small Arms Proliferation in India's North East" *Economic and Political Weekly, 6th* January 2001.
8. Linter in epic journey through immigrant Burma, documented in his book (1990) that he had met one of the first ULFA contingents under going training in the Kesan Chanlan Camp of the NSCN at their Oking headquarters in 1985.
9. During a discussion in Lok Sabha on 10th August 1995, the Minister of State for Internal Security admitted that "the growing nexus between the LTTE and the other militant organizations operating in North East-NSCN and ULFA - is bad for the country's security," Ved Marwah, Uncivil Wars: Pathology of Terrorism in India, Harper Collins, New Delhi 1995, 337.
10. Unable to withstand the counter-insurgency offensive by the army, both the ULFA and the NDAB abandoned their camps in Assam and found sanctuary in the dense jungles of Bhutan. Anindita Dasgupta: Small Arms Proliferation in India's North East" *Economic and Political Weekly,* 6th January 2001.
11. Cited in S.K. Ghosh's India's North-East Frontier Fifty Turbulent Years: Heavy Arms Traffic – A Menace to the Regions Stability, Titagarh, 1997, pp. 244-250.

12. Nepram Bina Lakshmi: *Society Under Seize – The Proliferation of Small Arms and Narcotics in India'*
13. *Ibid.*
14. *Ibid.*
15. Anindita Dasgupta: Small Arms Proliferation in India's North East. *Economic and Political Weekly*, 6th January 2001.
16. On February 11, 1998, the Indian Navy in an Operation Code named "Operation Week" intercepted a major shipment of contraband weapons off the coast of Andaman Islands. In the encounter six members Arakan Army, the Armed Wing of National United Party of Arakan, an ethnic insurgent group of Myanmar were killed and 36 were arrested along with 37 Thai fishermen who assisted them.

    That the Cox's Bazaar in Bangladesh is a transit point for illegal arms flows to India's Northeast and Myanmar was also corroborated by Indian Intelligence and Police Officers on field duty during a series of interviews with the author.
17. In 1995, in a joint operation code named "Operation Golden Bird", the Indian Army and Myanmarese Army intercepted a consignment of contraband arms near Saiha on the Indo-Myanmar border in Mizoram.
18. A media report quoting top military intelligence sources mentioned that photographs of ULFA's weapon taken in Bhutan camps and since seized by the Army showed shiny new arms which meant that despite.
19. Anindita Dasgupta: Small Arms Proliferation in India's North East. *Economic and Political Weekly*, 6th January 2001
20. *Ibid.*
21. A media report claims that the ULFA is negotiating to buy several tea gardens in Dibrugarh districts and along the Indo-Bangla broader in the Barak Valley. Although the ULFA would fund and manage the tea gardens, the purchase would obviously be in someone else's name. *The Sentinel*, Guwahati, June 9,2000.
22. Anindita Dasgupta: Small Arms Proliferation in India's North East. *Economic and Political Weekly*, 6th January 2001
23. Small Arms Abuse Rights in 100 Nations, Shillong Times, Shillong, January 10, 2001.
24. *Ibid.*
25. *Ibid.*

26. Nepram Bina Lakshmi: *Insurgency, Narcotics and Small Arms in India's North East,* (ii), The Sangai Express, Imphal, 30 September 2000.
27. Nepram, Bina Lakshmi: *Society Under Seize – The Proliferation of Small Arms and Narcotics in India's North East Region,* presented at the workshop organized by OXFAM VMAP on Aspects of the Conflict Situation in North East India held at ICSSR, NEHU, Shillong, 4-6-2001.
28. Ghosh, S.K.: *India's North-East Frontier Fifty Turbulent Years: Trafficking in Narcotic Drugs*, Titagarh, 1997, pp. 227-228.
29. Ibid.
30. *Satelliets to Chart Opium Belt*, The Telegraph, Guwahati, December 10, 2001.
31. "Narco Threat in Mizoram", *North East Sun*, June 1-14, 2001
32. Ibid.
33. Ibid.
34. Nepram Bina Lakshmi, *op.cit.*, p.12
35. Addicts who inject heroin by syringes into their veins are called SDVs sharing of syringes leads to HIV infection.
36. "Threat of AIDS Looming Large in the State", *Shillong Times*, Shillong, November 30,2001.
37. Nepram Bina Lakshmi, *op.cit.*, p.12
38. Ibid.
39. "Threat of AIDS Looming Large in the State", *Shillong Times*, Shillong, November 30,2001
40. "Drop in Manipur HIV Cases", *Shillong Times*, Imphal, November 30.
41. Ghosh, S.K., *op.cit.*, p.229
42. *Ibid.*
43. Nepram Bina Lakshmi, *op.cit.*, p.15
44. Stefano Drajani: "Inter-Relationship between Illicit Trafficking in Small Arms Trafficking and Terrorism Groups-African and European Issues" paper presented at Seminar organized by UNIDIR and SIDE.
45. Nepram Bina Lakshmi, *op.cit.*, p.11.

18

Some Geopolitical Aspects of the Question of Internal Security of Northeastern India

—R. GOPALAKRISHNAN

Insurgency, militancy, terrorism, etc. are all symptoms of socio-economic crisis and political uncertainty. These have irrevocably dominated the Post-1947 State and society. Struggle for improved material life conditions, growing uncertainty and uneasiness in participation and representation, perceived alienation and discrimination, have radically transformed the perception of the regional-national landscape. Confrontation and competition for power has become more of a rule than an exception. These have been translated at inter-group and inter-regional dimensions as well.

These instances of confrontation, frequently laced with ideology, have been successful in expressing societal contradictions, economic dilemmas, political opportunism and territorial paradoxes. In more than one way, this has encouraged entry of new actors and participants into confrontation - competition parameters. One can find a rationale for the human costs involved and reasons for economic stagnation. But it becomes difficult to evolve a framework of justification either for confrontation or continuation of stagnation.

Present day conflicts sans the romantic hues of the anti-Colonial struggle or anti-establishment movements. Neither do they mean to achieve their goals nor have the means to maintain status quo. Every instance of confrontation was a singular event in its history. Its continuation caused innumerable deaths, destruction of economically viable resources and perhaps led to exodus of many. People and territory became the enviable field. Their continuation while compelling socio-economic stagnation blurred the major issues (likewise compelling to restore status quo led to socio-economic neglect). Under these circumstances, one cannot but need to consider the individuals and their personalities, groups, the weight of history, etc., involved in the conflicts.

Uncertainty of unresolved conflicts makes the real issue its first casualty. This is followed by an intentional recourse to past events. These are relevant to the understanding of the complexities of issues of the conflicts. These are prerequisites to grasp the central fact about the Northeastern region, which is a region in revolt. Its past and present events are troubled. This suggests that indigenous factors of instability continued to remain significant. The rivalries and ethnic cleavages/differences were as obvious as the Colonial experience, which left its share of difficulties to the popst-1947 State. In doing so, though it created stable boundaries between different administrative units, the Colonial State laid the foundations of future conflicts in the Northeast.

Yet, despite the five decades of Independence, there has been a singular lack of information on (1) many of the revolts of the past-internal rivalries and anti colonial struggles in the various territories of the region; (2) on the traditional perception of the modern State among the populations of the region; and (3) of the people and their territory. Even the regional historians have explained what was only central to Assam valley-even here it falls short of explaining the existing predicaments.

The body of literature that now forms the base of images has emerged during the colonial times, which strengthened the distorted image that colonialism was synonymous with peace image. This is partially reinforced by the fact the colonial state faced several challenges to its authority and control but was successful in freezing many of the traditional rivalries, which were the features of the pre-colonial society because it disguised its fragility, and dangers of future unrest. Perhaps, such an understanding will help comprehension of the past values - a past untransformed by modernist introduction of alien culture and not marked by any change in the relationships between the various population groups.

The Northeastern Region delineated the rich geographical confusion of tribal groups within and across the frontiers. There also existed chronic conflict between hill and plain sections. Absence of effective central control encouraged revolts. Their forays in the plains were met with retaliation. Consequently, elements in the hills had little choice between the extremes of a wide degree of untrammeled authority and armed defiance of the Centre.

The available regional literature on these aspects indicates that:

> One, revolts were resistances to greater political control mounted by the centre that capacity and desire to manifest regional identity through revolt was one of the indices of survival and power of these identities.
>
> Two, a sense of distinctiveness from ethnic group to ethnic group remains the greatest historic feature of the region; the political boundaries and independence have accentuated the ethnic divisions and rivalries. This also suggests the impact of the ethnic-linguistic affinities and impact of historical associations.
>
> Three, Center-periphery conflicts
>
> Four, the revolts were aimed at restoring past values, untransformed by modernist introduction of Alien culture and were not marked by any change in the relationship between the groups.
>
> Five, internecine struggle was more frequent in a direct relationship to the weakness of the State. And whenever the individual emerged, the population of the sub-regions accepted the leadership of the individual. There were in terms of their expectations that such a

leader would transform their world, bring new era in which demands of the present would be satisfied through rich unreal promises of the future fulfilled or-a perceptive change emerged when the elite of these groups looked to the future. Supplanting the traditional approaches by programmatic ideologies, which urged revolt because of virtues of the future.

Six, initial revolts directed against administrative consolidation were with hopes of the capturing values of the past, untransformed by the modernist, introduction of alien culture and not marked by any change in the relationship between the ruler and the ruled.

Seven, the introduction of modernization processes and administrative consolidation /re-organization proceeded side by side were reinforced by specific policy measures. These allowed for disorientation to set in. This was favourable to traditional elite who commanded a general following amongst the derive peoples when the time came to revolt.

Administratively, regional political divisions frequently intensified diversions. There did exist distinct variations in geographic and administrative divisions between the sub-regions in the Northeast. However, the various sub-regions absorbed external influences more than diffusing their tradition, beliefs, etc. In a way, the various uprising during the British colonial period seems to have been almost entirely traditional in strategy and tactics.

All these sub-regions passed through the first five-decade of the 20th Century, with only suggestions of opposition to the Colonial establishment. This aggravated with the realization of imminent Colonial withdrawal from the Sub-Continent. This reinforced the problems of its divided society.

The way in which various societies in the region responded to the Partition and unification introduced new ethos; that is, replacing the traditional forms of appeals by the programmatic forms of appeals. This proved also the growing importance of political organization in pursuit of power. This brought into contact with the individuals belonging to the various sub-groups, who first served as members of labour battalions in France. This was significant as it increased political awareness throughout the region. These were translated through charismatic leaders who exploited the dichotomies between the traditionalists and nationalists. Yet what has been more important was the reservation which each of the various sub groups displayed toward the other, as well as different approach that each brought to bear upon the other increased the problems of developing membership and establishing viable and dynamic political organization. However, the groups in revolt that showed the possibility were able to exert continuous pressure of security forces through the 1950's and 1960's to eighties and early 1990's.

Thus the scale of revolts in the region was sufficient to disrupt the function .of the administration. It was in this administrative vacuum that insurgent groups were able to exploit and establish their influences. However, subsequent movements and the dominance of latest fragmentation tendencies among both the society and territories of the Northeast, made the situation more complex than it looks. The calm that prevailed till early 1950's and 1960's were enforced calm with federal power maintaining monopoly on force.

Further, deliberate policies of colonial power to restrict circulation, mobility and sharing of responsibility with the indigenous population cut the ground from those who sought gradualist solutions. Action and counter actions encouraged groups, which had the organizational ability of maintaining its existence. The protracted nature of these revolts and its alien responses provided a slow-acting catalyst, which brought into play a widely felt resentment of the sub-regional populations. In a way, lack of interferences by the colonial administration with the relationship between the traditional political authority structure and their populations, there was little opposition. from the less prosperous members of the society about the disadvantage of their position. This was applicable to the sub-regions. However, institutions, which aimed at transformation of the existing social environment, made major penetration of these societies' cultural relations.

Yet absence of revolt in majority of the region may perhaps be to the absence of effective administration in these far flung areas conditioned by distance accessibility parameters as well as by an absence of major problems of social disorientation-either through disruption of old patterns of society and in terms of preservation of traditional, social and political relationship. Viewing all events in retrospect, one can state that when unrest did set in the region, it was almost solely the perception or fear of being swamped or dominated that triggered of latest divisive tendencies. Yet within themselves, the relations in the traditional plural society were adequate to maintain status quo.

Yet, one does not fail to notice that the reasons for politically troubled region to have closer linkages with the happenings with the immediate borderlands. This to a substantial extent explains how the extra-mural forces and impulses encouraged many of the difficulties and problems that had continuously dominated the regional transaction (and in some instances undermined the regional power balances). The conflicts between inter and intra groups, major and minor or between lowland and highland did not disappear through administration and development. Yet, the changes that were introduced did bring frustration and disorientation that in post-1947 period revived the latent/dormant tendencies among the societies in the region. In a way, then, slow spread of modern education, limited exposure of the people to metropolitan, growing influence of cultural forces, specific policy measures, set the disruptive force to sufficiently influence the regional Governments. Economic limitations and absence of opportunities formed a part of the explanation for the endemic discontent that was and is the dominant activity today in the region. For every instances or outburst of resentment, casualties were the population, with the protagonists and the state, located at two extremities of the development-stagnation continuum.

Change is a gradual process. Inadequacies of the pre and post 1947 State(s) lay in their failure to adequately appreciate and establish a link between rapid change, discontent and disorientation on the one side and in the other between autonomy, stability, security and growth in the society and territory. It also suggested that were minimum efforts directed to explain the national discourse to the inhabitants. As a corollary, the impact of change in social, economic, cultural and political relations became singularly important. New political philosophy, greater individual (as a citizen) participation in the decision-making through defined system parameters, greater opportunities, etc., emphasized the contrasts between pre and post-colonial orders. New demands - political, social and economic, brought the prospects of change and development at the cost of marginalization of old economic systems and traditional values within the various societies. There were hardly any takers who were ready to accept this challenge(s).

At the same time, one can also notice that the Pre-1947 phase changes, which took place did not significantly influence the patterns and importance of traditional beliefs and attitudes. In fact, this development undermined the efforts of post 1947 developments. Subsequent programmes undermined the elite perception that craved for a status. With the experience and understanding gained through the participation earlier, the protagonists followed a policy of spatial expansion of dissent, isolation and control of far flung areas and isolate moderates to sustain a continued pressure on the state. In a way, they followed administrative and economic collapse with establishment of areas under their control and mobilizing the populations to present a common front against the State. These groups temporarily seized the initiatives to affect their dominance. In the process, they were able to tie down sufficient number of security forces for many years. They were successful to disrupt development and dealt severe blow to the region's economy.

Besides, the region indicated the presence of multiple sources of control. These co-existed with the ones established by the State. There were areas, which were politically under control but outside the purview of normal administrative machinery. Post-1947, efforts began first to minimize the anomalies and then remove these anomalies, so that a common administrative framework emerged in the region that was at par with the rest of the country. These steps were construed as reflection of continued dominance.

On the other hand, restoration of status quo was essential. Stalemate meant successes and failures for both the protagonists and the State. At a broader level, it became a matter of either perpetuating an arrangement in which political power came to be concentrated in the hands of elite, political party and bureaucracy with the majority, consisting of diverse groups and less advantaged with perceptibly less access to that power.

As a result, many were convinced of virtues of separate status but it would be wrong to attribute this to all of the populace. What appeared to be a common goal in initial stages was the membership will ensure all opportunity to be associated with the organization that would improve their material life conditions as well as provide alternative to the a state in which they had previously found themselves.

Thus insurgencies in the region began to reflect grandiose plans, perhaps unrealistic in the contemporary global and regional political developments. The insurgents passed beyond the first stage of their aims. Their effects till today continue that can be seen in terms of upkeep of large number of security and Para military forces on the one hand, while on the other, that compels the States to divert the much needed finances for development to meet law and order situations. Security measures and banning of insurgent outfits were some of the policy initiatives that allowed a diversion of finances for development.

Lessons, if any, that can be drawn from the events of the last five decades suggest that both the protagonists and the State had continuously reasserted there efforts; a) to dominate the populated areas and to build up a feeling of security. These led to an increasing communication; b) to break the system within the populated area, and c) to isolate and restrict the contestants from their sources of supply and either way, people, territory and economy were held to ransom.

Weapon sophistication, better intelligence and movement reinforced sanctuaries and access, made all these movements of protracted nature. One of the possible explanations can be lack of involvement of the people of their various sub-regions and their undefined role in the natural society as a whole. Moreover, elements within these societies could hardly garner effective support or were unable to protect the possible role, which their respective societies could play at the national level. Nor were any effort made to fully explain the position of the State. Besides, regional geopolitical compulsions required sufficient understanding of their compulsions and could have well been positively accommodated, had set the colonial policies were continued to a substantial extent.

Yet, success of these movements and counter-insurgency operations can be gauged from the emergence of Nagaland as an autonomous State in 1963 and the Northeastern Administrative Reorganization act in 1971, when composite State of Assam was reorganized.

Despite these developments, one still continues to ask reasons for continuation of the insurgency and its spread to other parts of the region. Is this due to the location and numerous neighbours that the region has? Or is it due to the political, social and economic predicaments, which the region has found itself into? Or is it a geopolitical heritage? These are some aspects that need to be enquired into for an understanding of the region which is in a state of revolt.

Index

H

I

J

❑❑❑